ATLAS

OF THE WORLD

This is a Parragon Publishing Book
This edition published in 2004

Copyright © Parragon 2003

This edition was created by
Starry Dog Books

Authors
Keith Lye and Philip Steele

Editorial consultant
Brian Williams

ISBN 1-40541-708-0

Printed in Indonesia

ATLAS
OF THE WORLD

p

INTRODUCTION

EUROPE

CONTENTS

THE AMERICAS

ASIA

AFRICA

OCEANIA

PLANET EARTH

The Earth is a huge sphere of rock, surrounded by air and partly covered by water. The North Pole is the point at the top of the sphere, while the South Pole is at the bottom. The imaginary line connecting the North Pole, the center of the Earth, and the South Pole is called the Earth's axis. It is tilted by about 23.5 degrees.

Another imaginary line runs around the Earth exactly halfway between the two poles. This line is called the Equator. It divides the world into two halves, called hemispheres. The Equator appears on globes, together with other lines that run around the globe parallel to the Equator. These are called parallels, or lines of latitude. Latitude is measured in degrees between the Equator (0 degrees latitude) and the poles (90 degrees latitude). The latitude of any place between them is the angle formed at the center of the Earth between the place and the Equator.

axis

prime meridian (longitude)

Equator (latitude)

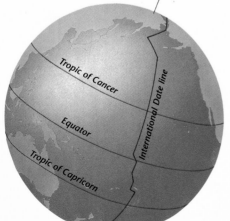

Tropic of Cancer

Equator

Tropic of Capricorn

International Date line

Other lines on the globe run at right angles to the parallels. These are called meridians, or lines of longitude.

◯ SPECIAL LINES OF LATITUDE
The hottest part of the world, called the tropics, lies between two special lines of latitude: the Tropic of Cancer, which is 23.5 degrees north and the Tropic of Capricorn, which is 23.5 degrees south. The coldest parts of the world lie north of the Arctic Circle, which is 66.5 degrees north, and south of the Antarctic Circle, which is 66.5 degrees south.

◯ FINDING THE WAY
Explorers use compasses to work out directions. Compass needles point toward the magnetic North Pole.

The prime meridian (0 degrees longitude) runs through Greenwich, in London, England. Other lines of longitude are measured 180 degrees east and 180 degrees west of the prime meridian. On athe opposite side of the world from the prime meridian, around 180 degrees east or west, lies the International Date Line.

○ MAPPING THE LAND

Land surveyors measure the positions and heights of places on the Earth's surface. Their measurements are used to make maps.

○ PETER'S PROJECTION

Map projections are ways of showing the Earth's curved surface on a flat piece of paper. The Peter's projection (top) shows the areas of land masses accurately, but distorts their shapes.

○ MERCATOR'S PROJECTION

No map projection is completely accurate. Gerardus Mercator's 16th-century projection shows directions accurately and ships' navigators used it to find their way. But this projection distorts areas.

To map any area, people called surveyors measure the exact latitude and longitude of a network of points on the Earth's surface. Then they measure the positions of all the land features between the points. With this information, they draw maps of the area. Drawing maps of large areas is made difficult by the fact that the Earth's surface is curved. World maps, which show the entire surface of the globe on a flat piece of paper, must be distorted to ensure that certain things, such as correct areas, distances, and directions, are preserved. The only true world map is the globe, because it has a curved surface.

○ TIME ZONES

Because the Earth rotates once every 24 hours, clocks in various parts of the world show different times. Time zones are measured east and west of the prime meridian. Canada and the United States each have six standard time zones.

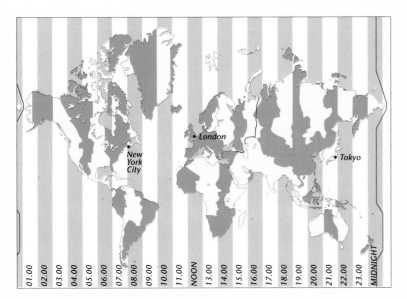

01.00 02.00 03.00 04.00 05.00 06.00 07.00 08.00 09.00 10.00 11.00 NOON 13.00 14.00 15.00 16.00 17.00 18.00 19.00 20.00 21.00 22.00 23.00 MIDNIGHT

New York City • London • Tokyo

THE EARTH IN SPACE

The Earth is a tiny speck in space. It is the fifth-largest of the nine planets that rotate around the Sun in the Solar System. The Sun is one of millions of stars that make up the Milky Way galaxy, which, in turn, is one of the billions of galaxies that form the Universe.

Most scientists believe that the Universe was formed between 10 and 20 million years ago, in a huge explosion called the Big Bang. The Sun was formed about 4.7 billion years ago, while the Earth and the planets were formed about 4.6 billion years ago from a flattened disk of gas and dust rotating around the Sun.

☾ GLOWING GALAXY
Galaxies are astronomical systems consisting of millions of stars. Our sun is one of the stars in a galaxy called the Milky Way. The Universe contains billions of galaxies.

1
2
3
4
5
6
7
8
9
10

☾ THE SOLAR SYSTEM
Nine planets and their moons rotate around the Sun. Together with other bodies, such as asteroids, comets, and meteors, they make up the Solar System.

1	Sun	6	Jupiter
2	Mercury	7	Saturn
3	Venus	8	Uranus
4	Earth	9	Neptune
5	Mars	10	Pluto

EQUINOXES AND SOLSTICES

On two days every year, on March 20th or 21st, and again on September 22nd or 23rd, the Sun is overhead at noon at the Equator. These two days are called equinoxes, a term meaning "equal night." This is because everywhere on our planet has 12 hours of darkness and 12 hours of daylight.

However, after March 21st, the northern hemisphere leans increasingly toward the Sun. On June 20th or 21st, the Sun is overhead at noon at the Tropic of Cancer. This day is called the summer solstice in the northern hemisphere and the winter solstice in the southern hemisphere.

After September 23rd, the southern hemisphere leans increasingly toward the Sun until, on December 21st or 22nd, the Sun is overhead at the Tropic of Capricorn. This is the summer solstice in the southern hemisphere and the winter solstice in the northern hemisphere.

Our planet is always on the move. It rotates on its axis once every 24 hours, giving us night and day. It also orbits around the Sun once every 365 days, 5 hours, 48 minutes, and 46 seconds. This is called the solar year. Our calendar includes some leap years of 366 days to allow for the difference between the solar and calendar year.

THE FOUR SEASONS
Places in the middle latitudes experience four seasons in the year as the Earth rotates once around the Sun.

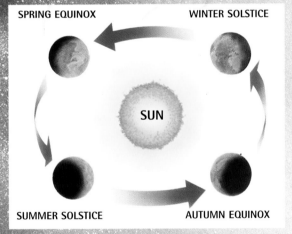

SPRING EQUINOX WINTER SOLSTICE
SUN
SUMMER SOLSTICE AUTUMN EQUINOX

SWIRLING CLOUDS
Photographs of our planet taken from space show swirling clouds and blue oceans. Water covers most of the Earth.

Neap tides occur when the Moon and Sun form a right angle with the Earth.

DAY AND NIGHT
The Earth spins on its axis, taking 24 hours, or one day, to complete one revolution. The term day is also used for the period when the Sun is shining on our part of the Earth. But the night, when it is dark because our part of the Earth faces away from the Sun, is also part of the whole 24-hour day.

TIDES
The gravitational pull of the Moon and, to a lesser extent, the Sun, causes bulges in the waters of the oceans. These bulges cause tides. Two high tides and two low tides occur every 24 hours and 50 minutes. The highest tides are called spring tides. These occur when the Moon, Earth, and Sun are in a straight line so the pull of the Moon and Sun is combined. The smallest tidal range (the difference between the levels of high and low tides) occurs when the Moon, Earth, and Sun form a right angle. The gravitational pull of the Moon and Sun are then opposed, causing neap tides. Spring and neap tides occur about twice every month.

SUN

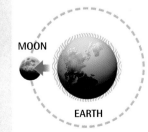
MOON EARTH

9

LAND AND SEA

Land covers about 29.1 percent of the Earth's surface. Most of the land is grouped into seven continents. Water covers nearly 71 percent of the Earth's surface. The largest of the four oceans is the Pacific, which covers about a third of the Earth's surface. People sometimes describe the waters around Antarctica as a fifth ocean, called the Southern or Antarctic Ocean. Most geographers, however, regard these waters as the southern parts of the Atlantic, Indian and Pacific oceans.

◊ CORAL ISLANDS

Oceanic islands rise from the deep ocean bed. These islands are active or extinct volcanic mountains. The tops of many ancient volcanoes are capped by coral. Coral is a hard rock built up by tiny creatures called coral polyps in warm, shallow seas. By contrast, continental islands, such as the British Isles, are parts of the continental shelf which lie above sea level.

North Atlantic Drift
Arctic Circle
Labrador Current
Oyashio Current
North Pacific Current
Gulf Stream
Canaries Current
Tropic of Cancer
Kuroshio Current
North Equatorial Current
Equator
Monsoon Drift
Australian Current
Tropic of Capricorn
Peru Current
Brazil Current
West Australian Current
Antarctic Circumpolar Current
Antarctic Circle

◊ INTREPID SUB

This submersible craft, called Alvin, has carried scientists down to the dark ocean floor. The scientists took photographs and collected samples. Unmanned subs are also used to explore the ocean bed. They collect video film for the scientists.

◊ MOVING SEAWATER

Seawater is always on the move. Waves, which make the water move up and down, are caused by the wind. Wind-driven currents carry warm water from the tropics toward the cold polar regions, while cold currents flow back toward the Equator. The Gulf Stream is a warm current which begins in the Gulf of Mexico. It runs up the coast of the eastern United States and then crosses the Atlantic toward Europe.

◊ AROUND A BLACK SMOKER

Hot water bubbles from a chimney on the ocean floor. Minerals feed tiny bacteria, which in turn provide food for giant clams and tubeworms.

Around most of the continents are shallow seas, covering areas called continental shelves. The continental shelves are flooded parts of the continents. The gently-sloping continental shelves end at the continental slope, which descends steeply to the abyss.

The abyss contains vast muddy plains and huge volcanic mountains, some of which rise from the ocean floor and emerge as islands. Other features are ocean ridges, which are long, underwater mountain ranges. In the middle of these ridges are rift valleys, where earthquakes are common. Scientists have discovered "black smokers" in the rift valleys. Black smokers are places where hot, mineral-rich water reaches the surface through cracks in the rocks. Minerals are deposited around the cracks to form tall "chimneys," around which strange creatures live. Molten lava also flows on to the surface in the rift valleys, creating new crustal rock. The other main feature of the oceans are enormous trenches. They are the deepest places in the oceans.

↻ **VOLCANIC ISLAND**
When an undersea volcano erupts, it may spell the birth of an island, if enough molten rock is flung up.

FACTS

MAJOR MOUNTAINS OF THE WORLD

AFRICA	
Kilimanjaro	19,340 ft
ANTARCTICA	
Vinson Massif	16,863 ft
ASIA	
Mount Everest	29,029 ft
AUSTRALIA	
Mount Kosciusko	7,310 ft
EUROPE	
Mount Elbrus	15,510 ft
NORTH AMERICA	
Mount McKinley	20,322 ft
SOUTH AMERICA	
Aconcagua	22,831 ft

↻ **THE OCEAN BED**
Running through the Atlantic Ocean from north to south is a huge, mostly submerged mountain range called the Mid-Atlantic Ocean Ridge.

continent

continental shelf

continental slope

abyssal plain

ocean ridge

oceanic crust

magma

THE CHANGING EARTH

⟳ PLATE PRESSURE
Earthquakes are most likely to happen where the edges of two plates that are moving in different directions grind against each other.

For millions of years after the Earth was formed, its surface was probably covered by molten rocks. Heavy elements, such as iron, sank to the center of the Earth to form a solid inner core and a molten outer core. Around the core was a thick mantle, composed of dense (heavy) rocks. Light material rose to the surface, while gases, released from the rocks by volcanic explosions, formed the beginnings of an atmosphere.

As the Earth cooled, the surface hardened to form a thin crust, while rain from the atmosphere filled hollows to form the first oceans and seas. The oldest rocks found on Earth are about 3.9 billion years old. No one knows exactly when life began.

⟳ CONTINENTAL DRIFT
About 280 million years ago, the land formed just one supercontinent, Pangaea.

⟳ By 180 million years ago, Pangaea began to split into Laurasia (to the north) and Gondwanaland (to the south).

⟳ About 65 million years ago, the Atlantic was widening, India was moving toward Asia, and Australia and Antarctica were still joined.

⟳ LIFE ON EARTH
Imagine all of the Earth's history compressed into 24 hours. On this scale, the first-known fossils would have formed at 05.45. However, the first creatures with backbones (the fishes) would not appear until 21.20. The first land plants would have appeared at 21.50 and the first land animals (amphibians) at 22.00. The first dinosaurs would have appeared at 22.50, but they would have become extinct at 23.40. People would have evolved only in the last 40 seconds!

million years ago	up to 540	540–505	505–433	433–410	410–360	360–286	286–245	245–202	202–144	144–65	65 mya – present

But the oldest fossils of simple organisms found so far were in rocks about 3.5 billion years old.

From a study of fossils, scientists have discovered that the surface of our planet is always changing. This is because the Earth's hard outer layers, consisting of the crust and the top, rigid layer of the mantle, are split into huge blocks called plates. These plates are moved around by currents in the partly-molten mantle beneath them. Plates do not move smoothly. Their jagged edges are locked together for most of the time. But pressure makes the rocks break. They then lurch forward, causing earthquakes.

◑ These very gradual plate movements have changed the face of the Earth, and are still going on today.

inner core

outer core

crust

mantle

◔ INSIDE THE EARTH
The Earth's crust is a thin shell, averaging 22 to 25 miles under the continents and 4 miles under the oceans. The crust encloses the 1,802-mile-thick mantle, the liquid outer core and the solid inner. The core is mostly iron.

◔ EARTHQUAKE HOT SPOT
The San Andreas Fault, California, is where the Northern Pacific plate and the North American plate are sliding past each other in opposite directions. There have been many serious quakes along this fault, including the devastating ones that hit San Francisco in 1906 and 1989.

The plates do not join up neatly. There are three main kinds of "join." Along the rift valleys in the ocean ridges, plates are moving apart. Molten rock, called magma, rises to fill the gaps and new crust is formed. Along ocean trenches, one plate is sinking beneath another. The edge of the sinking plate, called the subduction zone, melts into magma. The third kind of plate edge is called a transform fault, such as the San Andreas Fault in the western United States. This is a long crack between two plates that are moving alongside each other. Sudden movements along the fault cause severe earthquakes, with devastating results.

13

SHAPING THE LAND

Plate movements create land features. For example, chains of volcanoes form where one plate is sinking beneath another. Also, when two plates carrying land areas collide, the rocks along the plate edges are buckled upward into folds. Such collisions create long fold mountain ranges, such as the Alps, Himalayas, and Rockies. Plate movements also stretch and crack rocks, creating long faults. Sometimes, blocks of rock are pushed upward between faults to form block mountains. Blocks that sink between faults form steep-sided rift valleys.

↻ BUILDING MOUNTAINS
Plate movements form fold and block mountains. Dome mountains are pushed up by hot molten rock in the Earth's mantle.

↻ FOLD MOUNTAIN

↻ DOME MOUNTAIN

↻ FOLD MOUNTAINS
The Alps formed when plate movement squeezed rock up into folds.

The land is also shaped by erosion. For example, when water freezes in cracks in rocks, the ice occupies more space than the water. Constant freezing and thawing gradually enlarges cracks until the rocks split apart. Shattered rocks tumble downhill.

Some rock fragments are carried away by huge bodies of ice, called glaciers, which slide downhill. Rocks frozen in the base or sides of glaciers give the ice "teeth," enabling glaciers to wear away the land and carve out deep, U-shaped valleys.

Rivers also carry away rock fragments. They wear away V-shaped valleys as the moving rock fragments on the riverbed rub against the land, eroding other rocks.

↻ GRANITE
The ancient Egyptians mined granite and used it to build statues and other monuments. This igneous rock is hard-wearing and easy to carve.

↻ AMMONITES
Many fossil ammonites were formed after the dead animals were buried on the seabed. The remains decayed, leaving holes, or molds, in the rocks. The molds were later filled by minerals to form fossil casts.

14

Waves and currents create bays, headlands, cliffs, and caves along coasts. In dry areas, wind-blown sand scours rocks, whittling them into strange shapes.

Worn fragments of rocks, ranging from pebbles to fine particles of sand and mud, often pile up on the beds of lakes and seas. They squash together to make layers of rocks. These rocks often contain the fossils of ancient creatures that were buried at the bottom of the lake or sea.

Rocks formed from rock fragments are called sedimentary rocks. The other two main kinds of rocks

◑ SEDIMENTARY ROCKS
Most sedimentary rocks formed in layers at the bottom of the sea or a lake. Weathering forms them into shapely mountains.

◑ DEEP CANYON
The Yellowstone River has worn a deep, V-shaped valley in the Yellowstone National Park in Wyoming, USA.

◑ BLOCK MOUNTAIN

◑ GIANT'S CAUSEWAY, IRELAND
Basalt, a rock formed on the surface from molten lava, sometimes hardens to form six-sided columns.

are igneous and metamorphic rocks. Igneous rocks are formed from molten material. Some, such as granite, form when magma cools underground. Others, such as basalt, form when lava hardens on the surface.

◑ THE GREAT RIFT VALLEY
This valley, stretching from Turkey to Mozambique, was caused by plate movements.

Metamorphic rocks are rocks that have been changed by great heat or intense pressure. For example, heat and pressure change the sedimentary rock limestone into marble.

◑ MOVING ICE
Glaciers are rivers of ice that form in cold mountain regions. They carry pieces of rock called moraine, which wear away the land as they move along.

glacier

snout

moraine

meltwater

15

WEATHER AND CLIMATE

tundra

coniferous forest

temperate deciduous forest

savanna

grassland

rainforest

chaparral (scrubland)

desert

☼ SOLAR HEAT
The Sun's heat is most intense around the Equator. Near the poles, the Sun's rays are spread over a much larger area.

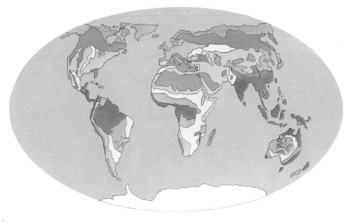

☼ LIVING COMMUNITIES
Scientists divide the world into several biomes—plant and animal communities that cover large areas. The largest influence on what lives in a biome is the climate. For example, the treeless tundra is a biome in the north polar region.

Weather is the state of the air around the Earth. It may be hot or cold, wet or dry, windy or calm. Most of the weather that affects us occurs in the lowest layer of the atmosphere—the troposphere. The troposphere is about 110 miles thick above the Equator and about 6 miles thick over the poles. It contains more than 75 percent of the air in the atmosphere.

The atmosphere includes other layers, such as the stratosphere, directly above the troposphere. The stratosphere contains a layer of a gas called ozone, which blocks out most of the Sun's harmful ultraviolet rays.

The atmosphere is always moving. Near the Equator, the Sun heats the ground and hot air rises. The rising air eventually cools and spreads out north and south. Around latitudes 30 degrees north and south, the air sinks back to the surface. Some of this air flows back to the Equator, forming trade winds, while some forms the westerly winds. These are called prevailing (main) winds. The other prevailing winds are the cold polar easterlies that flow from the poles.

☼ LAND AND SEA BREEZES
1. During the day, cool winds from the sea blow over the hot land.

2. At night, the land cools more quickly than the water and cool winds blow from the land over the warmer sea.

☼ EYE OF THE STORM
The center of a hurricane, known as the eye, is an area of calm surrounded by violent, swirling winds.

Air contains moisture in the form of invisible water vapor. Hot air can contain more moist water vapor than cold air. Hence, when warm air rises and cools, it releases the water vapor in the form of droplets of water or ice crystals. Billions of droplets and ice crystals form clouds.

Clouds are the source of rain and snow. Huge cumulonimbus clouds form in thunderstorms. Thunderstorms, which bring heavy rain, are the most common storms. Many occur in the rising air near the Equator. Others occur in the depressions that form along the polar front, the boundary between the cold polar easterlies and the warm westerly winds.

Other storms called hurricanes form over the oceans north and south of the Equator. When hurricanes reach land, they cause tremendous damage. The strongest winds of all occur in relatively small storms, called tornadoes.

SPLITTING THE SKY
Flashes of lightning are huge discharges of electricity in clouds. The intense heat created by lightning causes thunderclaps.

WEATHER SATELLITE
Satellites send back images of cloud systems and other weather information, such as temperatures in the upper air.

PREVAILING WINDS
Trade winds, westerlies, and polar easterlies are the world's prevailing winds. Around the Equator, winds blow from east to west. Local winds often blow in different directions from the prevailing winds.

rain cloud

river carries water back to ocean

FACTS

Climate is the usual, or average, weather of a place. The five main climatic types are tropical rainy climates, dry climates, warm temperate (or middle latitude) climates, cold forest climates, and polar climates. Each of these is further subdivided according to special features of temperature and rainfall. Some scientists recognize a sixth, mountain climate type, because on mountains temperatures fall the higher you climb. As a result, the tops of high mountains near the Equator are as cold as polar regions.

THE WATER CYCLE
There is only so much water on the Earth. Because we cannot make new water, clouds and rain are important parts of the water cycle. Heat from the Sun changes water from oceans, lakes, seas, trees, the soil, and other moist surfaces into water vapor, which forms the rain clouds. Most rain falls back directly into the oceans. The water that falls on land also finds its way back to the oceans in the end, by draining into rivers that lead to the sea. Then it is ready to go round the water cycle all over again.

17

PLANTS AND ANIMALS

Climate affects the soils, plants, and animals found in any area. Soils store heat, food, and water for plants. They also support plant roots. Scientists have divided the world into regions of different types of vegetation.

Around the icy polar regions are cold, treeless zones called tundra. Snow covers the tundra in winter, but during the short summer, the snow melts and plants grow in the swampy soil. Animal migrants, such as reindeer and caribou, arrive to feed on the plants. Birds also nest there, feeding on the swarms of insects that fill the air.

◑ MOUNTAINS
Temperatures fall at higher altitudes, so plant and animal habitats in mountain regions vary according to the height of the land.

◐ MOUNTAIN GOAT

◑ GRASSLANDS
Prairies are mid-latitude grasslands that are too dry for trees to grow.

◑ TROPICAL RAINFORESTS
Hot, steamy rainforests are rich in plant and animal species. Scientists believe that they contain many species yet to be discovered.

◑ GIRAFFE, AFRICAN SAVANNA

◑ TREE FROG

There are many different types of forest. In the far north, south of the tundra, there are vast, cold coniferous forests, which are home to evergreen trees such as fir, pine, larch, and spruce. The forests contain animals such as bears, mink, moose, and wolves. By contrast, warm temperate regions support forests of deciduous trees, such as ash, beech, chestnut, and oak, which shed their leaves in winter. Much forest has been cut down to create farmland, though wild boars, deer, foxes, and weasels survive in some areas. Mediterranean regions are covered with large areas of heathland, with their wiry grasses and trees such as cork oaks, myrtles, and olives. Tropical rainforests contain more than half of the world's species. Monkeys, snakes, and many birds live in the leafy canopy.

☉ CORAL REEFS

The world's coral reefs, which thrive in clean, warm seas, are threatened by human activities, including pollution and tourism.

☉ ANGELFISH

☉ CROCODILE

☉ WETLANDS

Lakes, rivers, and swamps form habitats for many plants and animals. Each species is adapted to its environment.

Savanna (grassland with scattered trees) borders the rainforests. The African savanna is especially rich in wildlife, including elephants, giraffes, lions, rhinoceroses, and zebras. Other kinds of grassland are much drier. They include the prairies of North America and the dry steppes of southeastern Europe and Central Asia.

Desert plants and animals must survive long periods without water. For example, cacti in North America's deserts store water in their swollen stems. Similarly, camels can go for several days without drinking.

☉ SAGUARO CACTUS

Mountains have varied plant and animal zones. Only sure-footed animals, such as yaks, ibexes, and wild sheep can scale the steepest rocky slopes. Other plant and animal regions include lakes and rivers, and the oceans.

☉ TUNDRA

During the short summer, the empty tundra becomes a breeding area for many migrating birds. In winter, the ground is frozen.

☉ POLAR BEAR

☉ DESERTS

Following a rare rain shower, a desert may be carpeted with flowers.

POPULATION

About 10,000 years ago, life on Earth was hard and most people lived by hunting animals and gathering plant foods. But once people had learned how to farm the land, food supplies increased and so also did the number of people.

◐ HUMAN EVOLUTION
Humanlike creatures evolved on Earth over the last four million years, but modern people appeared only recently.

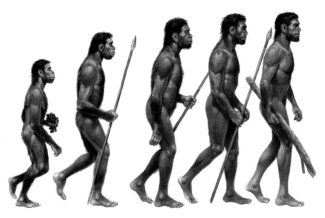

4–1.5 million years ago	2.5–1.5 million years ago	1.5 million–200,000 years ago	120,000–30,000 years ago	Modern man From 15,000 years ago

◐ IT TAKES ALL KINDS
The world's people are an exciting mix of different races, languages and cultures.

By 8000 BC, the world population was still only about eight million (today there are cities with more people than that!), but it steadily increased, reaching 300 million by AD 1000. The billion mark was reached in about 1850, and the two billion mark in the 1920s.

In 1975, the world population reached four billion, and the six billion mark was passed in 1999. The rapid increase in the 20th century, called the "population explosion," is expected to continue during the 21st century.

The world's people are divided by several factors, including race, language, and religion. All people belong to one species, called *Homo sapiens*. However, most people identify three main groups: Caucasoids (whites); Negroids (blacks); and Mongoloids, such as Chinese and Japanese. Racial discrimination has caused much conflict between peoples around the world.

САНКТ-ПЕТЕРБУРГ
ST.PETERSBURG

บางกอก
BANGKOK

Ηράκλειο
HERAKLION

አዲስ አበባ
ADDIS ABABA

東京
TOKYO

חיפה
HAIFA

مراكش
MARRAKESH

◐ OFFICIAL LANGUAGES
Europeans started traveling to other parts of the world from the 14th century. Later on, they set up colonies overseas. When such countries won their independence, they often adopted the language of the former colonial power as their official language. This is why English is now the official language of about 27 percent of the world's population. It is also the language for most international business. Other major official and business languages are Chinese, Hindi, Spanish, Russian, and French.

◐ URBAN LIFE
People in cities face many problems, including pollution, gridlock, and high crime rates. Yet cities are growing throughout the world, because city people usually get better jobs and services than their country cousins.

Language and religion also divide peoples. Experts argue about the number of languages in the world today, with estimates ranging between 3,000 and 6,500. The largest language group is the Indo-European family,

which includes most European languages, as well as Persian and Hindi in Asia. The second-largest language family is Sino-Tibetan, which includes Chinese.

The world's chief religions are Christianity (about 1.9 billion followers), Islam (about 1.1 billion), Hinduism (780 million), and Buddhism, which is followed by 324 million people.

◆ **POPULATION GROWTH**
In 1999, the world's population passed six billion. It is expected to level out at around 11 billion in 2200.

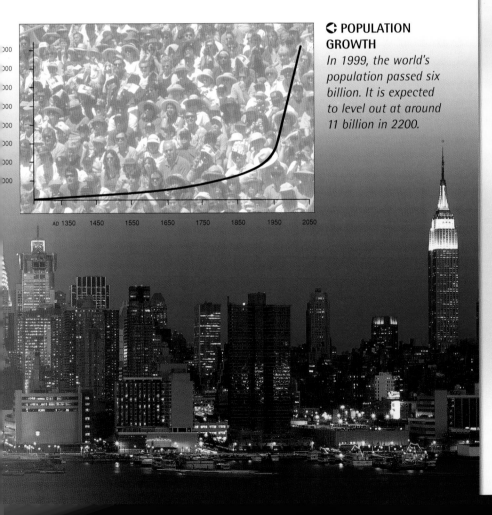

AD 1350	1450	1550	1650	1750	1850	1950	2050

FACTS

RELIGIONS OF THE WORLD

CHRISTIANITY
Christians believe in one God and in the teachings of Jesus Christ. Christianity is the chief religion of the Americas, Europe, and Australia.

ISLAM
Islam was founded by the prophet Muhammad in Arabia in AD 622. It is widely practiced in northern Africa and parts of Asia, and also has followers in North America and Europe.

HINDUISM
Hindus worship many gods. Hinduism is one of the world's oldest religions—it began 3,500 years ago. Today, it is the main religion of India.

BUDDHISM
Buddhism developed in India from the teachings of Gautama Buddha (the Enlightened One).

CONFUCIANISM AND TAOISM
Confucianism is based on the teachings of Confucius, a Chinese philosopher born about 550 BC. Taoism is another Chinese religion. It is based on the teachings of Lao Tzu about 300 BC.

JUDAISM
Judaism is an ancient "one-god" religion that developed in southwest Asia. Its followers are known as Jews.

SIKHISM
Sikhism was founded in India in the 1400s by Guru Nanak. The word "Sikh" means "disciple."

SHINTOISM
Shintoism is the oldest surviving religion of Japan. Shintoists worship forces in nature, including rocks and trees.

21

INDUSTRY AND ECONOMY

○ SAXON FARMERS
Until about 200 years ago, most people depended on farming. Even today, agriculture employs about half of the world's population.

Farming supplies most of the world's food and the raw materials to make clothes and other products. It is the world's biggest employer. But its relative importance has declined as manufacturing and the service industries have grown. The United States is the world's leading trading nation, followed by Germany, Japan, France, and the United Kingdom.

○ MINING
Some underdeveloped countries have large deposits of oil or valuable minerals. But only a few people benefit and many people remain poor.

One of the most important industries is mining. It produces fuels—mainly coal, oil, natural gas, and uranium for use in nuclear power plants—together with metals and many other materials used in manufacturing industries. When reserves run out, we may have to mine other planets or moons.

The modern world divides into developed countries, where many people live in luxury, and developing countries, where many people are very poor.

○ SUBSISTENCE FARMING
Many people in Africa and Asia produce little more than they need to support their families.

○ INDUSTRIAL REVOLUTION
The Industrial Revolution began in Britain in the late 18th century and spread rapidly. Today, manufacturing is a major employer, although in some countries it has become automated and employs fewer people. This has led to an expansion of the number of people in service industries.

FACTS

PER CAPITA GNPS

The per capita GNP, or gross national product, is the total value of all the goods and services produced by a country in one year, divided by the population. It is usually expressed in US dollars. The average per capita GNP in developed countries with high-income economies, such as the United Kingdom, is about US$23,500. In developing countries with middle-income economies it is $2,500. In developing countries with low-income economies, it is less than $400.

○ STOCK EXCHANGE

The economies of countries have become increasingly involved with each other because of trade and financial links.

○ STRUCTURE OF PRODUCTION

In India, agriculture (red), is still more important than industry (yellow). But services (blue) provide most income. In the United States, services and industry are far more important than agriculture.

INDIA

UNITED STATES

○ COMMUNICATIONS SATELLITE

Service industries such as television boomed in the 20th century.

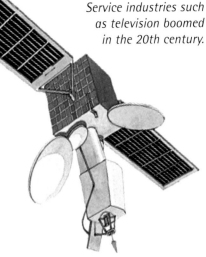

They may live in poor housing, often at some distance from a supply of clean water. Experts divide developing countries into those with middle-income economies, and those with low-income economies.

Developed countries with high-income economies import food and raw materials and export manufactured products. By contrast, developing countries with low-income economies have few manufacturing industries and most people work on farms, often at subsistence level. Countries with low-income economies include many nations, such as Mozambique (Africa) and Bangladesh (Asia), where per capita GNP (see panel) is less than US$500 a year. In a country such as Argentina, with a middle-income economy, GNP is around US$8,000 a year.

○ WHEN RESOURCES RUN OUT...

Biosphere was an artificial world created in Arizona, USA, to study how people might live within carefully controlled environments, such as a colony on the Moon.

GROSS NATIONAL PRODUCT

The map shows how countries are divided into poor developing economies, middle-income economies, and the wealthy high-income economies.

■ Low
$785 or less

■ Lower middle
$786–3115

■ Upper middle
$3,116–9,635

■ High
$9,636 or more

THE ENVIRONMENT

The development of the world's natural resources has brought great wealth to many people, especially in developed countries. However, economic development has caused great damage to the natural world. Because of the huge population explosion, people have flooded into areas of wasteland, cutting down forests and digging up grasslands to create farmland. This has led to soil erosion and massive reductions in wildlife. In some areas, fertile land has been turned into desert.

↻ MOUNTAINS OF RUBBISH
Unsightly refuse dumps can also be a health hazard. They provide homes for disease-carrying creatures, such as rats.

The growth of industrial cities has polluted the land, sea, and air. Rivers and lakes have been left lifeless by poisonous industrial wastes; air pollution has affected wildlife and caused health problems.

Gases released by factories, power plants, and cars have caused choking smog in cities. These gases are sometimes dissolved in water droplets in the air. This creates acid rain, which kills trees and most living things in lakes. The gases that pollute the atmosphere include carbon dioxide, which is released by the burning of fossil fuels—coal, oil, and natural gas. Carbon dioxide is called a "greenhouse gas," because it prevents the heat that rises from the ground escaping into space. As the amount of carbon dioxide in the air increases, so also does the temperature of the air. This process, called "global warming," has already begun to change world climates. In the future, it may melt the ice sheets around the poles and raise the level of the sea. Low-lying islands would disappear, and fertile or densely populated coastal lowlands would be flooded.

↻ FILTHY AIR
Car exhaust fumes pollute the air. Air pollution causes smog, which harms people and plants.

↻ FAREWELL TO THE FORESTS
The destruction of rainforests in South America, Africa, and Asia is a major environmental disaster.

⟳ WIND POWER

The burning of fossil fuels (coal, gas, and oil) causes pollution. Wind turbines can harness the power of the wind to produce "clean" energy.

⟳ SOLAR PANELS

Energy from the Sun can be harnessed by solar panels. In the future it may replace fossil fuels as a source of environmentally friendly power.

Gases called chlorofluorocarbons, or CFCs for short, have damaged the layer of ozone in the stratosphere, which protects the Earth from the Sun's burning ultraviolet radiation. Since the 1980s, governments have worked together to reduce the release of CFCs into the air to halt this danger. Such international action is required on many fronts to halt the damage being done by human activities to the Earth's fragile environment.

⟳ GREENHOUSE EFFECT

Greenhouse gases in the atmosphere retain heat that is reflected from the Earth's surface. This used to be a helpful thing, but the steady increase of these gases due to human activities has warmed the planet to dangerous levels over the last 150 years.

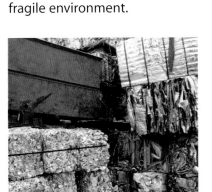

⟳ RECYCLING

Many waste materials, including metals, glass, and paper, can be recycled. Re-use reduces the amount of garbage that must be dumped or burned.

WORLD
FACTS

EARTH SEEN FROM SPACE

FACTS

THE PLANET EARTH

AGE: About 4,600 million years
DIAMETER: 7,926 miles
EQUATOR: 24,902 miles
MASS: 5,980 billion billion tons
TILT: 23.4° from the upright
DISTANCE FROM SUN: 92,000,000 miles
TIME TAKEN TO SPIN ON AXIS:
23 hrs 56 min
TIME TAKEN TO ORBIT SUN:
365 days 6 hrs
NUMBER OF MOONS: 1

FACTS

CLIMATE AND WEATHER

HIGHEST-KNOWN TEMPERATURE:
136°F (Libya, 1922)
LOWEST KNOWN TEMPERATURE:
-192°F (Antarctica, 1983)
WETTEST PLACE:
Mawsynram, India
(average rainfall of 467 inches a year)
DRIEST PLACE:
Atacama Desert, Chile
(average rainfall 0 inches per year)
MOST POWERFUL TORNADO:
280 mph (Texas,1958)

TORNADO

FACTS

SOARING PEAKS

1 Everest or Qomolangma, Himalaya
(29,029 ft)
2 K2 or Qogir Feng, Himalaya (28,251 ft)
3 Kanchenjunga, Himalaya (28,208 ft)
4 Lhotse, Himalaya (27,923 ft)
5 Yalung Kang, Himalaya (27,893 ft)
6 Makalu 1, Himalaya (27,788 ft)
7 Dhaulagiri 1, Himalaya (26,663 ft)
8 Manaslu 1, Himalaya (26,758 ft)
9 Cho Oyu, Himalaya (26,748 ft)
10 Nanga Parbat 1, Himalaya
(26,660 ft)

MOUNT EVEREST

PACIFIC OCEAN

FACTS

OCEANS AND SEAS

1 Pacific Ocean: 64,187,000 sq mi.
2 Atlantic Ocean: 33,420,000 sq mi.
3 Indian Ocean: 28,351,000 sq mi.
4 Arctic Ocean: 5,106,000 sq mi.
5 South China Sea: 1,149,000 sq mi.
6 Caribbean Sea: 1,063,000 sq mi.
7 Mediterranean Sea: 969,000 sq mi.
8 Bering Sea: 873,000 sq mi.
9 Sea of Okhotsk: 610,000 sq mi.
10 Gulf of Mexico: 596,000 sq mi.

NILE DELTA

FACTS

MIGHTY RIVERS

1 Nile, North Africa (4,160 miles)
2 Amazon, South America (4,049 miles)
3 Chang Jiang, China (3,964 miles)
4 Mississippi-Missouri, USA
(3,740 miles)
5 Ob-Irtysh, Russia (3,461 miles)
6 Yenisey-Angara, Russia (3,449 miles)
7 Huang He, China (3,395 miles)
8 Congo, Central Africa (2,900 miles)
9 Paraná, South America (2,796 miles)
10 Mekong, Southeast Asia (2,750 miles)

FACTS

A RESTLESS PLANET

WORST VOLCANIC ERUPTIONS:
Thíra, Greece (c.1500 BC)
Tambora, Indonesia (1815)
Krakatoa, Indonesia (1883)
HIGHEST ACTIVE VOLCANO:
Ojos del Salado, Chile-Argentina (22,595 ft)
MOST MASSIVE ACTIVE VOLCANO:
Mauna Loa, Hawaii, USA (1,500,875 cu ft)
HIGHEST GEYSER:
Waimangu, New Zealand (1,509 ft, 1903)
MOST POWERFUL KNOWN EARTHQUAKES:
Assam, India (Richter scale 9, in 1950)
HIGHEST TSUNAMI:
Alaska, USA (1,719 ft, in 1958)

VOLCANO

FACTS

EARTH'S LANDSCAPES

BIGGEST DESERT:
Sahara, North Africa (about 3,579,000 sq mi.)
BIGGEST RAINFOREST:
Amazon basin, South America
(about 965,000 sq mi.)
BIGGEST RIVER GORGE:
Grand Canyon, Arizona, USA
(277 miles long, about 5,300 ft deep)
LONGEST CAVE SYSTEM:
Mammoth Cave, Kentucky, USA
(about 348 miles)
HIGHEST WATERFALL:
Angel Falls, Venezuela (3,212 ft)

DESERT

COUNTRIES
OF THE WORLD

The world is divided into about 192 independent countries, which have control over their own affairs, and more than 40 dependencies, which rely to some extent on an independent country.

The largest independent countries are Russia, Canada, China, the United States, and Brazil. The smallest are Vatican City, Monaco, Nauru, Tuvalu, and San Marino. The numbers of independent countries and dependencies often change. For example, the Indonesian province of East Timor became an independent nation in 2002.

☉ AN EARLY MAP
This map shows the Americas in 1587, during the early days of colonization.

TIMELINE

RECENT CHANGES IN THE WORLD:

1991 The Soviet Union dissolved and divided into 15 nations

1991–2 The former Yugoslavia split into separate countries

1993 Czechoslovakia divided into the Czech and Slovak republics; Eritrea broke away from Ethiopia

1997 Hong Kong was reunited with China;

Zaire was renamed Democratic Republic of the Congo

1999 Portuguese Macao was reunited with China

2002 East Timor became an independent country

N
W — E
S

ICELAND

FINLAND

NORWAY

SWEDEN

SCOTLAND

ESTONIA

LATVIA

IRELAND

DENMARK

LITHUANIA

RUSSIA

WALES

NETHERLANDS

BELARUS

Key to Numbered Countries

1 LUXEMBOURG
2 LIECHTENSTEIN
3 SAN MARINO
4 VATICAN CITY
5 MONACO
6 ANDORRA

ENGLAND

BELGIUM

POLAND

GERMANY

1

UKRAINE

CZECH
REP.

FRANCE

SLOVAKIA

2

MOLDOVA

SWITZ.

AUSTRIA

HUNGARY

SLOVENIA

ROMANIA

6

CROATIA

SERBIA &
MONTENEGRO

PORTUGAL

3

BOS.-
HERZ.

5

ITALY

BULGARIA

4

SPAIN

MACEDONIA

ALBANIA

GREECE

MALTA

EUROPE

⬙ Oil rig,
NORTH SEA

⬙ Mt Triglav,
SLOVENIA

⬙ Bluebell wood,
BRITISH ISLES

⬙ Mt St Michel,
FRANCE

Europe's western shores face the North Atlantic Ocean. The restless sea has gnawed away at this coastline over the ages, creating chains of islands, headlands, and channels. Ocean currents warm the northwest of the continent, giving a moist and mild climate. Southern European lands border the Mediterranean and Black Seas, and are mostly warm and dry. However, Europe's northern borders are formed by the ice-bound coasts of the Arctic Ocean. In the east, the continental border with Asia runs overland along the Ural Mountains, the shores of the Caspian Sea, and the Caucasus Mountains. Europe and Asia are part of the same vast landmass.

Thousands of years of farming and hundreds of years of industrialization have completely changed the European landscape. Dense woodlands have been cut down and steppes (natural grasslands) have been given over to farming. Great cities and ports have grown up, linked by highways and railroads. Wilderness survives only in a few areas, such as the forests of the far north.

The European Union (EU), currently with 15 member nations, aims to bring increasing economic and political unity to the continent, particularly with the launch of a single currency, the euro. Europe is home to many different peoples, cultures, and languages. English, French, and Spanish are now spoken in many other parts of the world.

➩ GRAY
HERON

31

SCANDINAVIA
AND THE FAR NORTH

FACTS

DENMARK
Kongeriget Danmark
AREA: 16,638 sq mi.
POPULATION: 5.3 million
CAPITAL: Copenhagen
OTHER CITIES: Århus, Odense
HIGHEST POINT:
Yding Skovhøj (568 ft)
OFFICIAL LANGUAGE: Danish
CURRENCY: Danish krone

FINLAND
Suomen Tasavalta – Republiken
Finland
AREA: 130,559 sq mi.
POPULATION: 5.1 million
CAPITAL: Helsinki
OTHER CITIES: Tampere,
Turku
HIGHEST POINT:
Haltiatunturi (4,357 ft)
OFFICIAL LANGUAGES: Finnish,
Swedish
CURRENCY: Euro

Iceland is a northwestern outpost of Europe, lying just below the Arctic Circle. The island is volcanic, with warm springs and eruptions of lava in a bleak, moorland landscape.

◐ NORTHERN LIGHTS
The aurora borealis (northern lights) flicker eerily across the night sky in Arctic regions. They are caused by particles streaming from the Sun.

To the east, the Atlantic Ocean extends into the Norwegian and North Seas. The ocean sweeps on through the windy channels of the Skagerrak and Kattegat, into the shallow Baltic Sea. To the south lies Denmark, which takes in the flat lands of the Jutland peninsula and about 500 islands. The biggest of these are Sjælland, Fyn, Lolland, and Falster.

To the north lies the Scandinavian peninsula, occupied by Sweden and Norway. This stretches all the way to North Cape, beyond the Arctic Circle, where the sun lights up midsummer nights and the winters remain long and dark. Northern winters are severe, but southern regions have a more moderate climate. Lowland plains, covered in birch and spruce, rise to a backbone of rugged mountains. The landscape has been scarred by ancient glaciers. These have created many lakes, as well as the deep sea inlets or fjords that indent the Norwegian coast.

Finland lies on the freezing lands between the Scandinavian and Russian Arctic, with coasts on the Gulfs of Bothnia and Finland. Pitted with over 55,000 lakes, this is the most densely forested country in Europe.

☉ GUSHING GEYSERS
Iceland's geysers are caused by hot rock inside the Earth. The rock heats up pockets of water underground and makes spouts of steam gush up to the surface.

☽ NORWEGIAN FJORD
A fjord is a deep valley that was carved by a glacier during the Ice Age. When the glacier melted, the valley flooded with salty sea water.

ICELAND

SWEDEN

FINLAND

NORWAY

N
W   E
S

ICELAND

Grimsey
Raufarhöfn
Kópasker
Isafjördur
Olafsfjördur
Húsavík
Vopnafjördur
Thingeyri
Hólmavík
Saudárkrókur
Vatneyri
Blönduós
Akureyri
Myvatn
Seydhisfjördur
Eskifjördur
Neskaupstadur
ICELAND
HOFSJÖKULL
Djúpivogur
Olafsvik
Stykkishólmur
Hvitá
LANGJÖKULL
Hvítá
VATNAJÖKULL
Höfn
Borgarnes
Pjórsá
Akranes
Pingvallavatn
Porisvatn
Keflavík **Reykjavík**
▲ Hekla 1,491 m   ▲ Hvannadalshnúkur
Stokkseyri   2,119m
MYRDALSJÖKULL
Heimaey   Vík
Vestmannaeyjar
Surtsey

North Cape
Hammerfest
Polmak
Vadsö
Alta
Kirkenes
Utsjoki
Tromsö
Karasjok
Inarijärvi
Mt. Haltia
1,324m
L A P L A N D
RUSSIA
Narvik
Enontekiö
LOFOTEN VESTERALEN
Kiruna
Sodankylä
Mt. Kebnekaise
2,111m
Vittangi
Pelkosenniemi
Bodö
Gällivare
Rovaniemi
Jokkmokk
Tornio
Kemi
Boden
Mosjöen
Luleå
NORWEGIAN
SEA
Sorsele
Piteå
Oulu
Namsos   Grong
Storuman
Skellefte
Skellefteå
Kajaani
Steinkjer
Dorotea
Bygdeå
Kokkola
Trondheim
Umeå
Jakobstad
Outokumpu
SWEDEN
Ostersund
Ornsköldsvik
FINLAND
Kuopio
Joensuu
Kristiansund
Kramfors
Vaasa
Sunndalsöra
Ume
Seinäjoki
Ålesund
Röros
Sundsvall
Jyväskylä
Dombås
Ljusdal
Galdhøpiggen
Hudiksvall
Tampere
2,469m
Särna
Bollnäs
Port
Kouvola
NORWAY
Lillehammer
Mora
Söderhamn
Rauma
Hämeenlinna
Lahti
Voss
Gjøvik
Falun
Gävle
Hyvinkää
Kotka
Bergen
Borlänge
ÅLAND
Turku
Helsinki
Uskedal
Oslo
Västerdal
Uppsala
Mariehamn
Haugesund
Drammen
Västerås
Stavanger
Skien Fredrikstad
Karlstad
Örebro
Stockholm
Larvik
Eskilstuna
Södertälje
Egersund
Arendal
Strömstad Vänern
Norrköping
Kristiansand
Uddevalla
Linköping
Mandal
Trollhättan Vättern
GOTLAND
Skagerrak
Göteborg
Jönköping
Västervik
Boras
Visby
Älborg
Växjö
Borgholm
Kattegat
Halmstad
Kalmar
Holstebro Viborg
Karlskrona
JUTLAND Randers
Helsingborg
ÖLAND
Horsens
Århus
Kristianstad
Esbjerg
Helsingborg
Malmö
BALTIC SEA
DENMARK
Copenhagen
Ystad
Bornholm
Kolding
Odense
Trelleborg
Rønne
GERMANY

BEAVER

Scandinavia is one of the last strongholds of the European beaver. This species was once common in northern lands.

HELSINKI PORT

The Finnish capital has a fine natural harbor that has to be cleared of ice during the winter months.

DENMARK

DOWNHILL SKIING

Both Alpine (mountain) and Nordic (cross-country) skiing are popular during snowy Scandinavian winters. A wooden ski found in Sweden is believed to date back to about 2500 BC.

WOLVERINE

The wolverine lives in the forests of the cold north. It is a fierce predator, and will even attack deer or bear cubs.

33

ROYAL GUARD

A soldier stands guard outside the Amalienborg palace, Copenhagen. The palace is the home of the Danish royal family.

The term "Scandinavia" commonly refers to three northern European monarchies—Sweden, Norway, and Denmark—but it sometimes also includes the republics of Iceland and Finland. All these countries are democracies that have enjoyed a high standard of living in the last 50 years. Denmark, Sweden, and Finland are members of the European Union (EU). Denmark's self-governing overseas territories include the Faeroe Islands and Greenland, which geographically is part of North America. Norwegian territories include the Arctic islands of Jan Mayen and the Svalbard archipelago.

The development of these lands on the rim of Europe has been conditioned by harsh northern winters and by remote and difficult terrain, much of it covered in dense forests. The population is concentrated in the milder southern and coastal regions, where most

GRUNDTVIG'S CHURCH

This modern Danish church is named for Nikolai Grundtvig (1783–1872), who founded the Evangelical Lutheran People's Church of Denmark.

farming, industry, and trade is located. Only eight percent of Finland is suitable for agriculture, and only three percent of Norway. To the south, Denmark is a major producer of bacon and dairy items such as butter, cheese, and yoghurt. In volcanic Iceland, underground heat has been harnessed to warm greenhouses, where flowers and vegetables are grown for export.

The forests of northern Scandinavia provide timber for paper-making, construction, and furniture.

OIL FROM THE SEA

Large reserves of oil beneath the North Sea have made Norway Europe's largest oil producer. Norway also has major industries based on natural gas and petrochemicals.

LEGOLAND, DENMARK

Denmark exports the most famous toy in the world, Lego. Tourists flock to Legoland, where a tiny model of every major city has been built from the brightly coloured plastic bricks.

WIND TURBINES

Danish engineers pioneered wind turbine technology and today groups of windmills are a familiar sight in the Danish countryside. They may be up to 100 feet high, generating enough electricity for export as well as for local needs.

These lands also produce vehicles, machinery, and scientific and electrical equipment. Sweden has rich reserves of iron ore and uranium, and both Denmark and Norway have profited from North Sea oil and natural gas. Northern mountain streams and lakes generate hydroelectric power, and Denmark has been at the forefront of developing wind power. Fisheries have always provided food and a livelihood for people in each one of these northern lands.

Reykjavík, in Iceland, is the world's most northerly capital city. The capitals of the region are all old seaports that grew up on the trading routes between the Baltic, the North Sea, and the North Atlantic.

◯ TIMBER!
Timber is an important resource in Norway and Sweden. Some 65 percent of Finland is forested, and wood products make up 40 percent of Finnish exports.

◯ STOCKHOLM
Stockholm, the Swedish capital, lies on a strait between Lake Malar and the Baltic coast. The city's waterfronts also take in a number of small islands linked by bridges.

FACTS

ICELAND
Lyðveldið Ísland
AREA: 39,768 sq mi.
POPULATION: 0.3 million
CAPITAL: Reykjavík
OTHER CITIES: Kópavogur, Hafnarfjörður
HIGHEST POINT: Hvannadalshnúkur (6,951 ft)
OFFICIAL LANGUAGE: Icelandic
CURRENCY: Icelandic króna

NORWAY
Kongeriket Norge
AREA: 125,050 sq mi.
POPULATION: 4.5 million
CAPITAL: Oslo
OTHER CITIES: Bergen, Trondheim
HIGHEST POINT: Galdhøppigen (8,100 ft)
OFFICIAL LANGUAGE: Norwegian
CURRENCY: Norwegian krone

SWEDEN
Konungariket Sverige
AREA: 173,732 sq mi.
POPULATION: 8.8 million
CAPITAL: Stockholm
OTHER CITIES: Göteborg, Malmö
HIGHEST POINT: Kebnekaise (6,926 ft)
OFFICIAL LANGUAGE: Swedish
CURRENCY: Swedish krona

35

Scandinavia is home to several different peoples. The Saami have lived there since prehistoric times. Their modern homeland, known as Lapland, stretches through Arctic Norway, Sweden, and Finland and into Russia. Their language is related to Finnish and Estonian. Traditionally, the Saami are nomadic reindeer herders, but many now live and work in towns.

The Finns make up the majority of people living in Finland. They too speak their own language. Their ancestors moved into the region from what is now Russia, about 2,000 years ago. About the same time, other peoples were moving north into Scandinavia from Germany. These were the ancestors of today's Swedes (some of whom also live in Finland), Danes, Norwegians, and Icelanders. Swedish, Danish, Icelandic, and the two spoken versions of Norwegian (Bokmål and Nynorsk) are separate languages that have developed from similar Germanic roots.

About 1,200 years ago, the Scandinavians began to take to the sea to seek their fortune abroad. Known as Vikings or Northmen, they attacked coastal settlements all over the British Isles and Western Europe.

✪ STAVE CHURCH
During the 11th century, Christianity began to spread across Norway. About 600 wooden stave churches were built there during the Middle Ages. Today, only about twenty-four remain standing. They are named for their corner-posts, or staves.

✪ SAAMI TRIBESMAN
The Saami from Sweden still wear traditional costume for special occasions. The amount of Arctic pasture available for grazing has been greatly reduced in modern times, and only one-in-ten Saami still live by herding reindeer.

✪ A BRAVE LEADER
King Gustavus Adolphus of Sweden (1611–32) died after the battle of Lützen, in the Thirty Years' War. The Protestant Swedes were fighting Spain and the Holy Roman Empire.

✪ TOLLUND MAN
Discovered at Tollund Fen, Denmark, in 1950, the Tollund Man is over 2,000 years old. His body had been preserved in a peat bog since Iron Age times. The peat also dyed his skin brown.

✪ VIKING RAIDERS
The Vikings set sail from Scandinavia to trade, and also to raid the coasts of Europe. Armed with fearsome iron swords and axes, they looted towns, seized land, and took captives.

◔ GARDEN OF CULTURE
Tivoli pleasure gardens in Copenhagen provide the venue for open-air theaters, pavilions, and a concert hall. In daylight, the flowerbeds are a sea of color while at night, colored floodlights and firework displays brighten the sky.

TIMELINE

AD

c.200	Germanic tribes control most of Scandinavia; Finns settle Finland
c.750	The Viking age (until c.1100): overseas raids, trade, settlement
872	King Harald Finehair of Norway conquers Scandinavia
874	Norwegian Vikings settle Iceland
930	Establishment of Althing, one of the world's oldest parliaments, in Iceland
982	Danes colonize Greenland
1397	Union of Kalmar unites mainland Scandinavia under Danish rule
1523	Sweden leaves the Union
1540	Sweden rules Finland (until 1809)
1618	Thirty Years' War (until 1648): Scandinavia supports Protestants
1700	Great Northern War (until 1721): Sweden invades Russia, but is defeated
1809	Russia rules Finland (until 1917)
1905	Norway becomes independent
1919	Finland recognized as independent republic
1920	Iceland becomes independent
1939	World War II (until 1945): Germany invades Denmark and Norway; Sweden remains neutral; Finland invaded by Russia, allies itself to Germany in 1941
1944	Iceland becomes a republic
1973	Denmark joins EEC (later EU)
1994	Sweden and Finland vote to join EU; Norway votes against joining

◔ ST LUCY'S DAY
In Sweden, where northern winters are dark and long, it is small wonder that people like to honor St Lucy, a Christian saint associated with light. Her feast day falls on December 13th. Girls dress in white and wear a crown of fairy lights or candles.

They sailed westward to settle Iceland and Greenland, and even discovered North America. They founded new states in Russia and traded with the Arabs in the Middle East. By the 1100s the Viking homelands had become Christian kingdoms, which grew rich by trading in fish, timber, and furs.

In 1397 Sweden was united with Norway and Denmark by the Union of Kalmar. Sweden broke away in 1523 and over the next two centuries became a powerful nation. Norway regained independence in 1905 and Iceland in 1944. Finland was ruled by Russia from 1809 to 1917. After World War II (1939–45), Europe's far north enjoyed peace and increasing prosperity under a series of liberal governments. Most Scandinavian Christians are Protestants.

◔ CLEAN DESIGN
Scandinavian design is admired around the world for its unfussy look. This chair by Esko Pajamies was inspired by the renowned Finn, Alvar Aalto (1898–1976).

THE LOW COUNTRIES

FACTS

BELGIUM
Royaume de Belgique –
Koninkrijk België
AREA: 11,783 sq mi.
POPULATION: 10.3 million
CAPITAL: Brussels
OTHER CITIES: Antwerp,
Ghent
HIGHEST POINT: Botrange
(2,276 ft)
OFFICIAL LANGUAGES:
Flemish, French
CURRENCY: Euro

LUXEMBOURG
Grand-Duché de Luxembourg
AREA: 999 sq mi.
POPULATION: 0.4 million
CAPITAL: Luxembourg City
OTHER CITIES: Esch-sur-
Alzette
HIGHEST POINT: Buurgplatz
(1,843 ft)
OFFICIAL LANGUAGES: French,
German, Letzebuergesch
CURRENCY: Euro

NETHERLANDS
Koninkrijk der Nederlanden
AREA: 15,770 sq mi.
POPULATION: 16 million
CAPITAL: Amsterdam
OTHER CITIES: Rotterdam,
the Hague
HIGHEST POINT: Vaalser Berg
(1,053 ft)
OFFICIAL LANGUAGE: Dutch
CURRENCY: Euro

The Netherlands, Belgium, and Luxembourg lie in northwestern Europe, between France and Germany. They mostly enjoy a mild and moist climate.

The sand dunes of the West Frisian islands and the North Sea coast fringe a low plain. For thousands of years these marshy lands were flooded by the great rivers that spill across them—the Rhine, Schelde, and Meuse—and by wind-whipped tides powering in from the sea. Over the centuries, the peoples of the lowlands learned to build sea and river defences—dykes, dams, and barriers. They also became expert at draining marshes and flooded land. The large windmills that powered the drainage pumps may still be seen in many places. Areas reclaimed from the sea, known as polders, now form wide areas of green farmland. A network of canals crosses the countryside.

⊙ RIVER TOWN
On a wooded bend in the Sûre River, Luxembourg, is the old town of Esch-sur-Sûre, which attracts tourists and hikers.

To the south, the flat lands give way to sandy heaths and fertile plateaus, rising to the Ardennes. This wooded range of hills, some of which rise to over 1,970 feet, crosses southeastern Belgium, northern Luxembourg, and part of eastern France. Southern Luxembourg is taken up by rolling farmland, bordered by the Sûre and Moselle Rivers and crossed by the Alzette River.

⊙ DUTCH WINDMILL
As you cycle alongside Dutch canals, you are sure to see beautiful old windmills rising above the fields. Some are still in working order.

⊙ COPPER BUTTERFLY

⊙ GRAY HERON

◯ HOLDING BACK

At 20 miles long, the Afsluitdijk, between North Holland and Friesland, is the world's longest sea dam. Completed in 1935, it created a huge new lake, the IJsselmeer.

BELGIUM

NETHERLANDS

◯ THE AMSTEL RIVER

Amsterdam is the capital city of the Netherlands. It lies on the Amstel River, which has been channeled into canals to prevent flooding.

N
W — **E**
S

LUXEMBOURG

◯ SPACE-AGE LANDMARK

The Atomium was built for the World Fair, held in Brussels in 1958. It was a symbol of scientific progress.

◯ THE GRAND-PLACE

At the heart of Brussels, the Belgian capital, is the Grand-Place. Here, flower-sellers display their wares. Every other year a special floral display is held and the square is carpeted with begonias.

Map labels

West Frisian Islands
Ameland
Terscheling
Vlieland
Waddenzee
Leeuwarden
Texel
Barrier Dam
Sneek
Groningen
Assen
IJsselmeer
Emmen
North-East Polder
Alkmaar
Meppel
Markerwaard Polder (planned)
Zaanstad
Flevoland Polder
Zwolle
Almelo
Haarlem **Amsterdam**
NETHERLANDS
Hilversum
Enschede
Leiden
Amersfoort
Apeldoorn
IJssel
Gouda
Utrecht
The Hague
Arnhem
Delft
Lek
Rotterdam
Waal
Nijmegen
Dordrecht
Maas
GERMANY
s'Hertogenbosch
Oosterschelde
Breda
Tilburg
Vlissingen
Eindhoven
Westerschelde
Venlo
Zeebrugge
Ostend
Bruges
Antwerp
St. Niklaas
Genk
Roeslare
Ghent
Mechelen
Heerlen
Hasselt
Maastricht
Aalst
Brussels
Leuven (Louvain)
Kortijk
Vaalserberg 321m
Waterloo
Liège
Verviers
BELGIUM
Huy
Meuse
Tournai
Namur
Spa
Botrange 694m
FRANCE
Schelde
Sambre
Mons
La Louvière
Charleroi
ARDENNES MOUNTAINS
Dinant
GERMANY
Buurgplatz 559m
Bastogne
Libramont
LUXEMBOURG
Luxembourg
Esch-sur-Alzette

Belgium, the Netherlands, and Luxembourg are all small countries lying in a densely populated part of northern Europe. Together they are sometimes referred to as Benelux, the name of an economic union they formed in 1948. In 1957 the same three countries went on to become founder members of the European Economic Community (EEC), the ancestor of today's European Union (EU). All three are democracies. The Netherlands and Belgium are kingdoms, while Luxembourg is a grand duchy.

◑ MELT IN THE MOUTH
Belgium is famous for its luxurious chocolates. Each truffle is handmade, using the finest cocoa.

◐ LIGHT BULBS
Eindhoven is a major industrial center in the central southern Netherlands. It is dominated by Phillips, a Dutch-founded multinational firm that specializes in electrical goods for the home and in electronic technology.

The two most populous provinces of the Netherlands are North and South Holland, and the whole country is often referred to as Holland. The capital is Amsterdam, an old trading port where tall merchants' houses from the 1600s line the canals. It is a center of business and the arts, with a lively youth culture. The government sits at The Hague.

◐ TRAMS IN AMSTERDAM
Amsterdam's trams speed across the old city, crossing rings of canals. They connect Central Station, Dam Square, the old Mint, and the shops of Vijzelstraat, among other important sites.

The Netherlands is a wealthy country. It produces beers, vegetables, and dairy products, and is particularly well known for its cheeses. The fields are brightly colored with tulips in the spring. Bulbs and cut flowers are important exports.

◑ BELGIAN LACEMAKER
A Belgian lacemaker in traditional dress skillfully moves bobbins across a pillow. Cities such as Bruges have been famous for their lace since medieval times.

◑ BRUGES
Known as "the Venice of the north," the port of Bruges in northern Belgium has many picturesque canals and a thriving tourist industry.

◑ BELGIAN BEER
Belgium grows more than 400 tons of barley every year. Much of it goes to the brewing industry.

◑ ROTTERDAM PORT
Rotterdam, in the Dutch province of South Holland, was destroyed by bombing during World War II (1939–45). It was rebuilt and today is Europe's most important seaport.

◑ TULIP BULBS
In spring, when the tulips are blooming, the Dutch bulb fields take on the appearance of a child's coloring book. The Dutch passion for tulips dates back to the 1500s.

The industrial south produces household and electrical goods. Rotterdam is the world's busiest seaport, sprawling across a vast area of 40 sq miles.

◑ EUROPE UNITED
Luxembourg City is home to the EU Parliament and Court of Justice. The flags of EU members fly outside.

Belgium has been famous for its cloth since the Middle Ages and is still a major textile producer. It manufactures steel and chemicals, but coal mining is no longer the great industry it once was. Popular food products include beers, chocolates, and cooked meats from the Ardennes. The Belgian capital is Brussels—the chief administrative center of the EU.

Tiny Luxembourg is home to both the European Parliament and the European Court of Justice. In terms of income per head, it is the world's richest country. Its wealth comes from banking and finance. Wine-making is also important.

Most people in the Netherlands are Dutch, and the Dutch language is spoken everywhere. The Frisians, who live in the north and on the offshore islands, also speak their own language. Many Dutch cities are home to people whose ancestors came from countries formerly ruled by Holland, such as Surinam and the Dutch East Indies (now Indonesia), as well as workers from other parts of Europe.

◑ VINCENT VAN GOGH
The Dutch artist Vincent van Gogh painted this self-portrait after cutting off part of his ear. His landscapes and still-life paintings display the same boldness and original use of color.

◑ THE BIG RACE
The Elfstedentocht, or 11 Towns' Tour, dates back to the 1600s. At 124 miles, it is the longest ice-skating race in the world. It is also the biggest, with as many as 16,000 competitors. The race is normally held in the Netherlands, but if the weather is too warm, it is held somewhere else.

The two peoples native to Belgium are the Flemings of the north, who in their language and customs are very close relatives of the Dutch, and the French-speaking Walloons of the south. There have been violent clashes between the two communities over language and culture. French and German are widely spoken in Luxembourg, along with a local language called Letzebuergesch.

◑ A TRADING EMPIRE
The Dutch East India Company was founded in 1602. Its ships sailed to the Dutch East Indies (now Indonesia) to buy coffee, tea, and spices. On the way, the merchants would stop off at the Cape of Good Hope in southern Africa to stock up on supplies for their voyage.

In ancient times, this region of northern Europe was occupied by both Germanic and Celtic peoples, and lay on the edge of the Roman empire. In the 700s and 800s, it became part of the Frankish empire. During the Middle Ages, rule passed from one family of European nobles to another. As wars of religion tore Europe apart in the 1500s, the Protestant Dutch fought against rule by Roman Catholic Spain. By the 1600s the Netherlands was a wealthy, independent sea power, trading with the Far East. The year 1806 saw the region under French rule, but independence was soon restored.

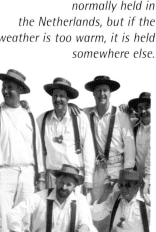

◑ GOUDA CHEESES
Round, yellow Dutch cheeses are laid out and weighed at Alkmaar in North Holland—a glimpse of tradition that is always popular with the many tourists that visit the area.

◑ LANGUAGE RIGHTS DEMONSTRATION
Language rights are a live political issue in Belgium. The Flemings of the north speak Vlaams or Flemish, a dialect of Dutch. The Walloons of the south are French-speakers.

✪ SOCCER CRAZY
Dutch soccer teams, such as Ajax, have won fans all over Europe and the national team is always a major contender in World Cup events.

Belgium broke away from the Netherlands in 1830, and Luxembourg in 1867.

Since the Middle Ages, the region has been a center of scholarship and the arts. Famous philosophers included Erasmus (1466–1536) and Spinoza (1632–77), while great painters included Pieter Breughel (c.1520–69), Rembrandt van Rijn (1606–69), Vincent van Gogh (1863–90), and Piet Mondrian (1872–1944).

✪ ANNE FRANK
Anne Frank (1929–45) was a young Jewish girl who spent two years living in a secret annexe in this house in Amsterdam, when the Germans occupied the Netherlands. In 1944 her family was discovered and deported. Anne died in a concentration camp. Her moving diary of the time spent in hiding has been published in at least 50 languages.

AD	
c.50	River Rhine becomes border of Roman empire
714	Franks rule most of Low Countries
922	Counts of Holland rule Low Countries (until 1384)
963	Luxembourg part of Holy Roman Empire
1384	Burgundy rules Low Countries and Luxembourg (until 1487)
1519	Low Countries part of Habsburg empire
1568	Start of Eighty Years' War against Spanish rule in Netherlands; Belgium remains Spanish
1602	Founding of Dutch East India Company
1648	Netherlands recognized as independent
1700	France rules Belgium (until 1713)
1713	Austria rules Belgium (until 1789)
1795	France rules Low Countries (until 1815)
1815	United Kingdom of the Netherlands
1830	Belgium breaks away from the Netherlands
1867	Luxembourg independent under Dutch monarch
1890	Luxembourg has its own grand duke
1914	World War I (until 1918): Germany invades Belgium; Netherlands neutral
1939	World War II (until 1945): Germany invades Belgium and Netherlands
1948	Benelux economic union formed
1957	Belgium, Netherlands, Luxembourg founder members of EEC (later EU)

EUROPE

THE BRITISH ISLES

The British Isles rise from a continental shelf, an underwater ledge of land extending into the Atlantic Ocean from northwestern Europe. They include about 5,000 small islands and two large ones, Great Britain and Ireland. Warm ocean currents keep the climate moderate, with winds bringing the heaviest rainfall to western coasts. The British Isles are occupied by two nations, the United Kingdom (a union of England, Scotland, Wales, and Northern Ireland) and the Republic of Ireland.

Southern England includes low chalk hills and plains of fertile clay. The River Thames flows into the North Sea, to the south of the flat lands of East Anglia. The rugged peninsula of Cornwall extends southwest toward the Scilly Isles. Northern England includes bleak moors rising to the Pennines—a chain of low mountains—and the Lake District of Cumbria.

To the west, Wales is a country of hills, green valleys, and mountains, bordering the Irish Sea. Across the Scottish border lie fertile lowlands, the island's highest mountain chains, and lakes known as "lochs." Scotland is fringed by the island chains of the Hebrides, Shetlands, and Orkneys.

Ireland is a land of lakes, river estuaries, peat bogs, and green farmland rising to low mountain chains. In the west, tall cliffs and long, sandy beaches meet the Atlantic breakers.

FACTS

UNITED KINGDOM
United Kingdom of Great Britain and Northern Ireland
AREA: 94,251 sq mi.
POPULATION: 58.8 million
CAPITAL: London
HIGHEST POINT: Ben Nevis (4,408 ft)
OFFICIAL LANGUAGES: English, Welsh
CURRENCY: Pound sterling

REPUBLIC OF IRELAND
Eire
AREA: 27,137 sq mi.
POPULATION: 3.8 million
CAPITAL: Dublin
OTHER CITIES: Cork, Limerick
HIGHEST POINT: Carrauntoohil (3,414 ft)
OFFICIAL LANGUAGES: Irish, English
CURRENCY: Euro

○ LOCHS AND ISLES
This castle lies on a tiny island in the middle of Loch Linnhe, on the west coast of Scotland, just south of Ben Nevis.

○ BLUEBELL WOODS
In early May, large areas of woodland in the British Isles are carpeted with sweetly scented wild flowers—bluebells.

44

⟳ THE FORTH BRIDGE

The Forth River flows from the Grampians down to the Firth of Forth. At the estuary, it is crossed by a cantilever railroad bridge, built in the 1880s, and a road suspension bridge completed in 1964.

UNITED KINGDOM

SCOTLAND

⟳ RED SQUIRREL

NORTHERN IRELAND

⟳ EUROPEAN BADGER

⟳ GREEN AND PLEASANT LAND

The county of Yorkshire in northern England has a landscape of rolling dales (valleys) and bleak moors.

ENGLAND

⟳ A ROAD INTO THE SEA

The rocky pillars of the Giant's Causeway, on the coast of Northern Ireland, are formed from a volcanic rock called basalt.

IRELAND

⟳ WARNING LIGHT

Lighthouses guard many reefs and rocks off the stormy coast of Wales.

WALES

45

The United Kingdom (UK) brings together the two kingdoms of England and Scotland, the principality of Wales, and the province of Northern Ireland. All are ruled by a single monarch and have a long history of democracy. In 1997 both Wales and Scotland voted to have their own parliaments.

✪ CROWN JEWELS
The Crown Jewels of the British kings and queens include a dazzling array of gold and precious stones dating back over 1,000 years.

The UK is a member of the European Union (EU). The Isle of Man and the Channel Islands are self-ruling states associated with the UK.

✪ PEAT BOG
Over many thousands of years, large peat bogs have formed in Ireland. This waterlogged turf is cut and dried for fuel in the home and for use in power stations.

The most densely populated area of the UK centers around the capital, London, in southeast England. London is home to about 6.8 million people. On the south coast, a rail tunnel links England with northern France. Other large industrial cities are found in the Midlands and the north. The traditional industries of these regions—coal, textiles, and shipbuilding—have all declined. The economy today is based on finance, services, chemicals, and telecommunications.

Wales is sheep-farming country. The capital, Cardiff, is in the industrialized south, where foreign-owned factories produce goods such as electronic components.

✪ PRIME BEEF
The Aberdeen Angus is a breed of cattle from northeast Scotland, prized for its meat. Its long coat protects it from the cold.

✪ BLACKPOOL LIGHTS
England's most popular seaside resort is Blackpool, on the northwest coast of Lancashire in northern England. Its attractions include the Blackpool Tower, the famous illuminations (lights) and many amusement parks.

☢ LIVERPOOL SKYLINE
Liverpool is a lively city on the River Mersey, in northwest England. During the 1800s and early 1900s it was one of the busiest seaports in the world.

◑ SCOTTISH TRAWLERS

At Mallaig harbor in Scotland, fishing boats return to unload the day's catch. Scottish trawlers bring in over 65 percent of all the fish and shellfish caught in the United Kingdom.

◑ ALL ABOARD!

Southern England and northern France, separated by the waters of the Channel about 10,000 years ago, were linked by a rail tunnel in 1994.

The Scottish capital is the city of Edinburgh. Heavy industry has always been based around Glasgow and the River Clyde. The most important resource is oil, drilled from under the North Sea. Important exports include salmon and Scotch whisky.

Northern Ireland has the industrial city of Belfast as its capital. The province has seen long years of conflict between those who wish to remain within the UK and those who wish to be part of the Republic of Ireland. A 1998 peace agreement set up a devolved Northern Ireland assembly.

◑ MILKING TIME

A cow is milked by hand on a small farm in Ireland. Irish dairy products include delicious butter and cheeses.

◑ SALMON LEAP

Scotland is famous for its freshwater fish. Wild salmon head upriver each year to their spawning grounds.

The capital of the Republic of Ireland is Dublin, on the River Liffey. Ireland's green fields are ideal for dairy farming, while the coasts and rivers provide fishing. Ireland's industries include brewing, glass-making, and computer manufacture. With a long history of poverty, the Irish economy has been transformed in recent years by membership of the EU.

FACTS

ENGLAND
AREA: 50,332 sq mi.
CAPITAL: London
OTHER CITIES: Birmingham, Manchester, Liverpool

NORTHERN IRELAND
AREA: 5,463 sq mi.
CAPITAL: Belfast
OTHER CITIES: Derry, Armagh

SCOTLAND
AREA: 30,406 sq mi.
CAPITAL: Edinburgh
OTHER CITIES: Glasgow, Aberdeen

WALES
AREA: 8,015 sq mi.
CAPITAL: Cardiff
OTHER CITIES: Swansea, Wrexham, Bangor

SELF-GOVERNING ISLANDS
Isle of Man, Guernsey (with six dependencies), Jersey

47

GODDESS OF THE CELTS
The Irish have a strong tradition of story-telling. Many myths date back to the days of the Celts. This statue shows the Celtic horse goddess, Epona, who was worshiped in Europe about 400 BC.

GLOBE THEATER
The Globe was originally built in 1599, on the south bank of the River Thames in London. Many of Shakespeare's plays were first performed there. Now a new Globe has been built.

The English are descended from the many different peoples who settled in the southern part of the United Kingdom over the ages—British Celts, Germanic peoples such as the Angles, Saxons, and Danes, and French-speaking Normans. The English language developed from Anglo-Saxon, but includes many words based on Latin and Norman French. It is the language of some of the world's greatest works of literature, such as the plays of William Shakespeare (1564–1616) and the poetry of John Keats (1795–1821).

The Welsh and Cornish are mostly the descendants of British Celts and are closely related to the Bretons. They have their own languages. Welsh is spoken by about half a million people in Wales and has a literature dating back about 1,400 years. Festivals of music and poetry called *eisteddfodau* are held throughout Wales, where there is a strong tradition of choral singing.

Scots are descended from both Gaelic and British Celts, from a people called the Picts, and from Norse invaders. The Scottish version of the Gaelic language may still be heard in the Highlands and islands, while the Anglo-Scots dialect of the Lowlands was the language of Scotland's national poet Robert Burns (1759–96).

A HINDU TEMPLE
Britain has many Hindu and Sikh temples, Islamic mosques, and Jewish synagogues in addition to its Christian churches.

THE GAME OF CRICKET
The game of cricket was invented in England in the 1700s. It spread from there to Australia, New Zealand, India, Pakistan, South Africa, and the Caribbean.

NATIONAL FLOWERS
Each country in the British Isles has its own national flower. There are the Scottish thistle (1), the Irish shamrock (2), the Welsh daffodil (3), and the English rose (4).

(1)

(2)

⟲ TOWERING ANGEL
Unveiled by artist Antony Gormley in 1998, the much-loved Angel of the North rises 65 feet into the sky. It is the largest sculpture in Britain.

⟳ WELSH ARTS FESTIVALS
At an eisteddfod, *poets, musicians, dancers, and actors of all ages compete in front of judges for honors.*

The Manx people from the Isle of Man, which lies midway between England, Ireland, Scotland, and Wales, are of mixed Celtic and Norse descent, while the Channel Islanders have English, Norman, and French roots.

The Irish are mostly descended from Gaelic Celts, along with some Viking, Norman, English, and Scottish ancestry. The Irish language, a version of Gaelic, is still spoken in some rural areas. Irish authors and poets have used both the Irish and English languages to great effect.

Many other peoples have settled the British Isles over the ages, contributing to the richness and variety of its culture. They include Roma (gypsies), Jews, Italians, Greek and Turkish Cypriots, Afro-Caribbeans, Chinese, Indians, Pakistanis, and Bangladeshis.

⟳ COWES WEEK
Cowes, on the Isle of Wight off southern England, is the setting for an annual yacht race, the Fastnet Cup.

⟳ CHINATOWN
Chinese people see in the Chinese New Year in style. Cities such as London, Liverpool, and Manchester all have lively Chinese districts.

⟳ MANX CAT
The Manx is a tailless breed of cat from the Isle of Man.

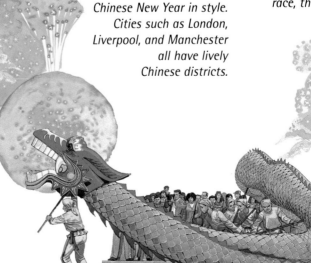

(3)   (4)

About 2,000 years ago, most of Great Britain was occupied by a group of Celtic tribes—the Britons. Picts lived in parts of Scotland, while Ireland was the home of another Celtic group, the Gaels. The Romans invaded in 55 BC and 54 BC and again from AD 43. They failed to conquer the far north and Ireland, but stayed for nearly 400 years.

⟡ SACRED STONES
Massive stones, lined up with the midsummer sunrise, were raised at Stonehenge in southern England between about 3200 and 2000 BC.

After the Romans left, the Britons came under attack from the west by groups of Gaels known as Scots, and from the south and east by Angles and Saxons—Germanic peoples who founded a number of small kingdoms that later became England.

⟡ THE BAYEUX TAPESTRY
In 1066 William, Duke of Normandy, defeated King Harold of England near Hastings. The story of the Norman invasion was recorded in the Bayeux Tapestry.

⟳ WARRIOR QUEEN
Boudicca was queen of a Celtic tribe called the Iceni. In AD 60 she led an uprising against the Roman conquerors of Britain. She captured London, but was then defeated in battle and killed herself.

Gradually the Britons were driven into Wales, Cornwall, and across the Channel to Brittany. Wales, Scotland, and Ireland flourished as centers of Celtic Christian civilization. Large areas of Britain and Ireland were later invaded by Vikings and then by Normans. The Norman kingdom founded in England in 1066 became very powerful, ruling large parts of France.

Wales was formally annexed by England in the 1500s, and the Scottish and English thrones were united in 1603. The United Kingdom, largely Protestant, tightened its grip on Roman Catholic Ireland, which was made part of the union in 1800.

⟳ EDINBURGH CASTLE
Edinburgh, the Scottish capital, was settled over 5,000 years ago. In 1997 the Scots voted to have their own parliament, based in Edinburgh.

By this time, the United Kingdom was becoming the world's first industrialized nation. It ruled a vast overseas empire, from India to Africa and Australia, which gave it raw materials and new markets. Not until the 20th century did the power of the British empire begin to fade, exhausted by two world wars (1914–18 and 1939–45).

TUDOR KING
Henry VIII (1491–1547) was the second Tudor king of England. He made himself head of the Church in England, and married six times.

Southern Ireland became a Free State in 1922 and a fully independent republic in 1949.

During the 1960s, most of Britain's remaining colonies became independent, as Commonwealth members. By 2000, the UK and Irish Republic had moved closer to their European trade partners, within the expanding European Union.

DEATH OF A KING
In 1649 the whole of Europe was shocked when Parliament ordered the execution of King Charles I, after the English Civil War. Britain returned to being a monarchy in 1660, when Charles II was restored to the throne.

POWER TO THE NORTH
After nearly 30 years of communal strife in Northern Ireland, a peace agreement in 1998 devolved power to a new Assembly, with members from Unionist and Nationalist parties.

EAMON DE VALERA
Eamon de Valera (1882–1975) took part in the Easter Rising in Dublin in 1916. He later became President of the Irish Republic.

DOMESDAY BOOK
In 1086 King William I (c. 1028–87) ordered a great survey of people and property in the lands he had conquered 20 years earlier. It was used for legal and taxation purposes until 1522.

51

FRANCE

FACTS

FRANCE
République Française
AREA: 212,936 sq mi.
POPULATION: 59 million
CAPITAL: Paris
OTHER CITIES: Marseille, Lyon
HIGHEST POINT: Mont Blanc
(15,770 ft)
OFFICIAL LANGUAGE: French
CURRENCY: Euro

MONACO
Principauté de Monaco
AREA: 0.75 sq mi.
POPULATION: 0.03 million
CAPITAL: Monaco
OTHER CITIES: Monte Carlo
OFFICIAL LANGUAGE: French
CURRENCY: Euro

France lies at the center of western Europe, between Germany and Spain. To the north it is bordered by the sandy shores and chalk cliffs of the Channel coast and the rocky headlands of Brittany. In the southwest, pine forests and dunes face the stormy Atlantic Ocean. The sun-baked hills of southern France descend to the Mediterranean Sea.

Along the Spanish border, the snowy peaks of the Pyrenees form a high barrier. The Alps, which straddle the border with Italy and Switzerland, soar to 15,770 feet at Mont Blanc. Northward lie the forested slopes of the Jura, Vosges, and Ardennes.

◑ CITY OF ARTISTS
The Montmartre district of the French capital, Paris, is famed for its street artists.

Most of northern France is a rolling plain, now cultivated. It is crossed by the winding River Seine. The volcanic rocks of the Massif Central dominate south-central France, to the west of the Rhône valley. The River Rhône flows south to form a delta on the southern coast, creating the wetland region of the Camargue. The Mediterranean island of Corsica is also French territory. It is mountainous, with olive groves and dry scrubland, called maquis.

Monaco is a tiny state on the Mediterranean coast, surrounded by France. It is a built-up zone, which includes new land reclaimed from the sea.

◑ WATER CARRIER
The Pont du Gard aqueduct in southern France was built 2,000 years ago by the Romans to carry water to the city of Nîmes.

◑ ISLAND OF THE MONKS
Mont-Saint-Michel is linked to the Normandy coast by a tidal causeway. Crowning the island is a Benedictine abbey, built in AD 966 and fortified by thick walls.

A SNOWY PEAK
Mont Blanc in the Alps is western Europe's tallest mountain. A 7.5-mile-long road tunnel was dug beneath the mountain in the 1960s.

ESTEREL, SOUTHERN FRANCE
The southern coast of France borders the Mediterranean. The inviting blue waters and sunny climates make the coast a popular tourist destination.

WILD BOAR

FRANCE

INSECT-EATER
The hoopoe, with its striking crest, is found in southern Europe. Its curved bill is tailor-made for teasing out insects from the bark of trees.

LOIRE RIVER
Straddling the Loire is the castle, or château, of Chenonceaux. The Loire is France's longest river. It stretches for about 630 miles from the Cévennes Mountains to the coast of Brittany.

MONACO

THE LAP OF LUXURY
One of the world's smallest countries, Monaco, attracts very wealthy visitors. The port of its capital, Monaco, is crammed with luxury yachts from around the world.

France is a democratic republic and a founder member of the European Economic Community (EEC), now the European Union (EU). It is one of the world's wealthier countries, and through its former overseas colonies, still has considerable international influence.

The capital, Paris, has a metropolitan population of over nine million people. It is in the center of northern France, on the River Seine. France's second city is Marseille, a large seaport on the coast of the Mediterranean Sea. The country is divided into 22 regions.

The coalfields of northern France have mostly run out. To generate power for industry, France depends heavily on nuclear power and hydroelectric schemes. Alternative energy sources that are harnessed include the sun and tides. French factories produce chemicals, aircraft, cars, and high-speed trains.

Traditionally, France is an agricultural country, and many people across the region still work as farmers. Normandy produces apples and dairy products.

☉ FASHION CAPITAL

A model at the Chanel catwalk show in Paris. Chanel was founded by the great French couturier, Coco Chanel (1883–1971).

☉ SUNFLOWERS

In the fields of southern France, bright yellow sunflowers ripen in the sun. The seeds of the flowers are harvested and then pressed to make sunflower oil.

☉ CHAMPAGNE

☉ HIGH-SPEED TRAIN

The TGV (train à grande vitesse) is a feat of French engineering. This high-speed train can top 310 mph.

☉ FINE WINES

The region of Bordeaux produces some of the world's finest red wines. Many vineyards are attached to a stately home, or château, which gives the wine its name.

The wide range of climates makes it possible to grow many kinds of crops, from wheat and maize to rice.

The warm hillsides of Provence in southern France provide flowers for the perfume industry, particularly lavender. The Loire, Burgundy, and Champagne regions are renowned for their fine wines. Forests in many areas provide timber and there are large fishing fleets in the west.

French cooking is generally thought to produce some of the best dishes in the world—indeed, French is the language of cooking. The catwalks of Paris are the

⟳ FATTENING UP
Pâté de foie gras is a rich pâté made from goose liver. The birds are fattened up on plenty of corn. Every region of France has its own pâté recipe.

⟳ SOFT CHEESES

ultimate achievement of any career as a fashion model. Tourists bring wealth to France too, visiting the Alpine ski resorts, the castles or châteaux of the Loire, and the beaches and yachting marinas of the south.

Although Monaco is such a small country, its tax laws attract many wealthy residents. It is a center of finance, tourism, and gambling, in the famous casino at Monte Carlo.

⟳ APPLES
In Normandy in northern France, farming is smallscale. Dairy farms and apple orchards predominate. The apples are used to make cider and calvados (apple brandy).

⟳ TIDAL BARRIER AT RANCE
France is a major exporter of electricity. Most is generated in nuclear power stations, but the French have also tried "greener" ways to make electricity. Here at St Malo, a massive tidal barrier harnesses the power of the River Rance.

⟳ INTO THE FUTURE
At Futuroscope, a theme park and high-tech college near Poitiers, French architects were given a free reign to create bold, imaginative designs for the 21st century.

⟳ FAST CARS
Motor racing is an important source of income to Monaco. Each year, the Monaco Grand Prix is held, with cars racing around its narrow streets.

EUROPE

The French are descended from many different peoples, including the ancient group of Celtic tribes known as Gauls, and the Franks, a Germanic people. The French language mostly comes from Latin, the language of the Roman empire. It is spoken everywhere in France, although there are great historical differences between French as spoken in the north and the Provençal version of the south.

Since the Middle Ages, the French language has been celebrated by poets, playwrights, storytellers, and philosophers. France has also produced great philosophers, movie-makers, painters, and composers.

☉ FATHER OF COMEDY
Jean Baptiste Poquelin (1622–73) was known as Molière. Many of his plays were performed for King Louis XIV.

☉ ENLIGHTENED TIMES
During the 1700s, France was a center of learning. The writer Denis Diderot (1713–84) compiled a massive 28-volume encyclopedia, which aimed to further all knowledge.

Playwrights such as Corneille (1606–84), Molière (1622–73), and Racine (1639–99), painters such as Monet (1840–1926) and Dégas (1834–1917), and composers such as Debussy (1862–1918) are admired around the world.

Within the French borders there are other peoples besides the French. The Basques and Catalans of the southwest have their own languages and traditions. The homelands of both these peoples extend across the border into Spain. The Corsicans have their own language, and along the eastern borders there are speakers of Italian and German.

The Bretons of the northwest are descended from British Celts who settled the region about 1,500 years ago. Their language is related to Welsh and Cornish.

☉ SACRÉ COEUR
Overlooking the French capital, Paris, is the domed Roman Catholic church of Sacré Coeur ("sacred heart"). Although France does not have an official state religion, most French people follow the Catholic faith.

☉ UP, UP AND AWAY
The Montgolfier brothers, Joseph and Jacques, pioneered the use of hot-air balloons in the 1780s.

A GAME OF BOWLS
Pétanque is a popular game played all over France; most towns have a square of gravel set aside for the game. Players aim to bowl their ball as close as possible to a smaller ball.

THE NAUGHTY NINETIES
In the 1890s, Paris had a reputation for being a city of fun, wild dances such as the can-can, pretty girls, artists, and poets.

The Normans are descended from Viking (Norsemen) invaders, who settled in the region of northern France that became known as Normandy.

Also living in France there are Roma (gypsies) and Jews. North Africans, descended from the citizens of France's former colonies, make up three percent of the French population. Many of these are Muslim, but nine-out-of-ten French people are Roman Catholic.

A hundred years ago the French were mostly a nation of country-dwellers. Today nearly 75 percent of the population live in towns and cities, leaving many rural areas deserted or given over to holiday homes and tourism.

MILITARY TRAINING
France has a military tradition dating back to the Middle Ages. Most men must spend some time in the army doing military service.

TOUR DE FRANCE
Every year, France hosts the world's most famous cycle race, the Tour de France. The grueling course stretches for about 2,500 miles and takes about three weeks to complete.

A TREASURE-TROVE OF ART
The Louvre museum, Paris, houses one of the world's greatest art collections. In the 1980s, a stunning pyramid of steel and glass was built at the entrance to the old museum.

● ICE AGE ART
There are about 600 cave paintings at Lascaux. They show the animals that prehistoric people hunted— bison, stags, and horses.

France has been inhabited since prehistoric times— cave paintings discovered at Lascaux date back to 15,000 BC. The ancient Greeks founded the port of Marseille in about 600 BC, when most of the country was home to a group of Celtic tribes known as the Gauls.

The Gauls were conquered by the Romans between 58 and 48 BC, and the Latin language became widely spoken. Germanic-speaking peoples from beyond the Rhine River began to attack the Roman empire, and by AD 476 it had collapsed. Power passed to the Franks, after whom the modern country is named.

● STANDING STONES
Sited at Carnac, on the coast of Brittany, over 3,000 stone monuments are arranged in avenues and circles. They were erected in Stone Age times.

The Franks beat back invasion attempts by the Moors (Muslim Berbers and Arabs) and founded a great Western European empire under Charlemagne (768–814). Vikings took control of Normandy in 911, but the French kings became very powerful during the later Middle Ages. They battled with their neighbors, especially the English, and expanded the frontiers of their kingdom. From the Middle Ages until the death in 1715 of Louis XIV, the "Sun King," France was seen as the center of European civilization, despite a series of fierce religious wars.

INTO BATTLE
Fierce Frankish armies defeated the Romans, Gauls, and Visigoths in their quest for land. By AD 540 they controlled most of Roman Gaul.

OFF WITH THEIR HEADS!
In the 1780s, the French people, tired of paying exorbitant taxes to their king, rose up in revolt. In the Reign of Terror that followed the Revolution, over 17,000 aristocrats were guillotined.

● BURNED AT THE STAKE
After hearing voices from God, Joan of Arc led the French into battle in the Hundred Years' War. The English burned her as a witch in 1431.

MEDIEVAL FRANCE
A code of fine manners, known as chivalry, grew up in the castles and great houses of France in the Middle Ages.

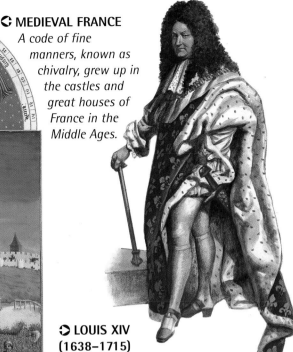

LOUIS XIV (1638–1715)
The "Sun King" ruled France for 72 years, during which time French power in Europe was at its height. He built the magnificent palace of Versailles near Paris.

France began to build up a large empire overseas, but injustice at home led to the outbreak of the French Revolution in 1789. Out of the ruins of this dream of freedom arose a Corsican general named Napoleon Bonaparte, who was crowned emperor in 1804. He led brilliant military campaigns from Spain to Russia and Egypt, but was finally defeated by British and Prussian forces at Waterloo in 1815.

France then suffered a series of invasions by Germany—in 1870, in 1914, and in 1940. After World War II, France lost most of its overseas empire, but encouraged economic and political union in Western Europe.

THE EMPEROR
From his revolutionary beginnings, Napoleon Bonaparte (1769–1821) became the most powerful ruler in Europe. He was a great soldier and law-maker.

GENERAL DE GAULLE
Charles de Gaulle (1890–1970) led the French resistance to the Nazi occupation in World War II.

WE WILL REMEMBER THEM
To this day, the fields of northeastern France are planted with poppies in remembrance of the soldiers who died there in the trenches during World War I. Millions of Allied and German soldiers lost their lives.

TIMELINE

AD

560	Frankish kingdom covers most of France
911	Vikings settle region of France now called Normandy
1297	Grimaldi dynasty rule Monaco
1337	Hundred Years' War against England (until 1453)
1491	France and Brittany united
1638	Birth of Louis XIV, France becomes major European power
1789	Start of the French Revolution
1804	Napoleon Bonaparte crowned emperor
1815	Napoleon defeated by British and Prussians at Waterloo
1848	France becomes a republic again
1852	France returns to being an empire
1870	Prussia defeats France. Revolution of the Paris Commune. The Third Republic
1914	World War I against Germany (until 1918)
1939	World War II against Germany (until 1945): France occupied 1940; Liberation 1944
1957	France founder member of EEC (later EU)
1958	Charles de Gaulle president until 1969
1968	Uprisings by students and workers
1995	Jacques Chirac becomes president

GERMANY

FACTS

GERMANY
Bundesrepublik Deutschland
AREA: 137,820 sq mi.
POPULATION: 82.3 million
CAPITAL: Berlin
OTHER CITIES: Hamburg,
Munich, Cologne
HIGHEST POINT: Zugspitze
(9,720 ft)
OFFICIAL LANGUAGE: German
CURRENCY: Euro

Germany is a country of contrasts. Famous for its busy cities and industrial regions, it also has some of Europe's most spectacular scenery with lakes, steep-sided river valleys, large forests, and snow-capped mountains.

Northern Germany, crossed by the rivers Weser and Elbe, lies on the windy coasts of the North Sea and the Baltic. These are linked by the Kiel Canal, which cuts through Schleswig-Holstein on the Danish border. The land is mostly a wide, flat plain. In central Germany rise the Harz Mountains and Swabian Jura, which drop away to sandy heath and flat farmland, part of the Great Plain that stretches eastward into Poland and Russia. Germany's eastern border lies on the rivers Oder and Neisse. The southwest of Germany is covered by woodland, the Black Forest, while the Bohemian Forest covers the southeast. The busy River Rhine winds northward from the French border, to be joined by the Main at Mainz and the Moselle at Koblenz. It flows through steep valleys covered in vineyards. In the far south are Germany's highest peaks—the Bavarian Alps—an extension of the Alps, the highest mountain chain in Europe. These mountains form a natural barrier between Germany and its southern neighbors.

The climate of the region varies greatly, being generally mild in the west, with harsh winters in the Alps and across the northeastern plains.

◯ ON THE PISTE
Skiing—both downhill and cross-country—is a very popular winter pastime in Germany. The winter resorts attract tourists from all over Europe.

◯ ALONG THE RHINE
The source of the River Rhine is high in the Swiss Alps. Flowing northwest, it passes through Germany and the Netherlands. It is Europe's busiest river. Here, the wine-producing town of Bacharach overlooks the river.

◔ NATURE'S PALETTE

Named for its dark spruces, the Black Forest also includes deciduous trees, that put on a colorful show each fall.

◔ EDELWEISS

GERMANY

NORTH SEA

BALTIC SEA

Sylt
Flensburg
Schleswig
Kiel Bay
Fehmarn
Rügen
Helgoland
Kiel
Mecklenburg Bay
Stralsund
Rendsburg
Neumünster
Rostock
Cuxhaven
Itzehoe
Lübeck
Wismar
Elmshorn
Norderstedt
Schwerin
Güstrow
Neubrandenburg
Wilhelmshaven
Bremerhaven
Hamburg
Emden
Buxtehude
Müritz Lake
Neustrelitz
Papenburg
Oldenburg
Bremen
Lüneburg
Uelzen
Wittenberge
Eberswalde-Finow
Delmenhorst
Weser
Elbe
Nordhorn
Vechta
Nienburg
Celle
Stendal
Berlin
Rheine
Hannover
Aller
Wolfsburg
Brandenburg
Frankfurt (an der Oder)
Osnabrück
Minden
Hildesheim
Brunswick (Braunschweig)
Potsdam
Gronau
Bielefeld
Salzgitter
Magdeburg
Eisenhüttenstadt
Münster
Hameln
Bad Harzburg
Bocholt
Hamm
Holzminden
Halberstadt
Dessau
Cottbus
Dinslaken
Dortmund
Paderborn
Göttingen
Halle
Hoyerswerda
Duisburg
Essen
Arnsberg
Kassel
Münden
Nordhausen
Leipzig
Krefeld
Wuppertal
Remscheid
Mühlhausen
Meissen
Görlitz
Mönchen-Gladbach
Solingen
Bergisch-Gladbach
Erfurt
Weimar
Freiberg
Dresden
Düsseldorf
Cologne (Köln)
Marburg
Jena
Gera
Chemnitz
Aachen
Bonn
Siegen
Alsfeld
Zwickau
Neuwied
Giessen
Fulda
Suhl
Plauen
Daun
Koblenz
Werra
Hof
Trier
Wiesbaden
Frankfurt am Main
Offenbach
Schweinfurt
Coburg
Bayreuth
Mainz
Darmstadt
Würzburg
Bamberg
Worms
Kitzingen
Ludwigshafen
Mannheim
Fürth
Nuremberg (Nürnberg)
Kaiserslautern
Heidelberg
Jagst
Regensburg
Saarbrücken
Karlsruhe
Heilbronn
Pforzheim
Stuttgart
Aalen
Ingolstadt
Passau
Baden-Baden
Tübingen
Danube
Reutlingen
Ulm
Augsburg
Braunau
Freiburg
Memmingen
Munich (München)
Rosenheim
Konstanz
Kempten
Lake Constance (Bodensee)
Zugspitze 2,963 m
Kufstein

GERMANY

NETHERLANDS
BELGIUM
LUXEMBOURG
FRANCE
POLAND
CZECH REPUBLIC
BOHEMIAN FOREST
SWITZERLAND
LIECHTENSTEIN
AUSTRIA

Ems
Rhine
Mosel
Saar
HUNSRÜCK
Rhine
Neckar
BLACK FOREST
SWABIAN JURA
Lech
Inn
Salzach
Main
STEIGERWALD
THURINGIAN FOREST
Main
Leine
HARZ MTS.
TEUTOBURG FOREST
Oder
Neisse
Elbe
Fulda

◔ WHITE GRAPES

Some of Germany's best wines are made from white grapes grown along the sunny banks of the River Rhine.

◔ KAFFEE UND KÜCHEN

Coffee and cakes like these are a special treat in cafés across Germany. A particular favorite is Black Forest gateau, which is coated with dark chocolate.

◔ FAITHFUL FRIEND

The German Shepherd dog is brave and loyal, which makes it an ideal breed for police work. Originally from Germany, it is now found worldwide.

◔ ALPINE HERDS

In spring, when the snows melt, cows are led up to graze the high Alpine pastures. In the fall they return to farms in the valleys.

◗ EAU DE COLOGNE

Germany is a democratic republic, with a federal system of government. This means that its regions, called Länder, have considerable local power. Until 1871 Germany was made up of many different small countries, and it was divided again from 1949 until 1990.

Germany has the strongest economy in Europe and was a founder member of the European Economic Community (today's European Union or EU). It produces electrical goods, optical instruments, chemicals, and cars, and is world-famous for company names such as Bayer, Bosch, Volkswagen, Mercedes, and BMW. German regions are known for their beers, white wines, and sausages.

Germany has to import much of its food. Most farms in Germany are small and run by part-time farmers, who have other jobs as well. The country's industrial growth in the 19th century was boosted by mining of coal reserves near the Ruhr River, but these reserves are almost used up, and Germany now relies on imported oil and gas for much of its energy needs.

◗ ROWS OF BEET
Sugar beet is a major crop in this part of Europe. Traditionally, farms in southern Germany are small family businesses, while on the plains of eastern Germany they are often very large.

◗ FRUIT OF THE VINE
Vineyards were planted in Germany in Roman times. The chief wine-growing areas are in the southwest and the sunny valleys of the Rhine and Moselle rivers.

◗ MEDIEVAL COSTUME
In Baden Württemberg, a festival in medieval costume celebrates the history of the region. Germany in the Middle Ages was made up of many small states.

◗ EUROPEAN GRAY WOLF
Once thought to be extinct in most central European countries, the European gray wolf is making a comeback in Germany. The wolves cross into the country from Poland across the Oder and Neisse rivers.

◐ ANTI-NUCLEAR PROTEST
German demonstrators protest against the transportation of nuclear waste. Environmental issues came to the fore in German politics between the 1970s and 90s, with a party called the Greens gaining wide support.

◑ COMPACT DISKS
Germany today is a major exporter of CDs, high-quality audio systems, radios, and electrical goods for the home, such as refrigerators.

◐ BEER FESTIVALS
Every October a famous beer festival is held in Munich, capital of Bavaria. Regional dress is still common in Bavaria—for women this is often a laced bodice, puffed sleeves, and a wide skirt, often decorated with ribbons.

The country has a fine network of railroads, including high-speed lines, and of highways (autobahns), the construction of which began in the 1930s. The River Rhine and a network of canals are used by freight barges, on a scale greater than anywhere else in Europe.

Germany has many large cities, such as Hamburg, Munich, Cologne, and Frankfurt am Main, which is a center of banking and international trade. Many foreign workers have sought employment in Germany, although the economy suffered from the high costs of reunification and modernizing East German industries in the 1990s. With the collapse of Communism in East Germany, Berlin once again became the capital of the whole country.

◐ THE VOLKSWAGEN
In German, Volkswagen means "people's car." Founded in 1936 to produce cheap, tough family cars, the company had worldwide success from the 1960s onward. Its works at Wolfsburg remain the world's largest.

○ THE PROTESTANT
Martin Luther (1483–1546) was a German monk who condemned corruption in the Roman Catholic Church and wrote a new translation of the Bible. He led the Protestant Reformation.

○ FOLK COSTUME
These dancers wear the traditional costume of Bavaria in southern Germany. The man wears lederhosen *(leather shorts) and the woman a dress called a* dirndl.

○ OBERAMMERGAU
In 1633 a terrible plague struck this village in Bavaria. The survivors vowed to thank God by staging a play about the sufferings of Christ. The play is still put on every 10 years.

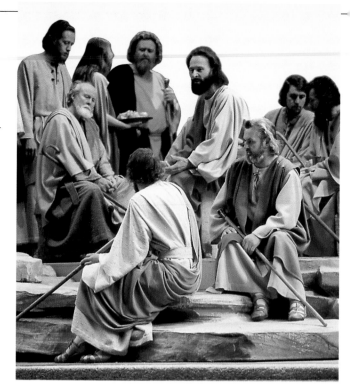

For a long time in its history, the German language was the only unifying element in German culture. German culture was thought of as being that of all those people who spoke German, and this included Austrians.

The standard form of the German language, called Hochdeutsch, is spoken throughout Germany, but there are also many regional dialects that vary greatly from north to south. In the last forty years or so, many workers from southern Europe and Turkey have also settled in German cities. The north is a stronghold of the Protestant faith, while the south is largely Roman Catholic. There are many traditional festivals and customs, with carnival being celebrated as a major festival from Cologne southward into Bavaria and Austria.

Germany has a long cultural history, dating from before the emergence of a single German state. It was the birthplace of the painter Albrecht Dürer (1471–1528), one of the great artists of the European Renaissance. Though German art has never rivaled that of France or Italy, German painters have produced works of striking individuality, among them those of the 19th-century Romantic painter Caspar David Friedrich and 20th-century Expressionists such as Max Beckmann.

○ LIFE OBSERVED
Fine detail characterizes the drawings of Albrecht Dürer, the greatest German artist of his day. Born in 1471, Dürer produced hundreds of paintings, engravings, and woodcuts.

SPEAK... GERMAN

hello	guten Tag
goodbye	auf Wiedersehen
thank you	danke
please	bitte
yes	ja
no	nein
school	schule
children	kinder

KARL MARX
Born at Trier in 1818, Marx showed how history is driven by economic forces and called on workers to seize power. His ideas inspired Communists long after his death in 1883.

Germany is particularly noted for its music. It has produced many of the finest composers: Bach, Handel, Beethoven, Mendelssohn, Schumann, Brahms, Wagner, and Richard Strauss. German orchestras, conductors, instrumentalists, and singers have achieved international renown.

Germany has also produced a number of great writers and thinkers, among them Kant (1724–1804), Goethe (1749–1832), and Schiller (1759–1805). In the 19th century, Germany was a center for new technology and new political ideas. The founder of Communist theory, Karl Marx, was German. So too were the pioneers of the motor car, Karl Benz and Gottfried Daimler, and Wilhelm Roentgen who discovered X-rays in 1895. In the field of medicine, Germany's Robert Koch made discoveries about the links between bacteria and disease.

PRINTING PIONEER
Johannes Gutenberg was a pioneer of printing with movable type. Born at Mainz in 1400, he moved to Strasbourg and set up a printing press there, perhaps as early as 1439.

THE YOUNG MOZART
German culture flowered outside what is today Germany. The composer Mozart, born in Salzburg (Austria) in 1756, spoke German. In the 18th century, imperial Austria with its rich artistic life at Vienna, where Mozart was court musician, began losing ground to Prussia, the emerging military power among the German states.

German architecture ranges from the medieval magnificence of cathedrals at Cologne and Ulm to the 20th-century innovations of the Bauhaus school, founded in 1919 by the architect Walter Gropius and influential far beyond Germany.

This region was once the home of Celtic tribes, but by about 550 BC they had mostly been driven out by Germanic peoples from the north and east. The Romans only succeeded in conquering parts of Germany, founding cities such as Cologne. It was Germanic tribes who finally broke the power of Rome in AD 476.

Germany lay within the Frankish empire, which was ruled by Charlemagne (742–814). After it broke up, a new Holy Roman Empire followed. Lasting from 962 to 1806, the empire encompassed a vast area of Central Europe—a patchwork of small kingdoms, principalities, and cities. These fell under the overall rule of the Austrian Habsburg family.

In the 1500s, parts of Germany became Protestant, following the teachings of a monk named Martin Luther. Bitter religious wars followed. The Thirty Years' War (1618–48) devastated most of the country.

✪ THE THIRTY YEARS' WAR

In 1618, a quarrel broke out between the Protestants in Bohemia and their Austrian rulers, who were Roman Catholic. This rapidly grew into a religious war that engulfed most of western Europe. Starvation and atrocities were common. Peace came with the Treaty of Westphalia, which recognized the rights of Protestants in Germany.

During the 1700s power shifted northward, as a state called Prussia built up a large, modern army. By 1871 the king of Prussia, Wilhelm I, was emperor of a united Germany.

✪ OTTO VON BISMARCK

Bismarck was a powerful Prussian statesman who engineered the Franco–Prussian War and created a united Germany in 1871.

During World War I (1914–18) Germany and Austria suffered disastrous defeat. Germany became a republic, but Communists and national socialists ("Nazis") fought each other on the streets. By the 1930s the Nazis were in power.

NAZI LEADER ✪

Adolf Hitler was born in Austria. Embittered by World War I, he preached violent and racist right-wing politics. He became leader of the Nazi Party and dictator of Germany, taking it to war in 1939.

✪ RIOTS IN BERLIN

1848 was the "Year of Revolutions" across Europe, and Berlin was one of the main centers of unrest. Women and children were attacked by Prussian soldiers as demands for reform and a united Germany were crushed.

○ GERMAN FOKKER E1
MONOPLANE

The Nazis annexed Austria, and German
troops invaded much of Europe during
World War II (1939–45). Their leader, a racist
dictator named Adolf Hitler (1889–1945),
ordered the murder of millions of Jews. Nazi
Germany was defeated by the Allies.

It was next divided into two countries, a
Federal Republic in the west, supported by
the United States and Western Europe, and a
Communist Democratic Republic in the east,
supported by the Russians. Germany was
not reunited until 1990.

○ **DRESDEN BOMBED**
*As World War II drew to a close,
German cities were relentlessly bombed
by Allied aircraft. The city of Dresden,
with its fine old buildings and priceless
works of art, was destroyed in a great
firestorm. Up to 130,000 people were
killed in the air-raids.*

↻ **END OF THE WALL**
*Germany was divided after World
War II. East Germans built a wall
across Berlin in 1961 and shot
anyone trying to escape. It was
finally knocked down in 1989.*

TIMELINE

AD

1282	Rise of Habsburg dynasty in Austria
1517	Luther starts the Protestant Reformation
1618	Thirty Years' War (until 1648)
1740	War of the Austrian Succession (until 1748)
1806	France defeats Prussia at Jena
1834	Prussia unites with small German states
1848	Revolution in Germany; failed
1870	Prussia defeats France
1871	Wilhelm I of Prussia, emperor of united Germany
1914	World War I (until 1918): Central powers (Germany, Austria–Hungary) defeated
1919	Weimar republic set up after emperor abdicates
1933	Hitler becomes German Chancellor
1938	Germany annexes Austria
1939	World War II (until 1945): Axis powers (Germany, Italy, and allies) invade much of Europe; defeated by Allies
1949	Germany is split into Federal Republic (West, capitalist) and Democratic Republic (East, Communist)
1957	German Federal Republic founder member of EEC (later EU)
1961	East and West Berlin divided by fortified wall (until 1989)
1990	Germany reunited after collapse of Communist rule in East Germany; Berlin is national capital again

IBERIAN
PENINSULA

The Iberian peninsula is a great block of mainland Europe that juts out into the Atlantic Ocean. It is narrowly separated from North Africa by the Strait of Gibraltar, and its southern shores border the Mediterranean Sea.

The peninsula is largely mountainous. The snow-capped Pyrenees run along the border with France. The Cantabrian ranges, which include the Picos de Europa, run parallel with the north coast, while southern ranges include the Sierra Nevada. Much of the central region is a sun-baked plateau called the Meseta. Major European rivers rise in the mountains. They include the Ebro, Guadalquivir, Duero, Tagus, and Guadiana.

Most of the Iberian peninsula is taken up by Spain. Portugal occupies the southwestern part, facing the Atlantic Ocean. Andorra is a little state high in the Pyrenees, while Gibraltar, a sheer rock guarding the entrance to the Mediterranean, is a British colony. Spain also takes in the Balearic island chain in the Mediterranean, the Canary Islands (geographically a part of Africa), and two ports on the coast of Morocco. Portugal governs Madeira and the Azores.

Although the northern Iberian coast is green and moist, most of the central region is hot and dry, with parts turning to desert.

⟳ IN THE PYRENEES
The Pyrenees Mountains run from the Bay of Biscay to the Mediterranean coast, a distance of more than 270 miles. Rushing streams descend from high peaks, which rise to 11,170 feet above sea level.

⟳ OLIVE GROVES
Olive trees thrive in the arid climate and dusty soil of southwest Spain and Portugal. The fruit are pressed to make oil or eaten whole.

FACTS

ANDORRA
Principat d'Andorra
AREA: 175 sq mi.
POPULATION: 0.1 million
CAPITAL: Andorra la Vella
HIGHEST POINT: Coma Pedrosa (9,665 ft)
OFFICIAL LANGUAGE: Catalan
CURRENCY: Euro

PORTUGAL
República Portuguesa
AREA: 31,515 sq mi.
POPULATION: 10.3 million
CAPITAL: Lisbon
OTHER CITIES: Porto, Setúbal
HIGHEST POINT: Estrela (9,721 ft)
OFFICIAL LANGUAGE: Portuguese
CURRENCY: Euro

SPAIN
Reino de España
AREA: 195,365 sq mi.
POPULATION: 40 million
CAPITAL: Madrid
HIGHEST POINT: Pico de Teide (Canary Islands, 12,198 ft)
OFFICIAL LANGUAGE: Spanish
CURRENCY: Euro

DEPENDENCIES
Gibraltar (UK)

⟳ BARBARY APE
A legend says that when the apes leave Gibraltar, so will the British.

⟳ CITRUS HARVEST

In spring, Seville is filled with the sweet scent of orange blossom. Seville's bitter oranges are used for making marmalade.

⟳ SPLIT TOWN

The old town of Ronda in Spain's Andalucia region is divided by a river gorge, El Tajo. Sheer rock faces drop for 426 feet. The two halves are linked by a stunning bridge.

ANDORRA

PORTUGAL

SPAIN

GIBRALTAR

Bay of Biscay

Cape Ortegal
Cape Peñas
La Coruña · El Ferrol
Carballo · Villalba · Oviedo · Gijón · Llanes · Santander
Cape Finisterre · Fonsagrada · CANTABRIAN · MOUNTAINS · Bilbao · San Sebastián
Santiago de Compostela · Lugo · Reinosa · Vitoria · Pamplona · PYRENEES · FRANCE
Sarria · Ebro · ANDORRA
Lalin · León · Osorno · Burgos · Logroño · Pico de Aneto 3,404m · Andorra la Vella
Vigo · Miño · Monforte de Lemos · Astorga · Villada · Soria · Saragossa · Cinca · Lérida · Figueras
Orenes · SIERRA CABRERA · La Gudina · Esla · Palencia · Arga · Gállego · Ebro · Manresa · Gerona
Braga · Baltar · Valladolid · Zamora · Duero · Caspe · Reus · Tarrasa · Costa Brava
Braganca · Mogadouro · Medina del Campo · SPAIN · Jalón · Tarragona · Barcelona
Porto · Vila Real · Tormes · Segovia · Tajuña · Tajo · Vinaroz · Cape Tortosa · Costa Dorada
Lamego · Douro · Salamanca · SIERRA DE GUADARRAMA · Guadalajara · Morella · Tortosa · Costa del Azahar
PORTUGAL · Avila · Alcalá de Henares · Teruel · Castellón de la Plana
Aviero · Viseu · Cuidad Rodrigo · MADRID · Aranjuez · Mijares · Sagunto
Guarda · SIERRA DE GREDOS · Béjar · Cuenca · Turia · Valencia · Menorca
Coimbra · Covilhã · Plasencia · Tajo · Toledo · Requena · Gulf of Valencia · Mallorca · Mahón
Leiria · Castelo Branco · MONTES DE TOLEDO · Júcar · Alcira · Ibiza · Palma · Manacor
Tomar · Tagus · Cáceres · Trujillo · Villarrobledo · Albacete · BALEARIC ISLANDS
Caldas de Rainha · Portalegre · Daimiel · Manzanares · Aimansa · Ibiza · Formentera
Santarèm · Badajoz · Don Benito · Guadiana · Ciudad Real · Alcaraz · Alcoy · Cape Neo
LISBON · Évora · Almendralejo · Puertollano · Valdepeñas · SIERRA DE SEGURA · Yecla · Alicante
Setúbal · Ardila · Pozoblanco · SIERRA MORENA · La Carolina · Moratalla · Elche · Costa Blanca
Azuaga · Linares · Cehegín · Orihuela
Beja · Guadiana · Constantina · Córdoba · Jaén · Segura · Murcia
Chança · Nerva · Guadalquivir · Martos · Lorca · Cartagena · Cape Palos
Lagos · Huelva · Seville · Puente Genil · Guadix · Baza · Aguilas · Costa Blanca
Faro · Algarve · Osuna · Genil · Granada · Huércal Overa · Costa Blanca
Cape Saint Vincent · Costa de la Luz · Las Marismas · Morón de la Frontera · Antequera · ▲ Mulhacén 3,478m · Almería
Gulf of Cadiz · Ronda · SIERRA NEVADA · Berja · Cape Gata
Jerez de la Frontera · SIERRA DE RONDA · Málaga · Motril · Costa del Sol
Cádiz · Marbella · MEDITERRANEAN SEA
Gibraltar (U.K.)
Algeciras
Strait of Gibraltar · Cueta (Spain)
Melilla (Spain)

⟳ PARDEL LYNX

BURROS ⟳

⟳ WHITE STORKS

⟳ THE ROCK

You can see the African coast from the 1,394-feet-high Rock of Gibraltar.

FISH AND FISHING
Fishing is a traditional part of the economy along the coasts of Spain and Portugal. In recent years there have been clashes with the fishing fleets of other EU countries over catch quotas.

CITY VISIONS
A sculpture of gold dazzles the eye in Barcelona, the chief city of the Catalonia region, Spain. Barcelona is famous as a center of culture and the arts.

The three independent Iberian nations are all democracies, although Portugal and Spain were dictatorships until the 1970s and Andorra was not fully democratic until 1993. Spain is now ruled by a king, while Portugal is a republic. Both have been members of the European Union (EU) since 1986. This has improved the standard of living, which in the past was generally very poor.

The warm climate means that a wide variety of crops can be grown, including oranges, lemons, olives, melons, and sunflowers. Portugal obtains cork from a kind of oak tree. Both Portugal and Spain have vineyards, and wines, sherries, and ports are produced. There are large fishing fleets. The catch includes sardines, tuna, anchovies, and cod. The food of the region includes spicy sausages, paella (a dish of rice mixed with seafood, chicken, or ham, vegetables and garlic) and all sorts of delicious snacks, or tapas.

There are reserves of iron, coal, and copper, and factories produce cars and textiles.

CASKS OF PORT
Port takes its name from Porto, a town in Portugal. It is a strong, dark, sweet wine that is aged in oak barrels, and is traditionally drunk after dinner.

SPANISH POLICE
Spanish mounted police exercise their horses. There are three police forces in Spain—the Guardia Civil, the Municipal Police, and the National Police. Each has different responsibilities.

○ ROPE-MAKING
Spain produces a large number of fiber crops, including cotton, flax, hemp, and esparto grass. These are used in the manufacture of rope, yarn, fabrics, textiles, and paper.

○ FORESTS OF CORK
Portuguese trees called cork oaks have a thick bark which can be harvested repeatedly to provide cork. This traditional industry is being threatened by the introduction of plastic stoppers for wine bottles.

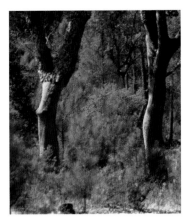

A major industry throughout the region is tourism, with northern Europeans flocking to the sunny beaches of Spain's Costa del Sol, Portugal's Algarve, the Canary Islands, and Majorca (the largest of the Balearic Islands).

About two-thirds of Portuguese are country-dwellers, but over three-fourths of the Spanish population now live in towns and cities. Many of the towns have historic centers with impressive castles, palaces, and cathedrals, and industrial suburbs. The Spanish capital is Madrid, which is located in the middle of the country, on the hot Meseta. Spain's second city is Barcelona, a lively cultural and commercial center on the Mediterranean coast. Lisbon, the Portuguese capital, is a seaport at the mouth of the River Tagus.

○ ON THE BEACH
Tourism has brought wealth to Spain, but has had a major impact on the Spanish environment. Hotels line the southern coasts and many remote regions are dotted with campsites.

○ PAELLA

○ INTREPID SAILOR
This statue celebrates the pioneering Portuguese navigator, Vasco de Gama (c. 1460–1524). He discovered a new route to the East around the southern tip of Africa.

○ INDUSTRIAL SPAIN
Spain is one of Europe's major producers of cars and other vehicles, with factories in Madrid, Barcelona, Valencia, and Saragossa. Vehicles are the country's most important export.

71

Spanish, officially based on Castilian, the form of the language spoken in the old kingdom of Castile, is spoken throughout Spain. Portuguese is spoken throughout Portugal. Both languages have spread around the world and are spoken in Central and South America. Many other languages and dialects may also be heard in the Iberian peninsula and its islands.

The Basques, who live in the northeast and in France, speak Euskara, which is not related to any other known language. They are a very ancient European people, with a history of seafaring. The Galicians of the northwest claim Celtic ancestry: their language, Galician, is related to Portuguese. The region of Catalonia is centered on Barcelona, and extends into Andorra and France. It also has its own language, Catalan. Roma (gypsies) have influenced the dance and music of Spain's Andalucia region. The Canary Islanders include descendants of the Guanche, a people related to the Berbers of North Africa.

☉ RED RAG TO A BULL
Bullfighting is a very ancient tradition in Spain and tens of thousands of bulls are still killed each year. It has many fans and many opponents.

☉ CERAMIC TILES
The Iberian peninsula is famed for its fine ceramics. These tiles grace the Plaza de España in Seville, which was built in 1929 for a large exhibition.

The modern national borders of the Iberian peninsula do not match those of the peoples and cultures. The Basques continue to call for independence. This has led to some power being devolved from central government, but a violent separatist campaign continues in the Basque country.

The Iberian peninsula has a rich cultural history. Its writers have included Portugal's greatest poet, Luis de Camões (1524–80), Miguel de Cervantes (1547–1616), who wrote the Spanish classic *Don Quixote*, the Spanish painter Francisco de Goya (1746–1828), and the Catalan architect Antonio Gaudí (1852–1926).

☉ FAIRYTALE ARCHITECTURE
The best-known example of Antonio Gaudí's surreal style of architecture is the Sagrada Familia church in Barcelona. He worked on this building from 1884 until his death in 1926.

☉ THE ALHAMBRA
This royal palace and fortress was built by the Moorish rulers of Granada, Spain, between the 1000s and the 1400s. It is one of the world's most beautiful buildings.

✪ SQUASHED TOMATOES

The town of Buñol in the eastern province of Valencia, Spain, holds an unusual festival every August. During the Tomatina, people pelt each other with tomatoes!

The region is strongly Roman Catholic, and everyday life is marked by colorful festivals in which statues of the Virgin Mary and saints are carried through the streets. Other festivals celebrate historical battles, trading fairs, horse-riding, and bullfighting. Traditional costume is worn for many of these events. Popular folk music includes the fiery flamenco music of Andalucia and soulful Portuguese songs known as fado.

✪ ART IN BILBÃO

The new Guggenheim Museum of Modern Art is in Bilbão, in the Basque country. The gallery's titanium exterior is designed to look like rolling waves. The collection inside includes works by Spanish-born Pablo Picasso (1881–1973).

✪ SWIRLING SKIRTS

The passionate flamenco is danced to the music of guitars, sometimes with castanets. It comes from around Seville and Cádiz.

✪ LIVING FAITH

The Iberian peninsula is strongly Roman Catholic. Almost every town or village honors its patron saint. Holy Week, the week before Easter, is marked with festivals (fiestas) and processions.

Prehistoric cave paintings at Altamira, in northern Spain, date back to 12,000 BC. Many different peoples settled in the region in ancient times, including Iberians from North Africa and Celts from Europe. They were followed in ancient times by Phoenicians, Greeks, Romans, and Jews. From about 200 BC until AD 475, Spain was a very important part of the Roman empire. Modern Spanish and Portuguese both developed from Latin, the language of ancient Rome.

�9 CAVE PAINTINGS
The prehistoric artists of Altamira painted the bulls, boars, and buffalo that they hunted. For color, they used red ochre from the soil and black soot.

�9 THE HEROIC KNIGHT
Rodrigo Díaz was born at Burgos in about 1043. He was a Christian knight who mostly fought against the Moors, although sometimes he fought for them. He captured Valencia in 1094, and became known as El Cid (from the Moorish Sidi, or "lord").

The next invaders were Germanic peoples, including Franks and Visigoths. From AD 711, they were pushed back to the far north by armies of Moors—Berbers and Arabs—invading from North Africa. The lands ruled by these Muslims became known as al-Andalus. Great cities with fine palaces and mosques were built. From the north, Christian armies began to fight to regain control—not completed until 1492.

The patchwork of small Catholic kingdoms gradually joined together during the Middle Ages.

Spain was united in 1512, and ruled Portugal, too, from 1586 to 1646. Seafarers from both countries led European exploration and colonization of the Americas, and traded with Africa and the Far East. They looted, fought, and traded around the world, and became very wealthy and powerful.

However, wars with other European nations weakened both countries. In the 1800s their American colonies mostly broke away from European rule.

Spain was torn apart by a bitter civil war between 1936 and 1939. A fascist dictator, General Franco (1892–1975), ruled Spain until 1975, when it became a kingdom once again.

Portugal, too, was ruled by dictators for 50 years, from 1926. It gave up its remaining colonies in Africa, and the region as a whole became seen once again as being central to the development of Western Europe, rather than as a backwater.

�9 PHILIP II
Born in 1527, Philip II became one of the most powerful and ruthless Spanish kings.

�9 THE REBEL
Spain lost its huge South American empire in the 1800s. Argentinean-born José de San Martín (1778–1850) helped to liberate his native country, as well as Chile and Peru.

◗ DEMOCRATIC PORTUGAL
After long years of dictatorship, Portugal celebrated its return to democracy in 1976.

◖ LISBON, 1755
In the early 1700s, the Portuguese capital was a wealthy city with many fine buildings. In November 1755 it was destroyed by a terrible earthquake just out to sea, which caused floods and fires. Ten thousand people died.

◔ FERDINAND MAGELLAN
This Portuguese seafarer, in Spanish service, set sail for the Americas in 1519. He sailed on to the Pacific, but was killed in the Philippines in 1521. His ship returned to Spain, becoming the first to sail around the world.

◔ THE GENERAL
In 1936 Francisco Franco launched an attack on Spain's government. After three years of civil war, assisted by Nazi Germany, he came to power in 1939.

TIMELINE

AD	
264	Germanic invasions
711	First Moorish invasion
1085	Christians capture Toledo
1086	Second Moorish (Almoravid) invasion
1143	Portugal an independent kingdom
1147	Third Moorish (Almohad) invasion
1212	Moors defeated at Las Navas de Tolosa
1278	Status of Andorra confirmed
1440s	Portugal expands overseas
1479	Kingdoms of Castile and Aragon unite
1492	Fall of Granada, last Moorish kingdom; Columbus sails to the Americas
1516	Carlos I, of the Austrian Habsburg dynasty, becomes king of Spain
1586	Portugal under Spanish rule (until 1646)
1701	War of Spanish Succession (until 1713)
1713	Gibraltar becomes British
1807	French begin occupation of Iberia (until 1814)
1919	Conflict with anarchists in Barcelona
1926	Dictatorship in Portugal (until 1976)
1936	Spanish Civil War (until 1939, when Franco becomes Spanish dictator)
1975	Spain becomes democratic monarchy
1982	Basque demands for independence
1986	Spain and Portugal join EEC (later EU)

75

ITALY
AND ITS NEIGHBORS

FACTS

ITALY
Repubblica Italiana
AREA: 116,324 sq mi.
POPULATION: 57.4 million
CAPITAL: Rome
OTHER CITIES: Milan,
Naples, Turin
HIGHEST POINT: Monte
Bianco (Mont Blanc)
(15,771 ft)
OFFICIAL LANGUAGE: Italian
CURRENCY: Euro

MALTA
Repubblika ta' Malta
AREA: 122 sq mi.
POPULATION: 0.4 million
CAPITAL: Valletta
OFFICIAL LANGUAGES:
Maltese, English
CURRENCY: Maltese lira

SAN MARINO
Repubblica di San Marino
AREA: 24 sq mi.
POPULATION: 0.03 million
CAPITAL: San Marino
OFFICIAL LANGUAGE: Italian
CURRENCY: Euro

VATICAN CITY
Stato della Città del Vaticano
AREA: 0.17 sq mi.
POPULATION: 1,000
CAPITAL: Vatican City
OFFICIAL LANGUAGES: Latin,
Italian
CURRENCY: Euro

AUSTRIA
Republik Österreich
AREA: 32,377 sq mi.
POPULATION: 8.1 million
CAPITAL: Vienna
OTHER CITIES: Graz, Linz,
Salzburg
HIGHEST POINT: Gross
Glockner (12,461 ft)
OFFICIAL LANGUAGE: German
CURRENCY: Euro

LIECHTENSTEIN
Fürstentum Liechtenstein
AREA: 61.78 sq mi.
POPULATION: 0.03 million
CAPITAL: Vaduz
HIGHEST POINT: Vorder-
Grauspitz (8,395 ft)
OFFICIAL LANGUAGE: German
CURRENCY: Swiss franc

The Alps form the highest mountain chain in western Europe. Switzerland, at the western end of this range, is a land of lakes, forests, high meadows, and icy summits. To the east lies the tiny state of Liechtenstein. The great Alpine peaks of Austria descend to fertile plains around the river Danube. Stretching southward is the Italian peninsula—a long, narrow strip of land jutting far out into the Mediterranean Sea.

In northern Italy, the mountains drop to a low-lying plain around the river Po, a patchwork of fields and towns fringed by coastal marshes and lagoons around the city of Venice. Flat lands also border Slovenia, to the east of the Dolomite range. The Apennine Mountains run down the spine of the peninsula, with fertile, vine-covered slopes descending to the coast. In the far south are dusty plains and scrub-covered hills. Earthquakes and volcanic eruptions are a danger.

Offshore lie a number of small islands, such as Elba, Ischia, Capri, and the Lipari Islands. There are two large islands as well, Sardinia and Sicily. Far to the south, between Sicily and the North African coast, are the islands which make up the small independent nation of Malta.

⊙ VENETIAN ROOFTOPS
Venice is built on a lagoon and is criss-crossed by canals. The only way to cross the city is on foot or by gondola, water taxi, or water bus.

⊃ TUSCAN LANDSCAPE
In Tuscany, a region in central Italy, medieval hilltop towns overlook fertile plains and rolling hills covered in vineyards and olive groves.

LIECHTENSTEIN

AUSTRIA

SWITZERLAND

VATICAN CITY

MALTA

SAN MArino

ITALY

Map labels: CZECH REPUBLIC, GERMANY, AUSTRIA, HUNGARY, SLOVENIA, SWITZERLAND, LIECHTENSTEIN, FRANCE, MONACO, Vaduz, Vienna, Passau, Linz, Krems, St Pölten, Baden, Bruck, Neusiedler See, Braunau, Wels, Steyr, Gmunden, Hallein, Salzburg, Wiener Neustadt, Kitzbühel, Innsbruck, Bremer, Leoben, Kapfenberg, Graz, Klagenfurt, Wolfsberg, Villach, Drava, Schaffhausen, Konstanz, Winterthur, St Gallen, Lake Constance (Bodensee), Basel, Baden, Zurich, Zug, Solothurn, Bern, Lucerne, Andermatt, Chur, Davos, Neuchâtel, Fribourg, Interlaken, St Moritz, Lake Neuchâtel, Zugspitze 2,963 m, Grossglockner 3,803 m, HOHE TAUERN, Lausanne, Montreux, Thun, BERNESE ALPS, LEPONTINE ALPS, Locarno, Bellinzona, Bolzano, Lake Geneva, Thonon, Geneva, Martigny, Zermatt, Matterhorn 4,478 m, Monte Rosa 4,634 m, Lugano, Mont Blanc 4,807m, Biella, L. Maggiore, Como, L. Garda, Trento, Borgo, Udine, Trieste, Lecco, Bergamo, Monza, Brescia, Verona, Vicenza, Piave, Treviso, Portogruaro, Venice, Turin, Milan, Pavia, Lodi, Cremona, Mantova, Padua, Chioggia, Ticino, Oglio, Po, Adria, Alessandra, Tanaro, Novi Ligure, Piacenza, Parma, Carpi, Panaro, Ferrara, Comacchio, Cuneo, Savona, Genoa, Reggio nell'Emilia, Modena, Reno, Ravenna, Gulf of Genoa, La Spezia, Carrara, Bologna, Rimini, Forlì, LIGURIAN SEA, Massa, Lucca, Pistoia, Florence, Arno, San Marino, Pesaro, Viareggio, Pisa, Livorno, Ancona, Caprala, Siena, Arezzo, Gubbio, Iesi, Macerata, Cortona, Piombino, L. Trasimeno, Perugia, San Benedetto, Elba, Grosseto, L. Bolsena, Terni, Teramo, Corno Grande 2,912m, Giglio, Pescara, Civitavecchia, Vatican City (in Rome), Vasto, Rome, Avezzano, Termoli, L. Varano, Latina, Agnone, Foggia, Isernia, Benevento, Otranto, Bari, Gulf of Gaeta, Naples, Melfi, Altamura, Vesuvius 1,227m, Ischia, Salerno, Potenza, Taranto, Brindisi, Gulf of Naples, Capri, Lecce, Gallipoli, Tricase, Gulf of Taranto, Belvedere Marittimo, Rossano, Cosenza, Crotone, Catanzaro, Salina, Stromboli, Vibo Valentia, LIPARI ISLANDS, Lipari, Vulcano, Reggio di Calabria, Cape San Vito, Palermo, Messina, Trapani, Alcamo, Mt. Etna 3,340m, Mazara del Vallo, Catania, Agrigento, Caltanissetta, Gulf of Catania, Pantelleria, Syracuse, Gulf of Gela, Ragusa, MALTA CHANNEL, MALTA, Corsica (France), Strait of Bonifacio, Asinara, Gulf of Asinara, Olbia, Alghero, Sassari, Nuoro, Gulf of Orosei, Sardinia, Tirso, Oristano, San Pietro, Cagliari, Gulf of Cagliari

○ BY THE SEASIDE
The fishing town of Positano lies on Italy's stunning Amalfi coast. Its buildings cling to the steep slopes.

○ A ROYAL RESIDENCE
This castle is home to the prince of Liechtenstein. It overlooks the capital, Vaduz. Parts of the castle date back to 1500s.

○ THE MALTESE CAPITAL
Since the 1500s, sailors entering the natural harbor of Valletta have been greeted by the dome of its cathedral.

○ AUSTRIAN TIROL
The province of Tirol in western Austria is a region of lush mountain pastures. In winter, these are buried under a thick blanket of snow.

☼ MOUNTAIN HOMES
Timber-built houses, called chalets, may be seen all over the Alps. They have broad roofs to protect against winter snowfall.

⟲ CITY OF STYLE
Milan is the fashion capital of Italy. Famous fashion houses include Gucci, Prada, Armani, and Valentino.

Switzerland is a neutral country. Both the Red Cross and the World Health Organization have their headquarters there. Its wealth comes from international banking, tourism, and making tools, instruments, chemicals, and cheese. Neighboring Liechtenstein is a democratic principality. It shares the same currency as Switzerland, and is also a center of banking and winter sports. Austria is a democratic republic. The mountain slopes provide timber for the mills and water for hydroelectric power. Vienna, the capital, is one of Europe's great historical cities.

The Republic of Italy occupies almost all the Italian peninsula, as well as Sardinia and Sicily. Its capital is the ancient city of Rome, on the River Tiber. Italy is a democratic country. It was the Treaty of Rome, signed in 1957, which set up the European Economic Community (today's European Union, or EU).

The wealthiest and most industrialized part of the country is the north, which is linked to the rest of western Europe by road and rail tunnels through the Alps. The south of the country remains poor. Over the years, many of Italy's workers have emigrated to northern Europe, the United States, Argentina, and Australia.

Nearly 70 percent of Italians are now city-dwellers, but agriculture is still very important.

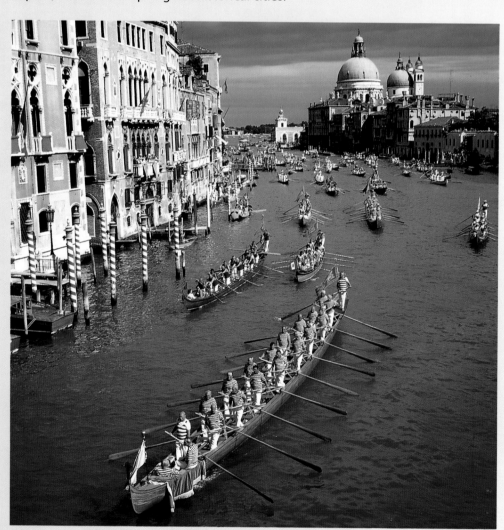

☼ VENICE REGATTA
Every year in September, Venice celebrates its history with a series of costumed regattas. Gondolas, gilded barges, and oared racing boats fill the Grand Canal.

FACTS

SWITZERLAND
Eidgenossenschaft Schweiz –
Confédération Suisse –
Confederazione Svizzera
AREA: 15,943 sq mi.
POPULATION: 7.1 million
CAPITAL: Bern
OTHER CITIES: Zurich,
Geneva
HIGHEST POINT: Monte Rosa
(15,203 ft)
OFFICIAL LANGUAGES:
German, French, Italian
CURRENCY: Swiss franc

⟳ SWISS GOLD
Bars of gold are stacked up in the vaults of a Zurich bank.

⟳ DOCK WORK
Malta's docks once serviced ships of the British navy, but now repair all kinds of merchant shipping.

Farms grow wheat, rice, corn, olives, and tomatoes. The vineyards of the Tuscany region produce world-famous wines. Indeed, Italy as a whole is the world's largest wine producer. Italian food, much of it based on pasta, risotto, polenta, or pizza dishes, has become a worldwide favorite.

Italy has few mineral resources, but has developed many successful industries, including plastics, textiles, leather goods, fashion, cars, computers, and household goods. Tourism in Italy dates back over 500 years. The country offers visitors winter sports, sunny beaches, ancient Roman and Etruscan sites, beautiful medieval cities, and stunning art treasures.

Set within Italy are two small patches of independent territory. The republic of San Marino, in the Apennines, was recognized as independent in 1631. It attracts many tourists. Vatican City, the world's smallest state, is part of the city of Rome. It serves as the world headquarters of the Roman Catholic Church.

Malta lies far to the south of Italy, on the ancient shipping lanes that cross the Mediterranean. It is a democratic republic and depends on tourism and ship repairs.

⟳ PERFECT PIZZA
Pizza has a delicious topping of tomato sauce, cheese, and chopped vegetables, meats, or fish.

⟳ BIRTH OF THE WEB
At the European Laboratory for Particle Physics (CERN), in Switzerland, a scientist tests magnets for a new accelerator. One spin-off of the research here was the development of the World Wide Web.

⟳ THE POLISH POPE
John Paul II became pope in 1978. He was the first non-Italian to hold the office in 450 years.

☪ ST NICHOLAS
December 5th is the Christian festival of St Nicholas. In the Lucerne region of Switzerland, this day is marked by a lantern procession and giving gifts.

About 65 percent of the Swiss people speak a regional dialect of German, 18 percent speak French, and you may hear Italian or a language called Romansch in the south. Switzerland is a conservative country, proud of its traditions. Geneva was one of the birthplaces of the Protestant faith.

Liechtenstein is largely Roman Catholic and German-speaking, with most people living in the capital city, Vaduz. Austria, too, is German-speaking. Its countryside is dotted with fine old castles, Catholic churches, and monasteries. Austria's cities have a long tradition of art, theater, and music.

Wolfgang Amadeus Mozart (1756–91) and Johann Strauss the Younger (1825–99) were both Austrian.

Italian, directly descended from the Latin language of the ancient Roman empire, is spoken all over Italy. The dialect spoken on the island of Sardinia is said to be the closest to the original Latin. In the far north there are a few speakers of French, German, and Slovenian. In the high Dolomites, a language called Ladin (related to Romansch) can also be heard.

☪ CLEVER HORSES
The days of the Habsburg emperors are recalled at Vienna's Spanish Riding School, where white Lippizaner horses perform elegant exercises to music.

☪ CATHOLIC AUSTRIA
About 300 years ago, the devout Roman Catholic faith of Austria inspired architects to erect beautiful churches and monasteries. This ornate building style is known as baroque.

Today's Italians are descended from all sorts of native peoples, settlers, and invaders. These included ancient Italian tribes, Etruscans, Romans, Greeks, Celts, Goths, Vandals, Lombards, Sards, and Normans. Today, the Italians' sense of identity depends more on the city or region in which they live than on their ancestry.

☪ PAVAROTTI
Italian is the language of opera. Luciano Pavarotti brought classical music to a wider audience when he formed the "Three Tenors," with Placido Domingo and José Carreras.

◒ ST FRANCIS OF ASSISSI

In 1205, Giovanni Bernadone (c.1181–1226)—Francesco— gave up his riches to become a monk, working with the poor and sick. He preached simplicity and a love for all creatures. Thousands followed his teachings and joined the Franciscan order of monks.

The traditional way of life in Italy is still strongly influenced by the Roman Catholic Church and the family. Many colorful festivals mark Christian saints' days and Holy Week.

Italy has probably contributed more to European civilization than any other country. Ancient Rome, heavily influenced by ancient Greece, was a center of literature and the arts, of philosophy and law-making, of engineering and technology. In later phases, the Italian city-states produced great poets such as Dante (1265–1321), artists such as Michelangelo (1475–1564) and Leonardo da Vinci (1452–1519), and composers such as Monteverdi (1567–1643). Opera is still very popular today, arousing as much passion as football.

The Maltese way of life has been strongly influenced by Italian traditions and sea-faring. The Maltese themselves are descended from the various peoples who, at one time or another in history, passed through their islands— including Greeks, Phoenicians, Arabs, Normans, and English, as well as Italians.

◒ DANTE ALIGHIERI

Born in 1265, Italy's greatest medieval poet wrote the Divine Comedy, a vision of heaven and hell.

◒ MALTESE CROSS

The Maltese cross is the badge of the Knights of St John, a religious fighting order based in Malta from 1530 to 1798.

◒ SOCCER MAGIC

Italian soccer clubs attract players from all over the world. Here, the Brazilian Ronaldo takes the field for Inter Milan.

◒ CARNIVAL TIME

Of all the world's carnivals, the one staged in Venice before the Christian period of Lent is the most elegant. People dress up (many in 18th century costume) and parade the city. Originally, carnival went on for two months!

81

☼ CELTIC ART
This Celtic figurine with a wheel symbol was found at Hochdorf in Austria. It dates to the 500s BC.

Austria, during the Middle Ages, was ruled as part of the Holy Roman Empire. Under the rule of the Habsburg family from 1282, it became one of Europe's strongest powers, its influence extending across central Europe. By the 1800s, following the Napoleonic Wars, Austrian power had weakened. It became a republic in 1918, after World War I.

Switzerland was created in the 13th and 14th centuries by cantons (provinces) uniting to throw off Austrian rule. It has been neutral in all wars since 1815. Liechtenstein was formed in 1719, when an Austrian prince bought two tiny states (Vaduz and Schellenberg) belonging to the Holy Roman Empire. It became an independent principality in 1866.

☼ MARIA THERESA
Born in 1717, Maria Theresa became empress and one of the wisest rulers of Austria. She died in 1780.

In Italy, legend tells, the city of Rome was founded in 753 BC. At this time the Etruscans ruled over central Italy, and Greek colonies were being founded in the south. Rome overthrew Etruscan rule in 509 BC. In the following centuries, the Romans conquered the rest of Italy and defeated a powerful rival, the city of Carthage, on the North African coast. They founded a great empire that stretched from Spain to Syria. By AD 476, the western half of this empire, including Italy, had been overthrown by Germanic invaders.

For the next 1,400 years Italy remained divided. There were invasions by Lombards and Byzantines. Normans carved out kingdoms for themselves in the south. The north fell under the rule of the Holy Roman Emperors, from across the Alps. The city of Rome, headquarters of the Roman Catholic Church, however, was still powerful as the center of the Christian world.

☼ IN THE ARENA
The Romans loved cruel spectacle. In arenas such as Rome's Colosseum amphitheater—the ruins of which still stand—huge crowds of up to 45,000 spectators watched fights to the death between gladiators (trained slaves or prisoners of war). Slaves were set against wild animals, too—roars of approval went up if a slave was torn apart.

☼ ROMAN COINS
Long before a single European currency was launched in 1999, most of Europe used the same coins—those of the Roman empire.

☼ TRAJAN'S COLUMN
Completed in AD 113, this marble monument records the triumphs of the Roman Emperor Trajan (AD 53–117).

☼ SALZBURG
The Austrian city of Salzburg is dominated by its fine medieval castle and the slightly later cathedral, built between 1614 and 1688.

A number of republics and cities grew up in the north during the Middle Ages. These became centers of commerce, and in Florence, in particular, learning and the arts flourished during the Renaissance.

Italy experienced periods of rule by the French, Spanish, and Austrians. During the 1800s, a movement grew up, under the leadership of Giuseppe Garibaldi (1807–82), to reunite the country. By 1871 Italy was a united kingdom.

Italy supported the Allies in World War I, but soon came under the rule of a fascist dictator, Benito Mussolini. It allied with Germany during World War II and in 1945 Mussolini was shot dead by rebel fighters.

In the years after the war, Italy was rebuilt. It enjoys democratic government, despite continuing problems with organized crime.

◑ CATHERINE DE' MEDICI

The powerful and ruthless Medici family ruled Florence and, later, Tuscany, from the 1400s to the 1700s. Catherine de' Medici (1519–89) married Henry II, king of France.

◔ MAFIA ON TRIAL

The Mafia is a criminal organization based in Sicily. Its leaders have been protected by corrupt police and politicians.

◑ GARIBALDI

In 1860, Giuseppe Garibaldi and his 1,000 "Red Shirts" began a military campaign to reunite Italy. He handed over the Kingdom of the Two Sicilies to Victor Emmanuel, who soon became king of a unified Italy.

TIMELINE

AD

117	Roman empire at greatest extent
568	Lombards invade northern Italy
917	Arabs capture Sicily
1090s	Normans invade Malta, Sicily
1291	Three cantons combine for defence to found the Swiss Confederation
1450	Height of the Renaissance
1494	France invades Italy
1530	Knights of St John (Malta) fight Turks
1631	San Marino independent
1719	Liechtenstein becomes independent
1798	France takes Malta
1800	French kingdom of Italy (until 1815); Britain takes Malta
1848	Revolution fails to end Austrian rule
1859	Austria loses most of its Italian possessions
1860	Garibaldi's patriots liberate Sicily
1861	Unification of Italy
1915	Italy joins Allies in World War I (until 1918)
1922	Fascist leader Mussolini seizes power in Italy
1938	Austria is annexed by Germany
1940	Italy joins World War II on German side; changes sides 1943; Mussolini is shot dead in 1945
1957	Italy founder member of EEC (later EU)
1964	Malta independent from British rule
1971	Women in Switzerland gain the right to vote
1995	Austria joins EU

CENTRAL EUROPE AND THE BALTIC

The northern part of Central Europe borders the Baltic Sea. Its eastern coast is low-lying, bordering sand dunes, bogs, heaths, and forests. Estonia and Latvia lie on the Gulfs of Finland and Riga, with Lithuania's short coastline stretching south to Kaliningrad, a small corner of Russian territory. Below the Gulf of Gdansk, the Baltic coast continues westward to Germany.

Most of Central Europe is far from the sea. The climate may be warm and sunny in summer, but the winters are long and cold. Much of Poland is a great plain, which stretches eastward into Belarus and Russia. Some parts are heavily forested or dotted with lakes; other parts are farmed or industrialized. In southern Poland the land rises to mountains along the borders of the Czech Republic and the Slovak Republic.

The Sudetes mountain range runs along the northern Czech border, while to the southeast the Bohemian Forest stretches into Germany. The Czech lands include wooded hills and rolling farmland, drained by the rivers Vltava, Elbe, and Morava. The Slovak Republic is more mountainous, with the Tatra range descending to fertile lowlands along the River Danube. Northern Hungary is a land of hills and low mountains, while the southeast forms a wide plain, with a rich, black soil that is ideal for farming.

◑ PRIENAI, LITHUANIA
Only one-in-three Lithuanians are now country-dwellers. Farmers grow potatoes, beet, and rye and raise pigs and chickens.

◑ BUDAPEST
Hungary's splendid Houses of Parliament lie at the center of the capital, Budapest, on the banks of the River Danube.

FACTS

CZECH REPUBLIC
Ceská Republika
AREA: 30,450 sq mi.
POPULATION: 10.3 million
CAPITAL: Prague
OTHER CITIES: Brno, Ostrava
HIGHEST POINT: Snezka (5,259 ft)
OFFICIAL LANGUAGE: Czech
CURRENCY: Koruna

ESTONIA
Eesti Vabariik
AREA: 17,400 sq mi.
POPULATION: 1.5 million
CAPITAL: Tallinn
OTHER CITIES: Tartu, Kohtla-Järve
HIGHEST POINT: Munamagi (1,042 ft)
OFFICIAL LANGUAGE: Estonian
CURRENCY: Kroon

HUNGARY
Magyar Köztársaság
AREA: 35,919 sq mi.
POPULATION: 10.2 million
CAPITAL: Budapest
OTHER CITIES: Debrecen, Miskolc
HIGHEST POINT: Kekes (3,330 ft)
OFFICIAL LANGUAGE: Magyar
CURRENCY: Forint

LATVIA
Latvija – Latvijas Republika
AREA: 24,900 sq mi.
POPULATION: 2.5 million
CAPITAL: Riga
OTHER CITIES: Jelgava, Daugavpils
HIGHEST POINT: Jaizina (1,020 ft)
OFFICIAL LANGUAGE: Latvian
CURRENCY: Lats

N W E S (compass)

ESTONIA (flag)

LITHUANIA (flag)

LATVIA (flag)

POLAND (flag)

CZECH REPUBLIC (flag)

HUNGARY (flag)

SLOVAK REPUBLIC (flag)

◯ LAKE BALATON

Central Europe's largest lake is surrounded by orchards and farms, and lies to the southwest of Budapest in Hungary's wine-producing region. In winter its shallow waters freeze over.

◐ IN BOHEMIA

Northern Bohemia, in the Czech Republic, is a region of woods and pretty old towns and villages. A day's hiking may be followed by a meal at a restaurant or a bottle of the famous Czech beer, Pilsener.

◑ CZECH CRAGS

Eroded into a fantastic pillar, Pravicky Cone can be seen in northern Bohemia, a mountainous region of the Czech Republic.

◑ IN THE TATRA MOUNTAINS

The mountains between Poland and the Slovak Republic are home to animals such as the Tatra chamois, an endangered species (shown here), and the European souslik.

Map labels:

ESTONIA, Tallinn, Kohtla-Järve, Hiumaa, Lake Peipus, Saaremaa, Tartu, Parnu, Munamagi 318m ▲, RUSSIA, LATVIA, Gulf of Riga, Ventspils, Jurmala, Gaizina 311m ▲, Saldus, Riga, Liepāja, Jelgava, Daugavpils, Siauliai, Panevezys, Utena, Klaipeda, LITHUANIA, Ukmerge, Nemunas (Neman), Kaunas, Vilnius, Kaliningrad (RUSSIA), 311 m ▲, Gulf of Gdansk, Gdynia, Gdansk, Kaliningrad, BELARUS, Kolobrzeg, Elblag, Olsztyn, Szczecin, NORTH EUROPEAN PLAIN, Bydgoscz, Bialystock, Gorzow Wielkopolski, Torun, Poznan, Plock, Warsaw, Kalisz, POLAND, Lodz, Odra (Oder), Glogow, Radom, Lublin, Kielce, Wroclaw, Czestochowa, Chelm, Walbrzych, SUDETES MOUNTAINS, Bytom, UKRAINE, Karlovy Vary, Prague, Katowice, Krakow, Rzeszow, Plzen, Pardubice, Tychy, Tarnow, BOHEMIA, CZECH REPUBLIC, Ostrava, Bielsko-Biala, Olomouc, MORAVIA, CARPATHIAM MOUNTAINS, Cesky Budejovice, Brno, Zilina, Rysy Paak 2,499m ▲, Presov, Trencin, Kosice, GERMANY, AUSTRIA, SLOVAK REPUBLIC, Miskolc, Nytra, Bratislava, Mt. Kekes ▲1,015m, Debrecen, Danube, Gyor, Budapest, Koros, ROMANIA, Tatabanya, Szombathely, HUNGARY, Bekescsaba, Tisza, Lake Balaton, Kaposvar, Szeged, Pécs, CROATIA, SERBIA & MONTENEGRO

From the 1940s until the years 1989–91, the Baltic states formed part of the Soviet Union (as Russia was then known), while Central Europe was ruled by Communist governments that supported the Soviet Union. Today, the entire region has broken free from Russian influence. Multi-party elections are held and the countries' economies are linked to the European Union (from 2004). All the countries of the region are republics. Before 1993, the Czech and Slovak republics formed a single state, Czechoslovakia.

◑ STAPLE CROPS
In Central Europe, staple crops —those that provide the basis of people's everyday diet— include wheat and rye, for making bread, and potatoes.

The Baltic states lack mineral resources and need imports to support their industries. They produce chemicals, textiles, and heavy machinery. The forests provide timber for making paper and matches. Many factories and mills are old-fashioned. Farms grow staple crops and raise cattle and pigs.

Poland has reserves of coal, sulfur, copper, silver, lead, salt, and natural gas. Shipbuilding and repair make up a major industry on the Baltic coast, and factories produce vehicles, heavy machinery, and footwear. Wheat and rye are grown and potatoes are a major crop.

When Czechoslovakia split in two, much of the industry lay on the Czech side of the border. It includes glass-making, iron, and steel. Slovakia depends more on farming. Hungary has reserves of bauxite, coal, and gas, and produces chemicals, plastics, aluminium, vehicles, and electrical goods. Its orchards grow cherries and other fruits for making jams.

◑ VISITING CENTRAL EUROPE
The tourist industry is growing rapidly in Poland, Hungary, and the Czech Republic. Here, visitors admire a waterfall at Souteska, northern Bohemia.

◑ THE TASTE OF PAPRIKA
The red fruit of a type of capsicum plant is dried and ground to make paprika. This peppery spice is used in dishes such as Hungarian goulash.

◑ ON THE MARCH
These Lithuanian soldiers are on parade to mark Independence Day. The country became an independent state in 1991.

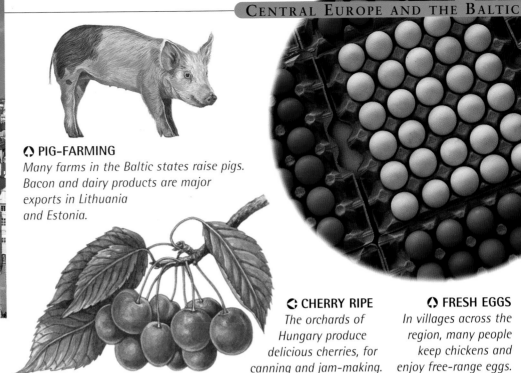

⟁ PIG-FARMING
Many farms in the Baltic states raise pigs. Bacon and dairy products are major exports in Lithuania and Estonia.

⟁ CHERRY RIPE
The orchards of Hungary produce delicious cherries, for canning and jam-making.

⟁ FRESH EGGS
In villages across the region, many people keep chickens and enjoy free-range eggs.

⟁ OLD PRAGUE
The Czech capital has many fine old buildings dating from the 1300s and 1400s, when the city was the center of the Bohemian kingdom.

Central Europe is famous for its delicious food, such as Hungarian goulash (a stew made of meat cooked with sour cream and paprika) and Polish *pierogi* (dumplings stuffed with mushrooms and meat). Alcoholic drinks include Polish vodkas, Czech beers, and strong red wines from Hungary.

Tourism is a growing industry in Central Europe. Major attractions include the old cities of Krakow, Prague, and Budapest, the Tatra Mountains, and the hot springs and health resorts of the Czech Republic.

⟁ SHIPBUILDING
Ship repair and construction is a traditional heavy industry around the Baltic coast, especially in the Polish port of Gdansk.

⟁ HUNGARIAN SPAS
Warm springs near Miskolc, in the north of Hungary, offer a chance to relax with friends. The water can be as hot as 86°F. Rich in minerals, it is said to cure many illnesses.

FACTS

LITHUANIA
Lietuva, Lietuvos Respublika
Area: 25,200 sq mi.
Population: 3.7 million
Capital: Vilnius
Other cities: Kaunas, Klaipeda
Highest point: Juozapines (964 ft)
Official language: Lithuanian
Currency: Litas

POLAND
Rzeczpospolita Polska
Area: 124,808 sq mi.
Population: 38.6 million
Capital: Warsaw
Other cities: Lodz, Krakow, Wroclaw
Highest point: Gerlachovsky Stit (8,714 ft)
Official language: Polish
Currency: Zloty

SLOVAK REPUBLIC
Slovenská Republika
Area: 18,924 sq mi
Population: 5.4 million
Capital: Bratislava
Other cities: Kosice,
Highest point: Rysy Peak (8,187 ft)
Official language: Slovak
Currency: Koruna

➲ STILL ON THE ROAD?

The traditional painted caravans of the Roma (gypsies) are a rare sight. In Central Europe, only ten percent of the Roma are still travelers.

➲ DRESSED FOR A FEAST

In Poland, traditional dress is still worn for folk dances and festivals. Bright colors and intricate embroidery are a feature of all the national costumes of Central Europe.

Peoples living on the east coast of the Baltic Sea include the Estonians, Latvians, and Lithuanians, each of whom have their own language. The Estonian language is related to Finnish and Hungarian. During the years that this region formed part of the Soviet Union, many Russians, Ukrainians, and Belarussians also settled there.

The Poles, Czechs, and Slovaks are all Slavic peoples, speaking languages that are separate but related to each other. The Magyar people, who invaded southern Central Europe about 1,200 years ago, make up 90 percent of the Hungarian population. Hungary is also home to small numbers of Germans and neighboring peoples such as Czechs, Serbs, Croats, and Romanians.

➲ PLUCKED STRINGS

The zither is an instrument used in Central European folk music. It has a flat soundbox and its jangling strings may be plucked with the fingers or a plectrum.

➲ MARIE CURIE

Born Marie Sklodowska (1867–1934), this great Polish physicist (on the left) researched into radioactivity and isolated the elements polonium and radium.

➲ A NEW THEORY

Nicolaus Copernicus (died 1543) was a Polish astronomer who proposed a revolutionary theory: that the Sun, and not the Earth, was at the center of the Universe.

PLANISPHÆRIVM
Sive
VNIVERSI TO-
EX HYPO
COPERNI
PLANO

COPERNICANVM
Systema
TIVS CREATI
THESI
CANA IN
EXHIBITVM

HORSEMANSHIP
A love of horses and riding was part of the Magyar way of life long before they settled in Hungary, and remains a tradition today.

Central Europe as a whole has a large Roma (gypsy) population, which has suffered from racism in many areas over the years. The region's large Jewish populations were scattered or murdered in terrible death camps during the occupation of the region by Nazi Germany during World War II (1939–45).

Central Europe is mostly Christian, with the Roman Catholic Church especially strong in Poland. The monastery of Jasna Góra at Czestochowa attracts many Catholic pilgrims, who come to see an icon (holy picture) known as the Black Madonna.

The region has contributed greatly to European culture. The musical composer Frédéric Chopin (1810–49) was Polish, and composer Antonín Dvořák (1841–1904) was Czech. Classical music has been much influenced by regional folk music and dances.

A LONG HISTORY
The Hungarian National Museum in Budapest celebrates a history that goes back to the 800s, when a legendary Magyar chief named Arpad conquered the region and set up a powerful kingdom.

CATHOLIC POLAND
Churches have been an integral part of the Polish landscape since AD 966, when the country became Christian. Ninety-five percent of Poles are Roman Catholic.

EGGSHELL PAINT
Hand-painted eggshells go on display in Budapest. Egg painting is an Easter tradition in Central and Eastern Europe, where it has become an art form.

MIXED NATIONALITY
Ceramic tiles adorn this chemist's shop in the old border town of Sopron. Allotted to Austria after World War I, Sopron voted to join Hungary in 1924.

⟳ PRAGUE, 1968

Soviet tanks rolled into Czechoslovakia in 1964 after the Czech government tried to introduce political reforms.

⟳ OUT OF THE WINDOW

An incident in Prague, in 1618, marked the start of the Thirty Years' War. The envoys of the Catholic Holy Roman Emperor were thrown out of a window by the Bohemian nobles, who were Protestant. They chose instead to be ruled by a German Protestant prince. Two years later, Catholic forces completely destroyed the Bohemian forces at the Battle of the White Mountain.

The flat lands lying between western and eastern Europe are hard to defend. Throughout history, they have been invaded from both the east and the west. Poland has probably changed its position on the map more times than any other country in Europe.

⟳ A STRONGHOLD

The medieval city of Kaunas in Lithuania built up strong defences during its long history of warfare.

About 2,700 years ago, the Celts flourished in the Czech and Slovak region and part of Hungary. They were displaced by Germanic tribes, but in the end it was Slavic peoples who controlled most of Central Europe, from the Baltic Sea to the River Danube. In about AD 800, the plains of Hungary were invaded by the Magyars—fierce horseback warriors from the East.

During the Middle Ages, powerful kingdoms grew up in the region. These included Poland (which united with Lithuania in 1382), Bohemia (capital at Prague), and Hungary. Central Europe came under attack from the east by Tartars and Turks; from the west, Germany's Teutonic Knights rode into Poland and the Baltic.

☐ THE MAGYARS

In about AD 800, hordes of nomadic warriors, the Magyars, poured across the Ural Mountains from Russia and conquered the plains of Hungary.

The Austrian empire spread eastward and had taken Bohemia by the 1500s and Hungary by the 1700s. Poland and the Baltic states were torn apart and invaded by the great powers of the day—Sweden, Russia, Austria, and the north German state of Prussia.

After World War I (1914–18), the nations of Central Europe were independent once again. However, German invasion during World War II (1939–45) brought terror and devastation to the region. Central Europe was liberated by local freedom fighters and by the army of the Soviet Union.

Post-war Communist governments in Central Europe were effectively controlled by the Soviet Union. There were uprisings against them, but in the end it was the collapse of the Soviet Union in 1991 that spelt the start of a new, post-Communist age for Central Europe and the Baltic states.

☐ WORKERS UNITED

In 1980 a trade union, Solidarity, was formed in Poland. It challenged the authority of the Communist government with a series of strikes in the Gdansk shipyards. Solidarity's leader, Lech Walesa, became Polish president in 1990.

☐ INDEPENDENT SLOVAKIA

This monument at Bankska Bystrica celebrates Slovak independence, gained when the country was part of Czechoslovakia. Today, it is independent in its own right.

☐ ON GUARD

A soldier stands on guard outside Prague Castle, once the capital of the powerful medieval kingdom of Bohemia.

TIMELINE

AD

500s	Slavs settle Central Europe
800s	Magyars seize Hungary
1237	Tartar invasions (until 1242)
1569	Poland, Prussia, Lithuania, and Livonia (Latvia) form a commonwealth
1618	Thirty Years' War
1648	Russia and Sweden seize Polish land
1699	Hungary under Austrian rule
1772	Poland partitioned between Russia, Austria, Prussia
1848	Hungary revolts against Austrian rule
1914	World War I (until 1918): Germany and Austria invade Poland
1918	Lithuania, Poland, Hungary, Czechoslovakia independent
1920	Latvia independent
1921	Estonia independent
1939	World War II (until 1945): Soviet Union annexes Baltic states 1940; Germany invades Central Europe and Baltic; massacre of Jews; Soviet Union pushes back German forces
1948	Communists take power in Central Europe
1956	Anti-Soviet uprising in Hungary
1968	Czech reforms crushed by Soviet Union
1990	Democratic elections in Central Europe
1991	Baltic states recognized as independent
1993	Czech and Slovak states separate

THE BALKANS

HERMANN'S TORTOISE

The Balkan peninsula extends southward into the Mediterranean Sea from Central and Eastern Europe. It is at its broadest in the north, where it stretches all the way from the islands of the northern Adriatic to the marshy delta of the River Danube, on the Black Sea. It narrows rapidly between the Ionian and Aegean Seas, where it breaks into the ragged headlands and island chains of Greece.

The only large plains lie in the north. The region as a whole is very mountainous, taking in the Carpathian ranges, the Transylvanian Alps, the Dinaric Alps, and the Balkan, Rhodope, and Pindus ranges. Even the largest of the Greek islands, Crete, is topped by a 8,060-foot-high peak named Mount Ida.

Winters can be cold and snowy in the northern Balkans, but are normally milder in the south. Summers are dry and hot, often fiercely so in Greece. Northern forests give way to scrub-covered rock and olive groves in the south. The Balkans lie in an extremely active earthquake zone.

The Balkans still include large areas of remote forest and mountain habitat, where wolves, brown bears, and wild boar live. The warmer regions have a wide variety of snakes and lizards. Many of the region's rare species are threatened by loss of habitat as forests are cleared and tourist resorts are built.

MT TRIGLAV

The Slovenian peak of Triglav rises dramatically to 9,393 feet. It is part of the Julian Alps range, on the border with Austria, and is 40 miles northwest of the capital, Ljubljana.

FACTS

ALBANIA
Republika e Shqipërisë
AREA: 11,100 sq mi.
POPULATION: 3 million
CAPITAL: Tiranë
OTHER CITIES: Durrës, Shköder, Elbasan
HIGHEST POINT: Korabit (9,026 ft)
OFFICIAL LANGUAGE: Albanian
CURRENCY: Lek

BOSNIA-HERZEGOVINA
Republika Bosnia i Hercegovina
AREA: 19,741 sq mi.
POPULATION: 4.0 million
CAPITAL: Sarajevo
OTHER CITIES: Banja Luka, Mostar
HIGHEST POINT: Maglic (7,831 ft)
OFFICIAL LANGUAGE: Serbo-Croat
CURRENCY: Marka

BULGARIA
Republika Bulgaria
AREA: 42,855 sq mi.
POPULATION: 8 million
CAPITAL: Sofia
OTHER CITIES: Plovdiv, Varna, Burgas
HIGHEST POINT: Musala (9,594 ft)
OFFICIAL LANGUAGE: Bulgarian
CURRENCY: Lev

CROATIA
Republika Hrvatska
AREA: 34,022 sq mi.
POPULATION: 4.4 million
CAPITAL: Zagreb
OTHER CITIES: Split, Rijeka
HIGHEST POINT: Troglav (6,005 ft)
OFFICIAL LANGUAGE: Serbo-Croat
CURRENCY: Kuna

GREECE
Elliniki Dimokratia
AREA: 50,949 sq mi.
POPULATION: 10.9 million
CAPITAL: Athens
OTHER CITIES: Thessaloníki, Lárisa
HIGHEST POINT: Olympus (9,570 ft)
OFFICIAL LANGUAGE: Greek
CURRENCY: Euro

CROATIA

☾ PELICANS
Rare Dalmatian and white pelicans breed in Balkan wetland regions.

☾ SLOVENIAN WORKERS
Slovenia escaped the worst of the region's strife in recent years. It hoped to prosper from EU membership.

SLOVENIA

BOSNIA-HERZEGOVINA

ALBANIA

ROMANIA

BULGARIA

☾ NEARER TO GOD
At Méteora, an area of Thessaly in central Greece, sheer pillars of rock rise to 1,800 feet. Some are topped by monasteries, the oldest dating from about AD 1100.

MACEDONIA

GREECE

SERBIA & MONTENEGRO

☾ THE EASTERN ADRIATIC
This beautiful Mediterranean shoreline attracted many visitors in the 1970s and 80s. Fighting in the 1990s destroyed the tourist industry there.

☾ CAPITAL CITY
Bucharest (Bucuresti) lies on the River Dambovit. It became the capital of Wallachia in 1698 and the capital of Romania in 1861.

Map labels

UKRAINE
Satu Mare
Botosani
Baia Mare
Iasi
MOLDOVA
Oradea
Somes
Cluj-Napoca
Mures
Bacau
MOLDAVIAN CARPATHIANS
Sifret
AUSTRIA
Triglav 2,863 m
Ljubljana
Maribor
HUNGARY
Tîrgu Mures
Alba Iulia
ROMANIA
SLOVENIA
Koprivnica
Arad
Muras
Deva
Sibiu
Brasov
Galati
Zagreb
Drava
Subotica
Tisza
Timisoara
Moldoveanu 2,543 m
Braila
Rijeka
Kupa
CROATIA
Osijek
VOJVODINA
Resita
TRANSYLVANIAN ALPS
Ploiesti
DOBRUJA
Pula
Sava
Prijedor
Novi Sad
Jiu
Sava
Bosna
Brcko
Belgrade
Craiova
Pitesti
Bucharest
Cres
Bihac
Banja Luka
Tuzla
Sabac
Smederevo
Dunarea (Danube)
Ruse
Constanta
Losinj
Gospic
BOSNIA-HERZEGOVINA
Valjevo
Negotin
Vidin
Dobrich
Zadar
DINARIC ALPS
Zenica
Srebrenica
Kragujevac
Mikhaylovgrad
Pleven
Iskur
Shumen
Balchik
Dugi I.
Livno
Sarajevo
Cacak
Morava
Vratsa
Lovech
Turgovishte
Kamchiya
Varna
Sibenik
Drina
Novi Pazar
Krusevac
Nis
BALKAN MOUNTAINS
Kazanluk
Split
Hvar
Brac
Vis
Mostar
Leskovac
Sofia
Sliven
Burgas
Korcula
SERBIA & MONTENEGRO
Pristina
Pernik
Stara Zagora
Yambol
Lastovo
Mljet
Dubrovnik
Podgorica
Pec
KOSOVO
Musala Peak Pasardzhik
Maritsa
BULGARIA
Shkoder
Urosevac
2,925 m
Plovdiv
Khaskovo
Drin Gulf
Mt Korabit 2,751 m
Tetovo
Skopje
RHODOPE MOUNTAINS
Smolyan
Orestiás
Durrës
MACEDONIA
Vardar
Drama
PIRIN MTS
Komotini
Tiranë
Prilep
Palikastron
Struma
Xanthi
Elbasan
Lake Ohrid
Bitola
Serrai
Kavála
Alexandroúpolis
Lake Prespa
Edhessa
Kilkis
Thessaloniki
Thasos
ALBANIA
Náousa
Samothrace
Vlorë
Ptolemaís
Aliakmon
Limnos
Gjirokaster
Mt Olympus 2,917 m
Mt Athos 2,033 m
GREECE
Ioánnina
Trikkala
Lárisa
Kérkira
Corfu
Parga
Volos
Skiathos
Skiros
Lesbos
Mitilíni
Arta
PINDUS MTS
Kardhítsa
Skopelos
Skiros
Pálairos
Lamia
Euboea
AEGEAN SEA
Leukas
Parnassus 2,547 m
Kimi
Chios
Astakós
Agrínion
Khalkís
Cephalonia
Ithaca
Pátrai
Mégara
Marathon
Andros
Sámos
IONIAN SEA
Amaliás
Lambia
Corinth
Athens
Tínos
Ikaria
Zante
Atlos
Pirgos
Argos
Piraeus
Kéa
Mikonos
Pátmos
Tripolis
Návplion
Láyrion
Kíthnos
Síros
Páros
Léros
PELOPONNESUS
Galatás
Sérifos
Naxos
Kálimnos
Kalamáta
Sparta
Sífnos
Íos
Astipálaia
Cos
Tílos
Areópolis
Néapolis
Mílos
Thíra
Rhodes
Rhodes Lindos
Cythera
SEA OF CRETE
Karpathos
Khaniá
Réthimnon
Iráklion
Crete
Mt Ida 2,456 m

During the 1990s there was civil war in the northwest as the Communist federation of Yugoslavia split up into separate countries. This were the new, smaller republics of Slovenia, Croatia, Bosnia-Herzegovina, Serbia & Montenegro, and Macedonia. Slovenia was later accepted as an EU member (from 2004).

In Romania, the people overthrew a self-styled Communist dictator, Nicolae Ceausescu (1918–89), in 1989. Communist rule collapsed in Bulgaria in 1990 and in Albania in 1992.

⚭ CROATS AND CONFLICT
An elderly Croatian man weaves canes into a basket. Between 1991 and 1995 Croatia fought the Serbs in both Yugoslavia and Bosnia. Many Serbs living in Croatia fled the country.

The Balkans are home to very many different peoples, including Serbs, Croatians, Slovenians, Montenegrins, Romanians, Bulgars, Turks, Roma (gypsies), Albanians, and Greeks. The region has had a very troubled political history, largely as a result of the neglect and division it experienced during the hundreds of years it was ruled by the Austrian and Ottoman (Turkish) empires.

⚭ THE WELDER
Serbian metal industries are based in Pancevo, Kragujeva, and Nis. The capital, Belgrade, is a center of both heavy and light engineering. Output has continued despite the political strife and warfare of the 1990s.

⚭ OCEAN HARVEST
Squid and octopus are an important ingredient in many Greek meals and snacks. They are served at coastal restaurants and bars during the summer months.

MACEDONIAN REPUBLIC
(Former Yugoslav Republic)
Republika Makedonija
AREA: 9,928 sq mi.
POPULATION: 2.0 million
CAPITAL: Skopje
OTHER CITIES: Bitola, Prilep
HIGHEST POINT: Korabit (9,066 ft)
OFFICIAL LANGUAGE: Macedonian
CURRENCY: Dinar

ROMANIA
România
AREA: 91,699 sq mi.
POPULATION: 22.4 million
CAPITAL: Bucharest
OTHER CITIES: Brasov, Constanta
HIGHEST POINT: Moldoveanu (8,360 ft)
OFFICIAL LANGUAGE: Romanian
CURRENCY: Leu

SLOVENIA
Republika Slovenija
AREA: 7,819 sq mi.
POPULATION: 2.0 million
CAPITAL: Ljubljana
OTHER CITIES: Maribor, Jesenice
HIGHEST POINT: Triglav (9,393 ft)
OFFICIAL LANGUAGE: Slovenian
CURRENCY: Tolar

SERBIA & MONTENEGRO
(Serbia-Montenegro)
Savezna Republika Jugoslavija
AREA: 39,449 sq mi.
POPULATION: 10.6 million
CAPITAL: Belgrade
OTHER CITIES: Novi Sad, Nis
HIGHEST POINT: Daravica (8,714 ft)
OFFICIAL LANGUAGE: Serbo-Croat
CURRENCY: Dinar

⚭ PETALS FOR SALE
Attar of roses—an oil product made from rose petals—is an important product of Bulgaria's Kazanluk district. It is used to make perfumes.

Greece has faced many problems, including a period of right-wing military rule from 1967 until 1973. It has also had long-running disputes with its eastern neighbor, Turkey, and with the new Slavic republic of Macedonia across its northern border.

The political troubles of the 1990s disrupted the Balkan economy. Greece, as a member state of the European Union (EU) since 1981, was one of the few countries in the region that was able develop peacefully.

The climate of the region is suitable for growing fruits, such as plums in the north and lemons and olives in the south, watermelons, corn, tobacco, and sunflowers. Bulgaria grows roses for the perfume industry. The Balkan lands produce iron and steel, chemicals, machinery, textiles, clothing, and footwear. Tourism is a major industry in Greece, which offers blue seas, island beaches, and pretty, whitewashed villages. Recent political troubles disrupted what had also been a thriving tourist industry on the coast and islands of Croatia.

◐ MELONS
The juicy red flesh of a Greek watermelon, or karpouzi, makes an ideal refreshment on a hot day.

◐ DEFENDING GREECE
The ceremonial uniform of the Greek national guard, the Evzones, includes a tasseled cap, a kilt, and white leggings. It is based on the dress of the mountain troops who fought against Turkey in the 1820s.

◑ A VOLCANIC ISLAND
The Greek island of Santorini, or Thira, lies just to the north of Crete. Today, it attracts thousands of tourists each year, but about 3,500 years ago it was the scene of one of the biggest volcanic explosions in recorded history.

◐ THRESHING CORN
Slovenian women thresh a harvest of wheat. Many people still work on farms in rural areas of the Balkans. Hi-tech machinery is rare on these small, family-run farms.

95

The early history of the Balkans is marked by the amazing civilizations that developed on the island of Crete from about 2500 BC until 1400 BC, and on the Greek mainland and islands from 1000 BC onward. The city-states of ancient Greece produced great playwrights and poets, sculptors, athletes, soldiers, traders, mathematicians, and thinkers. The idea of democracy—rule by a public assembly instead of by kings or dictators—was first tried out in Athens. Greek culture and ideas spread around the Mediterranean region as seafarers set up new colonies.

In 338 BC the northern kingdom of Macedonia conquered the rest of Greece, and a young ruler named Alexander the Great went on to found a vast empire which stretched southward to Egypt and eastward to India. This broke up after he died. In 146 BC Greece became part of the Roman empire, which soon swallowed up the whole Balkan region.

DRACULA'S CASTLE
The legend of Dracula, the vampire, is based upon Vlad IV, who ruled part of Romania in a reign of terror (AD 1455–62). He impaled his victims on pointed stakes.

MASK OF MYCENAE
This gold death mask comes from Mycenae, the citadel town in southern Greece that was the center of the Mycenean civilization between 1900 BC and 1100 BC.

The eastern part of the Roman empire survived after the western part collapsed, and this developed into the Byzantine empire, with its capital at Constantinople (modern Istanbul, in Turkey). The Byzantine empire became a center of Eastern Orthodox Christianity and of the Greek language and way of life.

ALEXANDER THE GREAT
Alexander (356–323 BC) conquered all the lands between Greece and India, and founded the Egyptian city of Alexandria.

THE BULL-LEAPERS
A wall painting from Knossos, on Crete, shows acrobats vaulting over the backs of bulls. About 3,500 years ago, Knossos was the capital of the Minoan civilization.

GREEK ARMIES
Ancient Greece was not a united state until 338 BC. When its armies did join forces, they defeated the mighty Persian empire. In the Greek state of Sparta, military training was strict and started from boyhood.

◐ A GREAT THINKER
Socrates was one of the greatest philosophers of ancient Greece. He was forced to commit suicide in 399 BC, as a punishment for encouraging people to think about good and evil, and disrespect the gods.

◐ A FATEFUL DAY
On June 28, 1914, the Archduke Franz Ferdinand of Austria and his wife were assassinated in Sarajevo, Bosnia. This incident triggered World War I.

The Byzantine empire fell to the invading Turks in AD 1453. Most of the Balkans remained under Turkish rule for over 400 years, with Austria–Hungary controlling parts of the northwest. World War I (1914–18) was started when a Serbian nationalist assassinated the heir to the Austrian throne in Sarajevo.

World War II (1939–45) brought Italian and German invasions of the Balkans and long years of guerrilla warfare, which continued after the war in battles between Communists and monarchists. Communists failed to gain control of Greece, but succeeded in the northern Balkans. All the Communist governments collapsed in the 1980s and 90s, and war followed.

◐ SOPHIA CATHEDRAL
Many Bulgarians belong to the Eastern Orthodox Church. The domed cathedral in Sophia shows the influence of the Byzantine empire.

◐ SLOBODAN MILOSEVIC
Serbian nationalist Milosevic rose to power in the 1980s. In the 1990s, he led ruthless campaigns against Bosnian Muslims and the ethnic Albanians of Kosovo.

TIMELINE

AD

330	Roman empire split: the eastern capital, Constantinople, goes on to become center of Byzantine empire
500s	Slavs invade Balkans (through 600s)
680	Bulgars invade Bulgaria
1396	Turks invade Bulgaria
1453	Turks capture Constantinople, then invade Balkans
1821	Greek War of Independence (until 1830)
1908	Bulgaria declares independence
1912	Balkan Wars (until 1913) drive Turks from most of Europe; Albanian independence
1914	World War I starts in Sarajevo: Turkey joins Germany and Austria; Greeks join Allies 1917
1918	Formation of Yugoslavia
1939	World War II (until 1945): 1940, Italy invades Albania; Greece invaded by Italy, Germany, Bulgaria
1946	Communist governments take power in Balkans; Greek Communists defeated in civil war (until 1949)
1967	Military coup in Greece
1975	Greece becomes a democratic republic
1981	Greece joins EEC (later EU)
1989	Revolution in Romania
1990s	Collapse of Communist governments in Balkans (through 1991); break-up of Yugoslavia; ethnic persecution
2001	Yugoslav leader Slobodan Milosevic tried for war crimes

◐ THE PARTHENON
The Acropolis in Athens is crowned by the Parthenon—a splendid temple to Athena, the goddess of the city. It was completed in 438 BC.

97

ALASKA
(U.S.A.)

C A N A D A

U . S . A .

N
W   E
S

BAHAMAS

MEXICO

CUBA
DOMINICAN REP.

HAITI
PUERTO
BELIZE   RICO
HONDURAS   JAMAICA
GUATEMALA
EL SALVADOR   NICARAGUA

COSTA RICA

PANAMA   VENEZUELA
GUYANA
SURINAM
FRENCH GUIANA

COLOMBIA

ECUADOR

B R A Z I L

PERU

BOLIVIA

PARAGUAY

CHILE

URUGUAY

ARGENTINA

98

⊙ HARLEY DAVIDSON
ELECTRA GLIDE

THE AMERICAS

◊ Disneyworld,
NITED STATES OF AMERICA

◊ Lake Moraine,
CANADA

◊ Amazon rainforest,
BRAZIL

◊ Toltec temple,
MEXICO

North and South America are two great continents, lying between the Atlantic and Pacific Oceans. They are linked by Central America, which narrows to a strip of land called the Isthmus of Panama. This is cut in two by the Panama Canal, which links the two oceans. Tropical Central America is bordered to the east by the Caribbean Sea, which is encircled by the islands of the Greater and Lesser Antilles.

North America is dominated by the mountain system called the Rockies, which runs from north to south. In the far north, frozen tundra yields to forest. To the south of the forest belt lie the prairies—rolling grasslands that are now used for grazing or are cultivated, part of a great plain drained by the Mississippi–Missouri river system. In the southern United States and Central America are rocky canyons, steamy wetlands, volcanoes, and deserts.

In South America, the Rockies are matched by the mighty Andes mountain chain. To the east, a maze of waterways flows into the River Amazon, which is surrounded by the world's largest tropical rainforest. South American grasslands include the llanos of Venezuela and the Argentinean pampas. There are windy plateaus and coastal deserts. The continent ends in the bleak island of Tierra del Fuego, which reaches out like a claw toward Antarctica.

◊ SAILFISH

CANADA

FACTS

CANADA
AREA: 3,558,096 sq mi.
POPULATION: 31 million
CAPITAL: Ottawa
OTHER CITIES: Toronto,
Montréal, Vancouver
HIGHEST POINT: Mount
Logan (19,524 ft)
OFFICIAL LANGUAGES: English,
French
CURRENCY: Canadian dollar

ST PIERRE AND MIQUELON
TERRITORIAL COLLECTIVITY OF FRANCE
AREA: 93 sq mi.
POPULATION: 6,500
CAPITAL: Saint-Pierre
OFFICIAL LANGUAGE: French
CURRENCY: Euro

☼ MUSK OX

Canada is the world's second largest nation in area. Its islands are scattered like pieces of a giant jigsaw puzzle across the Arctic, between the Beaufort and Labrador Seas. A wide expanse of northern Canada is covered by tundra, which has permanently frozen ground. During the brief summer, the snow on the tundra melts and lies in pools that attract insects and migrating birds.

Most of the Canadian mainland is covered by a broad belt of forests and glacial lakes. A vast slab of ancient rock, the Canadian Shield, borders Hudson Bay. In the west are the high peaks of the Mackenzie, Rocky, and Coast ranges, which descend to the moist green coast of British Columbia.

The southern border with the United States crosses the prairies and the Great Lakes. The St Lawrence River and Seaway link Lake Ontario with the Atlantic Ocean. Here, the warm Gulf Stream meets the cold Labrador Current, bringing fog to the waters off Newfoundland, Canada's Maritime provinces, and the little French islands of St Pierre and Miquelon.

☼ BATH TIME!
The moose can stand 7.5 feet at the shoulder. This one is pictured at Pukaskawa National Park, Ontario, on the north shore of Lake Superior.

☼ TAKKAKAW FALLS
Takkakaw means "wonderful" in the language of the Cree people. These mighty falls tumble over a drop of 833 feet in the Yoho National Park, British Columbia.

◑ TUNDRA LIFE

The Arctic tundra supports a wide range of wildlife, including birds such as ptarmigan and mammals such as caribou.

ARCTIC OCEAN

LINCOLN SEA

Ellesmere Island

Melville Island
Devon Island
BAFFIN BAY

Banks Island
Prince of Wales Island

BEAUFORT SEA

Victoria Island
Baffin Island

Davis Strait

FOXE BASIN

LABRADOR SEA

ALASKA (U.S.A.)

Dawson
Norman Wells
Great Bear Lake

▲Mt. Logan 5,951 m
Whitehorse
YUKON TERRITORY

NORTHWEST TERRITORIES

Southampton Island

Hudson Strait

HORN MOUNTAINS
Yellowknife
Dubawnt Lake

Coats Island
Mansel Island
Ungava Peninsula

Great Slave Lake
Fort Resolution

HUDSON BAY

Fort Smith

CARIBOU MOUNTAINS
Lake Athabasca

Churchill

Belcher Islands

Goose Bay

NEWFOUNDLAND

BRITISH COLUMBIA

Prince Rupert

CANADA

Reindeer Lake
Churchill
Nelson

La Grande Rivière

Gander
Newfoundland
St John's

QUEEN CHARLOTTE ISLANDS

Prince George

Peace River
ALBERTA

JAMES BAY
Akimiski Island

OTISH MOUNTAINS

Anticosti Island
Gulf of St. Lawrence

Edmonton
Red Deer

N. Saskatchewan
Prince Albert

MANITOBA

Severn

Péribonca

St Lawrence

PRINCE EDWARD ISLAND

Vancouver Island
Kamloops

Calgary
Saskatoon

Lake Winnipegosis
Lake Winnipeg

Albany

QUEBEC

NEW BRUNSWICK
Charlottetown
NOVA SCOTIA

Medicine Hat
S. Saskatchewan
SASKATCHEWAN
Regina

Lake Manitoba

ONTARIO

Quebec
Fredericton
St John
Halifax

Victoria
Vancouver

Winnipeg

Lake Nipigon

Montreal

ATLANTIC OCEAN

UNITED STATES OF AMERICA

Thunder Bay

Lake Superior

Ottawa

Georgian Bay

Lake Huron

Toronto
Lake Ontario

Hamilton
Niagara Falls

Windsor
Lake Erie

◑ IN THE ROCKIES

Moraine Lake may be visited in the Banff National Park, in Alberta. Its vivid blue color is caused by a silt known as "rock flour."

CANADA

◑ TUNDRA SOIL

A pingo is a mound of soil filled with a core of expanding ice. When the ice melts, the pingo collapses.

◑ THE BEAVER

Beavers live on many Canadian lakes. They use their powerful gnawing teeth to fell trees and shred wood.

101

FIGHTING THE BLAZE
A helicopter moves in to fight a forest fire. Canada's vast conifer forests stretch in a broad belt across central and northern regions, from British Columbia to the Laurentian Plateau.

LUMBERJACK YEARS
The loggers who felled the Canadian forests a century ago had few mechanical aids. They lived hard lives in remote camps.

The severe climate in the north of Canada has restricted settlement there. Seventy-seven percent of Canadians are town-dwellers, and the big cities are all in the south, where the climate is milder and transportation easier. The capital is Ottawa, a city in southeastern Ontario. The commercial centers are the much larger cities of Toronto and Montréal.

Canada is an independent nation, whose head of state is the British monarch. The country is organized on federal lines, with provinces and territories. Canada was a founder member in 1994 of the North American Free Trade Agreement (NAFTA), which strengthened economic ties with the United States and Mexico to the south.

The Canadian prairies supply wheat to the world and provide pasture for cattle. The great forests send timber to the sawmills. There are reserves of oil, natural gas, copper, gold, iron ore, and nickel, and there are plenty of rivers and lakes to provide hydroelectric power. Factories manufacture cars, paper, steel, and chemicals.

IN SEARCH OF COD
The Grand Banks are shallow waters off the coast of Newfoundland. They have attracted international fishing fleets for about 500 years, but stocks of cod have declined in recent years.

Food products include maple syrup, apples, cheese, and beer. Until recently Newfoundland on the east coast lay off one of the richest fishing grounds in the world.

SKY LEVEL
Toronto's CN Tower, at about 1,814 feet high, is one of the world's tallest structures. Its viewing platform is a dizzying 1,444 feet above the ground.

LOGGING TODAY
Canada has over 1,120 million acres of forest and is the world's leading exporter of forest products. These include timber in various forms, wood pulp, and paper.

OIL RIG, ALBERTA
Over 90 percent of Canada's reserves of oil and natural gas are found in Alberta province. Major production regions are at Lloydminster, Fort McMurray, and here, at Cold Lake.

However, overfishing has led to dwindling stocks and a ban on trawling until numbers recover.

Like the United States, Canada is a melting pot of peoples and cultures. For the last 30 years Canadian politics have been dominated by the future of Québec province, where a large number of French-speakers wish to break away from the rest of Canada altogether. English-speaking Canadians share many of the interests of their American neighbors—but are always keen to emphasize their own independent way of life.

IN MONTRÉAL
Montréal, capital of Québec province, is the chief city of French-speaking Canada and a center of commerce and the arts. Shop signs are often in French.

TORONTO SKYLINE
With a population of nearly five million, Toronto is Canada's biggest city. It is a national center of business and communications.

SPACE TECH
Canada has an important aerospace industry. It built this robotic lifting device, called the Canadarm, for use on American Space Shuttles.

SUGAR MAPLE
Maple syrup is boiled up from a sweet sap, collected from the maple tree. It was invented long ago by native peoples of the St Lawrence valley. Today it is popular in Canada and the United States, where it is poured over pancakes and waffles.

⟳ CHUCK WAGON RACE

These are a feature of North America's toughest rodeo, the Calgary Stampede. Held each year in mid-July, this celebration of cowboy skills dates to 1912.

⟳ DOGSLED, QUÉBEC

Teams of dogs still pull sleds in the Arctic as a means of transportation. Dogsled racing is a popular sport.

The first people to settle Canada were prehistoric peoples, who came via the Bering Strait "land bridge" from Siberia in Asia during the last Ice Age. Their descendants include the First Peoples, who live in Canada today—groups such as the Mohawk, Micmac, Innu, Cree, Dene, and Kwakiutl.

They were followed by waves of hunters—the ancestors of today's Inuit—who set up scattered settlements across the Canadian Arctic and Greenland. Except in Greenland, the descendants of all these native peoples are today greatly outnumbered by later immigrants. They have faced a long struggle to gain rights to their own land. A huge but very sparsely-populated area of Canada became the Inuit territory of Nunavut in 1999.

Vikings from Scandinavia were the first Europeans to arrive, about 1,000 years ago, but they did not stay—perhaps because of hostility from native peoples.

⟳ QUÉBEC INUITS, 1904

A hundred years ago, hunting met all the needs of the Inuit, providing meat, hides, and fur for clothing, bones for needles, and tools and gut for thread.

⟳ CANADIAN PACIFIC

This railroad was Canada's first continental crossing. It was completed in 1885 and ran between Montréal and Port Moody, Vancouver.

⟳ THE "MOUNTIES"

The Northwest Mounted Police, with their red coats and distinctive hats, were founded in 1873 to tame the "Wild West." In 1920 they became a national force, the Royal Canadian Mounted Police.

MONSTER MASH
In a different kind of stampede, heavy-metal racers with big tyres show off in Calgary, Alberta.

THE CHAMPIONS
Ice hockey was first played in Canada in the 1850s, and today is the country's most popular sport.

WINTERLUDE
The Winterlude festival is held each February in Ottawa. Events include sculpture in ice and snow, and skating on the Rideau Canal.

In the 1500s, English and French explorers arrived. The French colonized the lands around the St Lawrence River, while the British traded around Hudson Bay. Rivalry over trade brought the two nations into conflict with each other, and in the 1700s they fought for control of Canada. The British won. After the 1770s, families loyal to Britain poured into Canada from the newly independent United States.

Despite British control, the French retained their language and Roman Catholic faith. In 1867, Québec, Ontario, Nova Scotia, and New Brunswick were united as the Dominion of Canada—a part of the British empire. Many more peoples settled in Canada as the nation expanded across the prairies toward British Columbia.

People of British (especially Scots) and French descent make up a large percentage of the population. This also now includes Ukrainians, Dutch, Russians, Poles, Germans, Italians, Chinese, Indians, Vietnamese, and Afro-Caribbeans.

TOTEM POLES
Tall poles carved from cedarwood were erected in villages along Canada's Pacific coast by native chiefs. They represented guardian spirits and histories of the family or tribe.

ACROSS THE ARCTIC
Vehicles fitted with skis, such as skidoos, have become the most popular method of travel for the Inuit and other peoples of the north.

TIMELINE

AD
1497	John Cabot discovers Newfoundland
1534	Jacques Cartier explores the St Lawrence River
1608	Samuel de Champlain founds Québec
1642	Montréal founded
1670	Hudson's Bay Company established
1713	British gain Newfoundland
1759	British defeat French at Québec
1763	Canada becomes a British colony
1840	Act of Union joins Upper and Lower Canada
1867	Dominion of Canada: Ontario, Québec, Nova Scotia, New Brunswick
1870s	Manitoba, British Columbia, Prince Edward Island join Canada
1896	Klondike gold rush (until 1898)
1905	Alberta, Saskatchewan join Canada
1914	World War I (until 1918): Canada joins Allies
1939	World War II (until 1945): Canada joins Allies
1949	Newfoundland joins Canada
1959	St Lawrence Seaway opened
1968	Separatists demand free Québec
1994	Canada in North American Free Trade Agreement (NAFTA)
1995	Québec referendum rejects separatism
1999	Self-governing homeland for Inuit (Nunavut)

MAIZE

UNITED STATES OF AMERICA

FACTS

UNITED STATES OF AMERICA
AREA: 3,615,283 sq mi.
POPULATION: 286 million
CAPITAL: Washington DC
OTHER CITIES: New York City, Los Angeles, Chicago
HIGHEST POINT: Mt McKinley (20,320 ft)
OFFICIAL LANGUAGE: English
CURRENCY: US Dollar

BERMUDA
British Overseas Territory
AREA: 20 sq mi.
POPULATION: 0.06 million
CAPITAL: Hamilton
OFFICIAL LANGUAGE: English
CURRENCY: Bermuda Dollar

BALD EAGLE

The United States of America spans the whole of central North America. The only other territory in the region is a group of 150 small islands, lying 700 miles to the southeast of the state of New York, in the North Atlantic Ocean. These make up the British colony of Bermuda.

Forty-eight of the United States lie between the Canadian and Mexican borders. This is the American heartland. It has both North Atlantic and North Pacific coastlines. The land is amazingly varied, with long, straight highways cutting through deserts and mountains, farmland and forest, linking together the big cities of the east and west.

To the far northwest, separated from the US heartland by Canada, lies Alaska. This is covered by great areas of Arctic wilderness, and is the largest state of all. Its islands are inhabited by grizzly bears and its waters by schools of whales.

Far out to the west of the US mainland, in the Pacific Ocean, are the volcanic Hawaiian islands—an outlying state of the USA. Tourists come here to enjoy the warm climate and to see the island's spectacular volcanoes.

The United States is the fourth-largest country in area in the world, after the Russian Federation, Canada, and China.

CHIPMUNK

THE STATUE OF LIBERTY
This 302-foot-high statue overlooks the New York City harbor. A gift from the French, it was dedicated in 1886.

ORGAN PIPE CACTUS NATIONAL MONUMENT
Summer temperatures can soar to 106°F in this part of Arizona. Spiny cacti, bearing pink flowers in summer, line the Ajo Mountain drive.

ALASKA

ALASKA (U.S.A.)

◯ SEA COW
The rare manatee lives along the Florida coast.

◯ THE LARGEST STATE
Alaska is a land of misty shores, islands, towering mountains, glaciers, and remote, snowy wilderness.

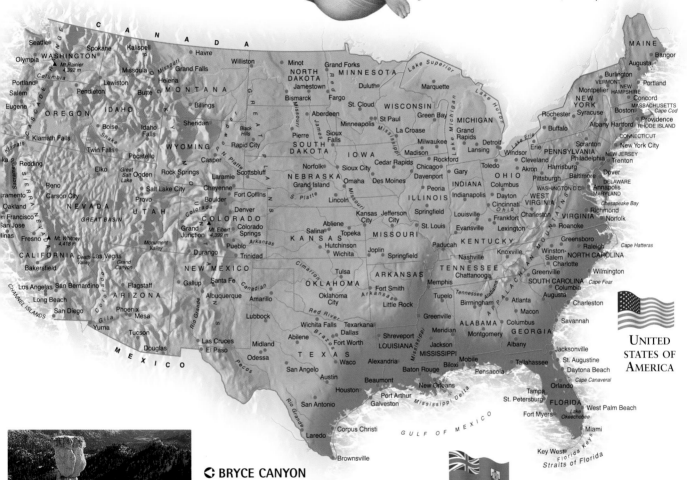

UNITED
STATES OF
AMERICA

BERMUDA

◐ BRYCE CANYON
Pink, orange, and buff-colored rocks have been eroded by wind, water, and ice into extraordinary pinnacles at this national park in Utah.

HAWAIIAN ISLANDS

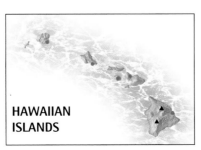

◯ NIAGARA FALLS
These spectacular waterfalls are on the United States–Canada border. They are not only a tourist attraction, but also a source of hydroelectric power.

THE EVERGLADES
The Everglades is a vast system of wetlands that drains southern Florida. Its wildlife includes alligators, tree snails, and egrets.

The northeastern United States is a temperate land of green river valleys, woodland, and rocky shores. The coastal plain is narrow in the north, but widens to the south of Chesapeake Bay, where it is fringed by long, sandy beaches. The flat lands rise to the Appalachian system, which includes the Green, White, Allegheny, and Blue mountain ranges. In the far southeast, the sunny peninsula of Florida ends in a string of small sandy islands, known as keys. Here, the calm can be shattered by violent hurricanes.

FIRE WARNING
A notice in Bryce Canyon, Utah, warns of the danger of forest fires. America's vast forests are often devastated by blazes.

To the south of the Great Lakes lies a broad plain, drained by the Missouri and Mississippi rivers. The latter forms a muddy delta where it enters the steamy Gulf of Mexico. Flat, dusty farmland stretches westward, a danger zone for sudden and devastating tornadoes. The American prairies, once a great sea of grass stretching to the badlands at the foot of the Rocky Mountains, are now patchworked with fields of crops, farm buildings, and ranches.

Beyond the massive peaks of the Rockies lie dazzling salt flats and rocks worn into bizarre shapes by the wind and weather. The Colorado River has cut the world's most impressive gorge, the Grand Canyon. The deserts of the southwest shimmer in the heat.

NIGHT-RAIDER
The raccoon, with its banded eyes and tail, often raids garbage cans by night.

CLIFF CASCADE
Beautiful waterfalls roar down the cliffs of California's Yosemite Valley. This is the upper part of the Yosemite Falls, the world's second-highest, with a drop of 2,424 feet.

LAVA FLOW
This slow-moving lava from a Hawaiian volcano is known as pahoehoe.

TORNADO TWISTERS
Raging tornadoes, also called twisters, are common in the Prairie states. They can spin at more than 300 miles per hour, sucking up anything in their path.

The Coast, Cascade, and Sierra Nevada ranges of the far west act as a barrier to rain-bearing winds from the ocean. However, the western slopes catch the rain, making the forests of the northwest cool, moist, and green. The north of California has a pleasant climate when not shrouded in fog from off the ocean. The south is hotter and drier.

Alaska stretches high into the deep-frozen Arctic and includes empty wilderness, icy shores, and some of the highest peaks in the Americas.

The 126-or-so Hawaiian islands are the tops of a broad chain of very high submarine volcanoes.

◐ THE COLORADO ROCKIES
The Rocky Mountains National Park is entered from the town of Estes Park, Colorado, on the Big Thompson River. The massive ranges of the Rockies form the backbone of the North American continent.

◐ GRAND CANYON
In Arizona, the Colorado River has carved out the world's biggest gorge. In parts, it is nearly a mile deep.

◐ THE COLORS OF THE FALL
In New England—the far northeastern region of the United States—the leaves of the temperate woodland trees turn to beautiful reds, oranges, and browns before they drop off in the fall.

◑ SEA LIONS
Graceful in the water, comical on land, sea lions live on many of the islands off the coast of California. The males can be much bigger than a grown man—nearly 10 feet long.

◐ GOLDEN GATE BRIDGE
This is California's most famous landmark. Opened in 1937, the bridge crosses a strait that connects San Francisco Bay with the open Pacific Ocean.

◑ OKEFENOKEE SWAMP
This wildlife refuge lies on the Georgia–Florida border. It is a maze of waterways, marshes, and floating islands. Its bald cypress trees are draped with Spanish moss.

109

During the last 75 years the United States has become the world's most powerful nation, and one of the richest.

It is a democratic republic, which works on a federal system; its states have powers to make their own laws. The head of state is the president, who is elected for a term of four years.

In addition to its 50 states, the USA also governs various island territories in the Pacific Ocean and the Caribbean Sea.

The United States is one of the world's great food producers, growing wheat, soya beans, corn, citrus fruits, and vegetables. Coasts and rivers produce large catches of fish. Milwaukee is famous for its beers, Kentucky for its bourbon, and California for its wines.

The United States has great mineral wealth. It drills for oil and natural gas in Texas, the Gulf of Mexico, and Alaska. It is the world's largest producer of coal. It has gold, uranium, copper, and iron ore. Dammed rivers and lakes are used to produce hydroelectric power. Managed forests provide timber, with the far northwest a major center of logging.

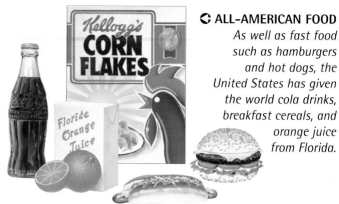

◐ ALL-AMERICAN FOOD
As well as fast food such as hamburgers and hot dogs, the United States has given the world cola drinks, breakfast cereals, and orange juice from Florida.

◐ A HOLLYWOOD STAR
Stars are inset in the pavement in Hollywood, California, as a tribute to the big names of movies. Walt Disney (1901–66) is honored as the creator of Mickey Mouse.

◑ BEFORE SEPTEMBER 11, 2001
This photo shows the New York City skyline before September 11, 2001. On that day, the twin towers of the World Trade Center (right of picture) were destroyed by terrorists.

◑ EARLY SKYSCRAPERS
The world's first high-rise buildings were built in Chicago and New York City. Better known as the "Flat Iron," because of its shape, New York's 20-storey Fuller Building was erected in 1901.

◑ HARLEY DAVIDSON ELECTRA GLIDE, 1988

◑ DISNEYWORLD
This famous Florida theme park opened in 1971—the second one to be dreamt up by the pioneer of animated film, Walt Disney. It attracts many thousands of visitors each year from all over the world.

TEXAS OIL
Texas built its wealth on cattle, cotton, and oil. Today, the United States ranks as the world's second-largest oil producer.

American factories make a wide range of household goods, textiles, and garments. California is the world center of computer technology and software, and also the center of the movie and television industry. The United States is the leading manufacturer of airplanes and spacecraft. The city of Detroit makes cars.

Services such as banking, finance, and insurance are now more important to the American economy than manufacturing. New York City's Wall Street is the center of the American financial world. The United States, with neighboring Canada and Mexico, set up the North American Free Trade Agreement (NAFTA) in 1994.

Although the United States has such great economic power, it too has its problems. Its industries face competition from other countries, where costs are lower.

◯ SHOP TILL YOU DROP!
American ways of buying and selling have spread around the world. Shopping malls are an American invention.

◯ KENNEDY SPACE CENTER
Cape Canaveral, Florida, is the launch site for many US space missions. Space shuttle flights began in 1981. Two shuttles have been lost in accidents, in 1986 and 2003.

◯ CYBER SUCCESS
The world computer revolution of the 1980s and 90s was spearheaded in "Silicon Valley," California.

◯ BIOSPHERE 2
This experimental base was set up in the Arizona Desert. Inside, all of the Earth's habitats are recreated in miniature. It is a practice-run for future space bases on other planets or on the Moon.

◯ MOUNT RUSHMORE
Completed in 1941, these giant heads show the four former US presidents Washington, Jefferson, Roosevelt, and Lincoln.

⟳ HOME RUN
Baseball is one of America's most popular sports. It has been played since the 1840s.

⟳ IN CHINATOWN
Since the 1800s, the United States has had a large population of Chinese descent. In the Chinatown district of New York's Lower East Side, signs are in Chinese and shops sell Chinese food.

Three-fourths of all Americans live in towns and cities. Hispanic and African-Americans make up the two largest minority groups.

The nation's first peoples (Native Americans, Inuit, and Aleuts) now make up only one percent of the population. There has been a strong revival of interest in their traditional cultures.

The USA has no official religion, but religion plays an important part in everyday life. Eighty-five percent of the population is Christian, with Protestants outnumbering Roman Catholics two-to-one. Two percent of Americans are Jewish, and two percent are Muslim. English is the official language, but Spanish is also widely spoken.

⟳ HOT GOSPEL
Christian churches from the African tradition developed the choral sound known as gospel music, which has also influenced popular music. This singer is a New York City policewoman.

⟳ RIDING SCHOOL, NEW MEXICO
Horse-riding has been part of the American way of life since the days of the Wild West.

⟳ HAWAIIAN DANCE
The Hawaiian islands became a state of the Union in 1959. The islanders' dances and traditional costume of grass skirts and flower garlands belong to the Polynesian culture of the Pacific.

⟳ AFRICAN–AMERICANS
America's large black population is of African descent. Afro-Americans have played an important part in the advancement of civil rights and in American culture. They invented many popular musical forms, including jazz and the blues.

⟳ NATIVE AMERICAN TRADITIONS

The first peoples still face many social and economic problems, but they have retained a fierce pride in their traditions and customs.

⟳ SKATING IN CENTRAL PARK

A haven for relaxation, Central Park lies at the heart of New York City's busy Manhattan district. It is a place to walk, jog, rollerblade, or picnic.

The majority of the population is white, of European descent. These include English, Scots, Welsh, Irish, French, Italians, Germans, Dutch, Swedes, and Poles. About nine percent are Hispanics, Spanish-speaking people originally from Mexico, Central America, or the Caribbean. There are Jews, Chinese, Japanese, Koreans, and Vietnamese. There are Polynesians from Hawaii and Samoa. About 12 percent of Americans are blacks, of African and Caribbean descent, whose ancestors were enslaved by the European settlers during the first 300 years of settlement.

The minority peoples of the United States, from the Native Americans to the Afro-Americans, have all experienced racism and poverty. And yet the real wealth of the nation lies in its rich mixture of cultures, and the broad spectrum of styles found in music and dance, writing, art, customs, beliefs, food, and festivals. American writers, artists, musicians, and movie-makers have had a great influence on the world during the last 100 years. The most popular sports—baseball, basketball and American football—are supported by millions of fans across the country.

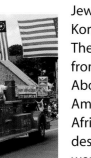

⟳ 4TH OF JULY

The United States marks its independence, won from Great Britain in 1776, each July 4. This parade is taking place in the New England state of Maine.

⟳ FREE PRESS

The United States has many famous city-based newspapers, including the Washington Post and the New York Times.

⟳ AMERICAN FOOTBALL

Fast and exciting, American football is popular both at college and at professional level. Superbowl contests have been known to attract world television audiences of over 138 million.

○ WARRING STATES
Flags of the Confederacy and the Union, the two conflicting sides in the American Civil War (1861–65).

The Native Americans are descended from prehistoric peoples who crossed into North America from the Asian region of Siberia sometime after 30,000 BC. They developed many different cultures in different parts of the Americas.

In the 1500s, English, Dutch, Spanish, and French colonists began to explore and settle the east and south. At first they made alliances with the Native Americans (whom they called "Indians"), but they soon fought bitter wars with them and with each other. Many Europeans bought African slaves to plant tobacco and cotton on the lands they had seized.

○ FORT PITT
Nineteenth-century traders meet Native Americans at Fort Pitt. The Native Americans lost their lands and their way of life as European settlers moved West.

○ A BITTER CONFLICT
Over 360,000 Union (Northern) troops were killed during the Civil War, and 260,000 Confederate (Southern) troops. Thousands of civilians also died.

The British colonists revolted against rule from London, declaring their independence in 1776. They defeated the British troops and founded a new republic. This survived a bitter civil war between the northern and southern states, which lasted from 1861–65 and brought an end to slavery.

Pioneers pushed west into "Indian Territory," seizing land and killing the Native Americans. Vast areas of land were purchased from the French, Spanish, and Russians (who governed Alaska until 1867).

○ PILGRIMS
The most famous European settlers were a group of Puritans, religious refugees from England, who founded a colony at Plymouth Rock, Massachusetts, in 1620.

THE RUSH FOR GOLD
In 1848 gold was discovered on the American River, in California. Soon prospectors were arriving from all over the world in the hope of making their fortunes.

The east became industrialized, railroads crossed the continent, gold was found in California. Thousands of poor people left Europe in search of fame and fortune in this new land.

The United States fought alongside the Allies in World War I (from 1917 to 1918). After the boom years of the 1920s came an economic crash in 1929 and years of hardship. The United States entered World War II in 1941, when Japan bombed the naval base at Pearl Harbor, Hawaii. After the end of the war in 1945, relations with one former ally, the Communist Soviet Union, went from bad to worse. During the "Cold War" that followed, the two rival superpowers remained on the brink of hostilities until the late 1980s.

MARTIN LUTHER KING
This great campaigner for civil rights won the Nobel Peace Prize in 1964. He was murdered in 1968.

AMERICA MOURNS
John F Kennedy, a young and dynamic president, was assassinated in 1963. Here he is mourned by his wife Jackie and his brother, Robert.

POLITICAL PARTIES
The two most powerful political parties are the Democrats and Republicans. Here, Democrats hold their convention in Chicago.

WESTWARD BY WAGON
In the 1840s, thousands of pioneers headed west along routes such as the Oregon Trail, which stretched for 2,000 miles.

TIMELINE

AD

1565	Spanish found St Augustine, Florida
1607	English found Jamestown, Virginia
1620	Pilgrims found Plymouth colony
1700s	Height of slave trade
1773	"Boston Tea Party"
1775	American Revolution
1776	Declaration of Independence
1783	Britain loses colonies
1789	George Washington first president
1791	Bill of Rights
1803	Louisiana Purchase
1812	War with Britain (until 1814)
1819	Florida bought from Spain
1846	War with Mexico (until 1848): California and New Mexico gained
1861	Civil War (until 1865)
1865	President Lincoln assassinated
1867	Alaska bought from Russia
1876	Battle of Little Big Horn
1898	Spanish–American War
1917	USA joins Allies in World War I (until 1918)
1929	Wall Street Crash
1941	Japan bombs Pearl Harbor; USA enters World War II (until 1945)
1950s	Cold War (until 1990)
1961	Vietnam War (until 1973)
1969	US astronauts land on the Moon
1963	President Kennedy assassinated
1994	USA enters North American Free Trade Agreement (NAFTA)
2001	Terrorist attacks on World Trade Center and Pentagon

MEXICO
AND CENTRAL AMERICA

MONARCH BUTTERFLY

FACTS

BELIZE
Republic of Belize
AREA: 8,867 sq mi.
POPULATION: 0.2 million
CAPITAL: Belmopan
OTHER CITIES: Belize City, Dangriga
HIGHEST POINT: Victoria Peak (3,681 ft)
OFFICIAL LANGUAGE: English
CURRENCY: Belize dollar

COSTA RICA
República de Costa Rica
AREA: 19,730 sq mi.
POPULATION: 3.9 million
CAPITAL: San José
OTHER CITIES: Limón, Alajuela
HIGHEST POINT: Chirripo Grande (12,533 ft)
OFFICIAL LANGUAGE: Spanish
CURRENCY: Costa Rican colon

EL SALVADOR
República de El Salvador
AREA: 8,124 sq mi.
POPULATION: 6.2 million
CAPITAL: San Salvador
OTHER CITIES: Santa Ana, San Miguel
HIGHEST POINT: Monte Cristo (7,933 ft)
OFFICIAL LANGUAGE: Spanish
CURRENCY: Salvadorean colon

GUATEMALA
República de Guatemala
AREA: 42,042 sq mi.
POPULATION: 11.6 million
CAPITAL: Guatemala City
OTHER CITIES: Puerto Barrios, Quezaltenango
HIGHEST POINT: Tajumulco (13,845 ft)
OFFICIAL LANGUAGE: Spanish
CURRENCY: quetzal

Mexico's northern border runs along the banks of a long river known in the United States as the Rio Grande and in Mexico as the Rio Bravo del Norte. It passes through hot, dusty desert.

A long, thin peninsula, Baja (Lower) California, extends southward from Tijuana into the warm, blue Pacific Ocean. The Western and Eastern Sierra Madre ranges enclose a high central plateau, which includes deserts, lakes, swamps, and smoking volcanoes. Violent earthquakes are common. Southern ranges include the Southern Sierra Madre and the Chiapas Highlands. In the far southeast, the Yucatán Peninsula forms a broad hook around the Bay of Campeche. In the south of the country, the vegetation includes lush tropical forest.

The seven small countries of Central America lie to the south of the Isthmus of Tehuantapec. The landmass snakes from northwest to southeast, reaching its narrowest point at the Isthmus of Panama. Its backbone is a series of peaks, including many active volcanoes, and high plateaus or mesas. This highland chain is broken only by the expanse of Lake Nicaragua, which covers an area of 3,250 square miles. The Caribbean coastal strip is low-lying and flat, with swamps and lagoons. The Central American climate is tropical and often hot and humid.

TEMPLE OF THE WARRIORS
This imposing temple, now ruined, was built by the fierce Toltec warriors who conquered the Maya of Chichén Itzá in AD 987.

◑ HOWLER MONKEY

Some species of these large, noisy monkeys are threatened by the loss of tropical forests in Central American rainforests.

MEXICO

◑ PANAMA CANAL

This vital shipping link was opened in 1914. It cuts through the Isthmus of Panama to link the Atlantic and Pacific Oceans.

◑ TOUCAN

This bird uses its huge bill to eat tropical fruits.

◑ CHICHÉN ITZÁ

The ruined city of Chichén Itzá in Mexico's Yucatán peninsula was a center of the Mayan and Toltec civilizations between AD 800 and 1180.

BELIZE

HONDURAS

GUATEMALA

◑ IN BELIZE

The low-lying, swampy coast of Belize is fringed by coastal shallows and islands called cays. Hurricanes are common in August and September.

NICARAGUA

◑ UNDER THE VOLCANO

Costa Rica is a mountainous country. The Arenal volcano, in the Cordillera de Guanacaste, last erupted in 1968.

EL SALVADOR

PANAMA

COSTA RICA

◑ SAGUARO CACTUS

The saguaro of Mexico's northwestern deserts is the world's biggest cactus, growing to 50 feet or more.

◑ AFTER THE HURRICANE

Much of Central America, including the Honduran capital, Tegucigalpa, was devastated by Hurricane Mitch in 1998.

◑ DOWN IN ACAPULCO

Tourists flock to Acapulco in southwestern Mexico for the beaches and fishing. The city has one of the best natural harbors in the Pacific.

◑ MARKET TRADITIONS

Bargain-hunters throng an outdoor market in Mexico City. The modern city is built on the site of the ancient Aztec capital, Tenochtitlán, which held vast, open-air markets.

◑ COFFEE BEANS

Coffee is a major export of Central American countries such as Nicaragua and Costa Rica.

Mexico is normally considered as part of North America, although its southern regions have more in common with the Central American countries to the south. It is a federal democratic republic, and in 1994 signed up to the North American Free Trade Agreement (NAFTA) with Canada and the USA.

Mexico has large oilfields in the Gulf of Mexico, as well as silver, lead, gold, and uranium. Ninety-five percent of its mineral resources are still to be mined. It manufactures fertilizers, petrochemicals, vehicles, and machines. Mexican farmers grow cotton, coffee, tropical fruits, and vegetables. There is a large fishing industry.

Mexico has the highest foreign debt of any developing country. Many of its people are very poor; over the years, large numbers have crossed illegally into the United States in search of work. Mexico City has more than 20 million people, and is probably the most polluted capital city in the world.

◑ TACOS, GUACAMOLE DIP, AND CHILLI PEPPERS

Mexico's problems are mirrored in the Central American republics of Guatemala, Belize, Honduras, El Salvador, Nicaragua, Costa Rica, and Panama. Over the last 50 years, extreme right-wing dictators in Central America have used death squads to silence any opposition. The United States—eager to prevent Communism in the region—sometimes backed their governments, who faced prolonged attack from left-wing revolutionaries. Central America also saw bitter border disputes. The root of all these conflicts has been poverty. The warfare has now mostly ended, but the rebuilding process is slow. Poverty and foreign debt remain the chief problems. The regional economy depends on coffee, bananas, cotton, sugarcane, corn, fish products, and seafood. Exports include textiles and handicrafts.

◑ SEA HARVEST

A Mexican fisherman casts his net. Sardines are by far the largest catch in these waters, followed by anchovies, tuna, and prawns.

◑ BLUE WATERS

Off Cajún, in northeast Yucatán, tourists can see the wonders of a tropical coral reef through glass-bottomed boats.

◔ BANANA TRADE

Bananas are packed for export before they ripen. The Central American countries compete fiercely with their Caribbean neighbors for their share of the world market.

◑ MINING FOR TIN

Mexico has rich mineral reserves, including tin, silver, antimony, mercury, and fluorite. Its most valuable reserves are of oil and natural gas.

◑ WOVEN BY HAND

The region is famous for its brightly colored, patterned textiles. Traditionally, these are woven on simple backstrap looms, tensioned around a fixed post.

◔ MEXICO CITY

The Mexican capital and its sprawling suburbs are home to nearly 25 million people. It is the most populous city in all the Americas and is a center of business, finance, industry, and communications.

FACTS

HONDURAS
República de Honduras
AREA: 43,277 sq mi.
POPULATION: 6.5 million
CAPITAL: Tegucigalpa
OTHER CITIES: San Pedro Sula, Choluteca
HIGHEST POINT: Cerro Las Minas (9,275 ft)
OFFICIAL LANGUAGE: Spanish
CURRENCY: Lempira

MEXICO
Estados Unidos Mexicanos
AREA: 756,066 sq mi.
POPULATION: 100 million
CAPITAL: Mexico City
OTHER CITIES: Guadalajara, Monterrey, Puebla de Zaragoza
HIGHEST POINT: Citlatépetl (18,700 ft)
OFFICIAL LANGUAGE: Spanish
CURRENCY: Mexican peso

NICARAGUA
República de Nicaragua
AREA: 50,193 sq mi.
POPULATION: 4.9 million
CAPITAL: Managua
OTHER CITIES: León, Granada
HIGHEST POINT: Cordillera Isabella (7,998 ft)
OFFICIAL LANGUAGE: Spanish
CURRENCY: córdoba

PANAMA
República de Panamá
AREA: 29,157 sq mi.
POPULATION: 2.9 million
CAPITAL: Panama City
OTHER CITIES: San Miguelito, Colón, David
HIGHEST POINT: Volcán Baru (11,400 ft)
OFFICIAL LANGUAGE: Spanish
CURRENCY: Balboa

119

THE AMERICAS

◑ AN OLMEC HEAD
This colossal stone head was carved about 3,000 years ago by the Olmec people of ancient Mexico.

From about 1200 BC onward, Mexico and Central America saw the rise of some great civilizations founded by indigenous (native) peoples—the Olmecs, Maya, Toltecs, and Aztecs. Ruined cities, stepped pyramids, and large temples may still be seen. When the Spanish invaded the region in AD 1519, they were awestruck by the wonders of the Aztec capital, Tenochtitlán (today's Mexico City).

The indigenous peoples, whom the Spanish called "Indians," were skilled astronomers, mathematicians, writers, musicians, and craftspeople. But lacking firearms, they were soon defeated by Spanish guns. The region became part of Spain's overseas empire for the next 300 years or so.

◔ MITLA RUINS
Mitla, in southern Mexico, was an ancient holy site. It was occupied by the Mixtecs about 1,000 years ago. The ruins still bear traces of the original paint, made from berries.

◑ TEXTILE WEAVING
Skeins of brilliant colored wools for hand weaving are piled high ready for sale in this Guatemalan market.

After independence in 1823, power in Mexico remained in the hands of a few wealthy landowners. The country lost large areas of territory to the United States in the 1840s, and from 1910 until 1917 it was torn apart by revolution and civil war.

After the Central American nations gained independence, they at first tried to unite in a federation, but went their separate ways in 1838. Here, too, the people remained poor, while a few landowners grew very rich. Belize was a British colony—British Honduras—from 1862 to 1981.

◔ AN AZTEC HEADDRESS
The Aztecs were fine craftworkers, producing beautiful feather cloaks and headdresses, intricate jewelry, and patterned textiles.

◔ THE MAYA
The classic period of Mayan civilization lasted from about AD 250 to 900. It was marked by the building of cities with great stone temples and pyramids. The homeland of the Maya stretched from Mexico's Yucatán peninsula southward into Guatemala and Belize. Their descendants still live in these regions today.

The peoples of the region enjoy a rich culture. Some are of European descent, and many more are mestizos, people of mixed native and Spanish descent. Indigenous peoples living in the region include large groups of Maya, as well as Otomi, Tarascan, Zapotec, Mixtec, Tarahumara, Nahua, Miskito, Guaymi, and Cuna. The Garifuna, who live in Belize, Honduras, and Nicaragua, are descended from Africans and from an indigenous people—the Caribs. The whole region is Spanish-speaking. Indigenous languages are also spoken and English is heard in Belize and on Nicaragua's east coast.

◑ COLONIAL ARCHITECTURE
Spanish-built churches may be seen in Taxco de Alarcón, Mexico. The region was a center of mining before the Spanish arrived in 1528.

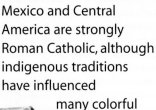

◑ MIXED TRADITIONS
Ancient Mayan rituals have influenced the Christian worship of the Quiché Maya of Guatemala.

Mexico and Central America are strongly Roman Catholic, although indigenous traditions have influenced many colorful religious festivals and processions.

◑ DAY OF THE DEAD
Mexicans commemorate their dead each year on November 1st. Altars are laden with food offerings, papier-mâché skeletons, photographs, and flowers.

TIMELINE

BC

| c.2600 | Origins of Maya civilization in Yucatán |
| c.1000 | Origins of Zapotec civilization |

AD

300s	Mayan empire (until 900s)
c.1325	Aztecs build great city of Tenochtitlán
1400s	Height of Aztec empire
1519	Spain invades Aztec empire (conquers by 1521)
1600s	Pirate attacks on Atlantic coast
1810	Revolt against Spanish rule in Mexico
1821	Collapse of Spanish rule in Central America
1823	United provinces of Central America (by 1838): Honduras, Costa Rica, El Salvador, Guatemala, Nicaragua
1846	Mexican War with USA (until 1848): loss of California and New Mexico
1862	British Honduras (Belize) a British colony
1911	Mexican Revolution: political reform
1914	Panama Canal opens
1970s	Political violence in Guatemala
1978	Nicaraguan Revolution
1981	Belize independent
1985	Earthquake, Mexico City
1994	Uprising in Chiapas, Mexico
	Mexico enters North American Free Trade Agreement (NAFTA)
2001	Third Summit of the Americas discusses a wider Free Trade Area

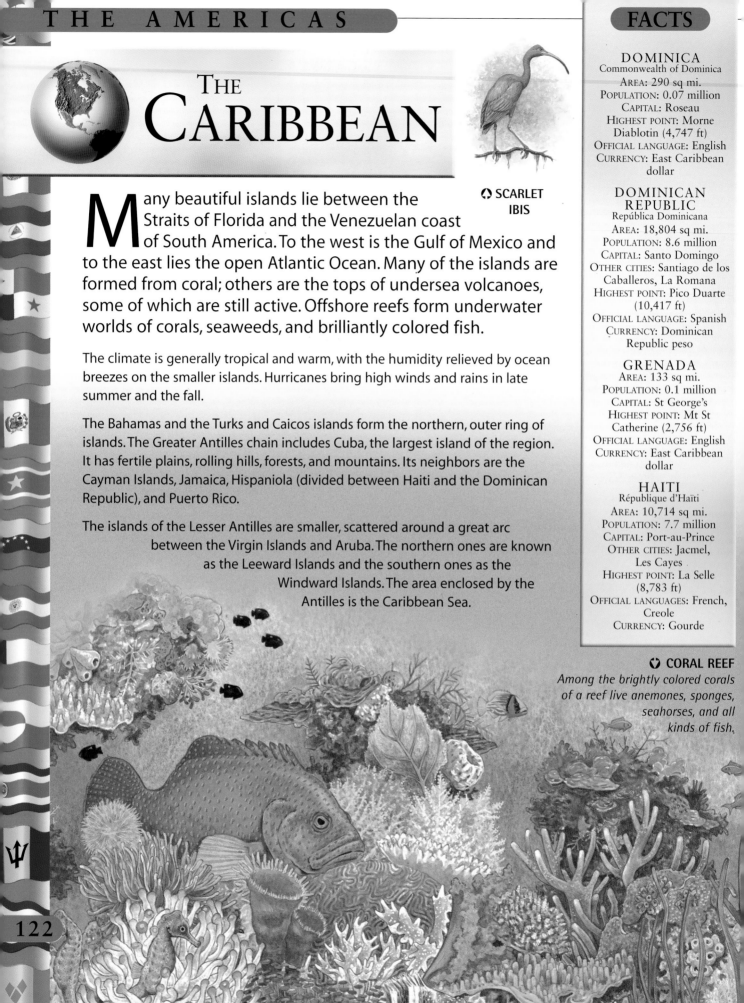

THE CARIBBEAN

◊ SCARLET IBIS

Many beautiful islands lie between the Straits of Florida and the Venezuelan coast of South America. To the west is the Gulf of Mexico and to the east lies the open Atlantic Ocean. Many of the islands are formed from coral; others are the tops of undersea volcanoes, some of which are still active. Offshore reefs form underwater worlds of corals, seaweeds, and brilliantly colored fish.

The climate is generally tropical and warm, with the humidity relieved by ocean breezes on the smaller islands. Hurricanes bring high winds and rains in late summer and the fall.

The Bahamas and the Turks and Caicos islands form the northern, outer ring of islands. The Greater Antilles chain includes Cuba, the largest island of the region. It has fertile plains, rolling hills, forests, and mountains. Its neighbors are the Cayman Islands, Jamaica, Hispaniola (divided between Haiti and the Dominican Republic), and Puerto Rico.

The islands of the Lesser Antilles are smaller, scattered around a great arc between the Virgin Islands and Aruba. The northern ones are known as the Leeward Islands and the southern ones as the Windward Islands. The area enclosed by the Antilles is the Caribbean Sea.

DOMINICA
Commonwealth of Dominica
AREA: 290 sq mi.
POPULATION: 0.07 million
CAPITAL: Roseau
HIGHEST POINT: Morne Diablotin (4,747 ft)
OFFICIAL LANGUAGE: English
CURRENCY: East Caribbean dollar

DOMINICAN REPUBLIC
República Dominicana
AREA: 18,804 sq mi.
POPULATION: 8.6 million
CAPITAL: Santo Domingo
OTHER CITIES: Santiago de los Caballeros, La Romana
HIGHEST POINT: Pico Duarte (10,417 ft)
OFFICIAL LANGUAGE: Spanish
CURRENCY: Dominican Republic peso

GRENADA
AREA: 133 sq mi.
POPULATION: 0.1 million
CAPITAL: St George's
HIGHEST POINT: Mt St Catherine (2,756 ft)
OFFICIAL LANGUAGE: English
CURRENCY: East Caribbean dollar

HAITI
République d'Haïti
AREA: 10,714 sq mi.
POPULATION: 7.7 million
CAPITAL: Port-au-Prince
OTHER CITIES: Jacmel, Les Cayes
HIGHEST POINT: La Selle (8,783 ft)
OFFICIAL LANGUAGES: French, Creole
CURRENCY: Gourde

◊ CORAL REEF
Among the brightly colored corals of a reef live anemones, sponges, seahorses, and all kinds of fish.

ANTIGUA AND BARBUDA
AREA: 171 sq mi.
POPULATION: 71,000
CAPITAL: St Johns
HIGHEST POINT: Boggy Peak (1,329 ft)
OFFICIAL LANGUAGE: English
CURRENCY: East Caribbean dollar

BAHAMAS
Commonwealth of the Bahamas
AREA: 5,382 sq mi.
POPULATION: 0.3 million
CAPITAL: Nassau
HIGHEST POINT: Cat Island (207 ft)
OFFICIAL LANGUAGE: English
CURRENCY: Bahamian dollar

BARBADOS
AREA: 166 sq mi.
POPULATION: 0.26 million
CAPITAL: Bridgetown
HIGHEST POINT: Mt Hillaby (1,115 ft)
OFFICIAL LANGUAGE: English
CURRENCY: Barbados dollar

CUBA
República de Cuba
AREA: 42,803 sq mi.
POPULATION: 11.0 million
CAPITAL: Havana
OTHER CITIES: Santiago de Cuba, Camagüey
HIGHEST POINT: Turquino (6,578 ft)
OFFICIAL LANGUAGE: Spanish
CURRENCY: Cuban peso

⟳ PALM TREES
Everyone's image of the Caribbean is of beautiful palm trees swaying in the breeze. Here, on the sunny island of Jamaica, coconuts are growing in trees that can be as tall as 80 feet.

⟳ STORMY WEATHER
Satellites in space track the progress of a hurricane. These devastating, whirling storms sweep across the Caribbean between August and October each year.

BAHAMAS

ST KITTS AND NEVIS

ANTIGUA AND BARBUDA

CUBA

PUERTO RICO

DOMINICA

JAMAICA

HAITI

ST LUCIA

DOMINICAN REPUBLIC

TRINIDAD AND TOBAGO

BARBADOS

ST VINCENT AND THE GRENADINES

GRENADA

⟳ DONKEY TRAFFIC
Donkeys are a traditional way of getting around in the mountainous countryside of the Dominican Republic.

⟳ TROPICAL BEACH, ST LUCIA
St Lucia is a volcanic island lying in the Windward Islands. Its white sand beaches and spectacular scenery attract many tourists.

123

☾ CHE GUEVARA
Argentinian-born Ernesto "Che" Guevara played an important part in the Cuban revolution (1956–59). He was killed in Bolivia in 1967.

☾ BOAT BUILDING
A wooden hull is constructed in Barbados. Boats are still built by traditional methods on many Caribbean islands.

FACTS

JAMAICA
AREA: 4,244 sq mi.
POPULATION: 2.5 million
CAPITAL: Kingston
OTHER CITIES: Spanish Town, Montego Bay
HIGHEST POINT: Blue Mountain Peak (7,402 ft)
OFFICIAL LANGUAGE: English
CURRENCY: Jamaican dollar

ST KITTS – NEVIS
Federation of St Christopher and Nevis
AREA: 104 sq mi.
POPULATION: 0.04 million
CAPITAL: Basseterre
HIGHEST POINT: Liamuiga (3,793 ft)
OFFICIAL LANGUAGE: English
CURRENCY: East Caribbean dollar

ST LUCIA
AREA: 617 sq mi.
POPULATION: 0.16 million
CAPITAL: Castries
HIGHEST POINT: Mt Gimie (3,145 ft)
OFFICIAL LANGUAGE: English
CURRENCY: East Caribbean dollar

ST VINCENT AND THE GRENADINES
AREA: 150 sq mi.
POPULATION: 0.11 million
CAPITAL: Kingstown
HIGHEST POINT: La Soufrière (4,173 ft)
OFFICIAL LANGUAGE: English
CURRENCY: East Caribbean dollar

TRINIDAD AND TOBAGO
Republic of Trinidad and Tobago
AREA: 1,980 sq mi.
POPULATION: 1.3 million
CAPITAL: Port-of-Spain
OTHER CITIES: San Fernando, Arima
HIGHEST POINT: Aripo (3,084 ft)
OFFICIAL LANGUAGE: English
CURRENCY: Trinidad and Tobago dollar

☾ RADIO TELESCOPE
The world's biggest single-unit radio telescope is located near Arecibo, on the island of Puerto Rico.

There are 13 independent nations in the Caribbean region. Some are democratic republics, some still have European monarchs as their heads of state. Economic links are strengthened by the Caribbean Community and Common Market (Caricom, founded in 1973). Most of the Caribbean's 11 other territories remain dependencies of other countries by choice, because it brings them wealth and security. Some are governed as if they were part of mainland France.

Cuba, the largest Caribbean island, has had a Communist government since 1959, and until 1991 had vital trading links with the Communist countries of Central and Eastern Europe. Since the collapse of Communism in Europe, Cuba has had to struggle against a strict United States ban on trade.

Political violence and corruption have a long history on some islands, such as Haiti. On other islands, the problem has been one of alliances. For example, Anguilla refused to join the federation of St Kitts–Nevis when it became independent, and Aruba pulled out of the Netherlands Antilles. Other islands have been hard hit by natural disasters, such as hurricanes or volcanic eruptions.

Many of the Caribbean islanders are poor. Cash crops produced for export include spices, tropical fruits such as bananas, mangoes, and limes, sugarcane and cotton. Cuba is famous for its rum and tobacco. Many islanders fish and grow their own food. Popular local dishes are made from saltfish, pigeon peas, coconut, chilli peppers, and cornmeal.

☾ CHANGING TIMES
St Lucia's Rodney Bay was once a swampy coastline with a couple of fishing villages. In the 1940s it was transformed into a US naval airbase. Today it is a tourist center, with a yachting marina and many hotels.

☾ MARKET DAY
What's on sale in a Caribbean market? Lush tropical fruits, coconuts, saltfish, seafood, and vegetables. Snacks on offer are sure to include rotis—pancakes wrapped around curried chicken and vegetables.

↺ Fidel Castro
The leader of Cuba's revolution was Fidel Castro. He overthrew the regime of Fulgencio Batista in 1959.

Manufacturing is limited, but Trinidad produces oil and natural gas. The region's blue seas and beaches of white sand fringed with palms have made tourism a major industry in many islands. Other islands, such as the Caymans, have passed tax laws that allow international finance companies and banks to set up their headquarters there. The wealth made from tourism and offshore banking often fails to benefit the local people.

↻ CARIBBEAN VILLAGE
Most Caribbeans live in simple, one-storey homes. White walls reflect the sun and keep the interiors cool despite the fierce heat outside. Up to four generations of the same family may live together in one or these small houses.

↻ WORLD-CLASS CIGARS
Cuba has long been famous for the finest quality cigars and for rum, made from sugarcane.

FACTS

Caribbean dependencies

ANGUILLA
British Overseas Territory
AREA: 35 sq mi.
POPULATION: 9,000
CAPITAL: The Valley
OFFICIAL LANGUAGE: English
CURRENCY: East Caribbean dollar

ARUBA
Self-governing island of the Netherlands
AREA: 75 sq mi.
POPULATION: 0.08 million
CAPITAL: Oranjestad
OFFICIAL LANGUAGE: Dutch
CURRENCY: Florin

CAYMAN ISLANDS
British Overseas Territory
AREA: 102 sq mi.
POPULATION: 0.03 million
CAPITAL: George Town
OFFICIAL LANGUAGE: English
CURRENCY: Cayman Islands dollar

GUADELOUPE
Overseas region of France
AREA: 658 sq mi.
POPULATION: 0.4 million
CAPITAL: Basse-Terre
OFFICIAL LANGUAGE: French
CURRENCY: Euro

MARTINIQUE
Overseas region of France
AREA: 425 sq mi.
POPULATION: 0.4 million
CAPITAL: Fort-de-France
OFFICIAL LANGUAGE: French
CURRENCY: Euro

◐ THE SLAVE TRADE
From the 1500s to the 1800s, slaves were brought to the Caribbean from Africa and were sold at markets. Families were separated, and punishments were harsh, often fatal.

◑ SUGAR PLANTATIONS
Sugarcane was the mainstay of the Caribbean economy from the 1600s until recent times. Sugar was shipped to Europe and North America. Slaves imported from West Africa worked the European-owned plantations.

FACTS

Caribbean dependencies

MONTSERRAT
British Overseas Territory
AREA: 39 sq mi.
POPULATION: 6,000
CAPITAL: Plymouth
OFFICIAL LANGUAGE: English
CURRENCY: East Caribbean dollar

NETHERLANDS ANTILLES
Self-governing islands of the Netherlands
AREA: 308 sq mi.
POPULATION: 0.2 million
CAPITAL: Willemstad
OFFICIAL LANGUAGE: Dutch
CURRENCY: Netherlands Antilles guilder

PUERTO RICO
Commonwealth territory of the USA
AREA: 3,427 sq mi.
POPULATION: 3.8 million
CAPITAL: San Juan
OFFICIAL LANGUAGES: English, Spanish
CURRENCY: US dollar

TURKS AND CAICOS ISLANDS
British Overseas Territory
AREA: 166 sq mi.
POPULATION: 0.01 million
CAPITAL: Cockburn Town
OFFICIAL LANGUAGE: English
CURRENCY: US dollar

VIRGIN ISLANDS (BRITISH)
British Overseas Territory
AREA: 58 sq mi.
POPULATION: 0.02 million
CAPITAL: Road Town
OFFICIAL LANGUAGE: English
CURRENCY: US dollar

VIRGIN ISLANDS (USA)
Unincorporated Territory of the USA
AREA: 134 sq mi.
POPULATION: 0.1 million
CAPITAL: Charlotte Amalie
OFFICIAL LANGUAGE: English
CURRENCY: US dollar

In prehistoric times the Caribbean islands were settled by indigenous people from the American mainland. By the time Columbus sailed to the islands in 1492, there were two main groups of peoples on the islands—the Arawaks and Caribs. The Arawaks were savagely treated by the Spanish. They were enslaved, murdered, or infected with diseases. The Caribs, who had a fearsome reputation among the Europeans, resisted longer. In the end, however, few communities survived.

The Spanish took over many islands. As their fleets shipped back plundered treasures from the mainland (the "Spanish Main"), they were preyed on by British, French, and Dutch pirates. Soon these countries too seized islands and planted them with tobacco and sugarcane. They imported slaves from Africa to work the land. Cruelly treated, some slaves escaped and there were violent revolts in Jamaica and Haiti in the 1700s. In the 1800s, Haiti became the first independent Afro-Caribbean republic.

◑ CARNIVAL
Carnival in Trinidad is a time for dressing up in costumes, dancing, steel-band music, and verses called calypsos.

◓ THE SANTA MARIA
Christopher Columbus' ship reached San Salvador, in the Bahamas, in 1492—a turning point in American history.

◑ PIRATE WOMEN
Two notorious women pirates, Anne Bonny and Mary Read, went on trial in Jamaica in 1720. Caribbean coasts had long been terrorized by pirates and buccaneers.

⟳ BACK TO AFRICA
Rastafarians look back to their African roots and honor Haile Selassie (1891–1975), former emperor of Ethiopia.

After the abolition of slavery (mostly in the 1830s) many European settlers left the region they called the West Indies. People from India and Southeast Asia were hired to work on some islands, such as Trinidad. Most Caribbean islands remained colonies until the 1960s.

Today's Caribbeans are descended from many peoples—Native Americans, Africans, Spanish, English, Irish, French, Dutch, and Asians. The two largest ethnic groups are of Afro-Caribbean and Hispanic descent. Spanish, English, and French are widely spoken, often in Creole dialects influenced by African languages.

Christianity is strong. On Haiti, some people practice Voodoo, an African spirit religion. The Rastafarians of Jamaica are inspired by African spirituality.

Caribbean music and dance styles—from salsa to reggae—have become popular all over the world. Music comes to the fore in the region's famous carnivals. Popular sports include cricket, soccer, and baseball.

⟳ STEEL BAND
Steel drums called pans make the typical sound of Trinidad.

⟳ THE MUCH-LOVED GAME OF CRICKET
West Indian cricket teams have been world-beaters since the 1960s. It is a hugely popular sport in the Caribbean islands.

⟳ HAITIAN VOODOO
Drums and dancing send people into a trance at Cap Haitien. Voodoo, known as Vodun in the Creole dialect of Haiti, is based on an African belief in spirits called loas. It inspired the slave revolts on Haiti and is still popular today.

TIMELINE

AD

c.200	Native American settlement: Ciboney people expelled from Cuba by the Taíno
c.1000	Arawak and Carib migrations and wars
1492	Christopher Columbus lands in the Bahamas
1496	First Spanish settlement, Santo Domingo (Hispaniola)
1511	Spanish settle Cuba
1523	Slave trade with Africa
1655	British capture Jamaica
1660s	Piracy widespread (until 1720s)
1697	French gain control of Haiti (Hispaniola)
1804	Haiti independent republic under black rule
1838	Abolition of slave trade in some parts of the region
1868	Independence movement defeated in Cuba (by 1878)
1895	Uprising in Cuba (until 1898)
1898	Puerto Rico ceded to USA
1952	Fulgencio Batista seizes power in Cuba
1959	Fidel Castro overthrows Batista in Cuba
1961	Barbados independent
1962	Cuban Missile Crisis: clash with USA over siting of Soviet missile base. Jamaica, Trinidad independent
1973	Bahamas independent
1983	USA invades Grenada
1995	Series of volcanic eruptions on Montserrat

127

NORTHERN ANDEAN COUNTRIES

○ BIRD WITH SNAKE
Beautiful stone carvings were made at San Augustín, Colombia, about 2,000 years ago.

FACTS

BOLIVIA
República de Bolivia
AREA: 424,164 sq mi.
POPULATION: 8.5 million
CAPITALS: La Paz, Sucre
OTHER CITIES: Santa Cruz, Cochabamba
HIGHEST POINT: Nevado Sajama (21,463 ft)
OFFICIAL LANGUAGE: Spanish
CURRENCY: Peso boliviano

COLOMBIA
República de Colombia
AREA: 440,831 sq mi.
POPULATION: 43 million
CAPITAL: Bogotá
OTHER CITIES: Medellín, Cali, Barranquilla
HIGHEST POINT: Cristobal Colón (19,029 ft)
OFFICIAL LANGUAGE: Spanish
CURRENCY: Colombian peso

ECUADOR
República del Ecuador
AREA: 178,176 sq mi. (including Galápagos Islands)
POPULATION: 12.8 million
CAPITAL: Quito
OTHER CITIES: Guayaquil, Cuenca
HIGHEST POINT: Chimborazo (20,702 ft)
OFFICIAL LANGUAGE: Spanish
CURRENCY: Dollar

PERU
República de Peru
AREA: 496,225 sq mi.
POPULATION: 26 million
CAPITAL: Lima
OTHER CITIES: Callao, Arequipa, Chiclayo
HIGHEST POINT: Nevado Huascarán (22,205 ft)
OFFICIAL LANGUAGES: Spanish, Quechua, Aymará
CURRENCY: Nuevo sol

The Andes mountains run the length of South America, from Colombia in the north to Tierra del Fuego in the south—nearly 4,000 miles. The mountains are very high, very beautiful, and very valuable, for they contain precious silver, tin, and other minerals.

The Andes range includes massive snow-capped volcanoes, gleaming glaciers, and wide, cool plateaus. Titicaca, the world's highest navigable lake, occupies 3,200 square miles of the plateau on the border between Peru and Bolivia. To the north, the Andes drop to low-lying plains around the humid Caribbean coast. To the west, they are bordered by a coastal strip along the Pacific Ocean. In parts this is humid and fertile, but in Peru much of it is dusty desert, made dry because cold ocean currents make it more difficult for the air to fill with moisture and form rain.

Far out west in the Pacific is the Galápagos island chain, which belongs to Ecuador. In eastern Ecuador, the peaks and sunlit plateaus of the Andes descend through misty foothills and sheer-sided valleys into the vast rainforests of central South America. Streams rising on the eastern slopes drain into the great Orinoco and Amazon river systems.

○ BAÑOS, ECUADOR
This small town lies in the eastern Andes, on the route to El Oriente, Ecuador's province in the Amazon River basin.

COLOMBIA

○ ANDES WATERSHED
South America is divided into two by the Andes range. Some rainfall drains into the Pacific Ocean, but the rest flows eastward into the distant Atlantic.

○ LAKE TITICACA
This is the largest lake in South America. It is really made up of two smaller lakes, Chucuito and Uinamarca, which are linked by a narrow strait.

ECUADOR

○ ONE MORE RIVER TO CROSS
The Urubamba rises in the Andes and flows through deep gorges. It eventually joins up with the Apurímac to form the Ucayali, which in turn drains into the mighty Amazon.

PERU

Map labels
Point. Gallinas
Barranquilla
Cartagena
Cristobal Colón 5,775 m
PANAMA
VENEZUELA
Cauca
Magdalena
Cape Corrientes
Medellín
Manizales
Pereira
Ibagué
Bogotá
Meta
COLOMBIA
Buenaventura
Cali · Neiva
Nevado del Huila 5,750 m
Pasto
Guaviare
Point Galera
Quito
ECUADOR
Chimborazo 6,267 m
Caquetá
Putumayo
Guayaquil
Gulf of Guayaquil
Iquitos
Amazon
Marañón
Point Aguja
Piura
BRAZIL
Chiclayo
Trujillo
Ucayali
Nevado Huascarán 6,768 m
Chimbote
PERU
Callao
Huancayo
Lima
Cuzco
Paracas Pen.
Volcán El Misti 5,842 m
Nevado Ancohume 6,550 m
Mamoré
Guaporé
Nazca
Arequipa
Lake Titicaca
La Paz
BOLIVIA
Cochabamba · Santa Cruz
Oruro
PACIFIC OCEAN
Lake Poopó
Sucre
Potosí
Pilcomayo
CHILE
ALTIPLANO
PARAGUAY

BOLIVIA

○ EASTERN BOLIVIA
These village huts are in the Las Yungas region of eastern Bolivia, where the Altiplano (high plateau) drops to the humid, forested lowlands of the Amazon basin.

○ CONDOR

N
W E
S

○ HIGH ALTITUDE
The Chacaltuya ski lodge near La Paz, Bolivia, is the world's highest. It overlooks the tablelands of the Altiplano.

○ RIVER OF ICE
In Peru, the Andes divide into three main sections. The highest peaks rise in the Cordillera Blanca. Here, snow-capped peaks tower above glaciers such as Pastoruri, at 17,390 feet above sea level.

○ FISHING
The Aymara and Uru peoples of Lake Titicaca fish in the deep lake for catfish, trout, and killifish.

○ COCAINE PATROL
A plane hunts for secret plantations of coca. The coca plant is processed to make the drug called cocaine.

The four countries of the northern Andes are all republics. The army has often seized power in this region, or controlled governments behind the scenes. There have been long years of guerrilla warfare, fueled by widespread poverty and social injustice. There have been murderous activities by the criminal gangs who export cocaine. This illegal drug is made from the coca plant, which has been grown by poor peasants in the region for thousands of years.

The northern Andes region has great mineral wealth in the form of oil, copper, emeralds, silver, tin, zinc, lead,

○ GATHERING REEDS
Tall, tough reeds called totora grow on the shores and islands of Lake Titicaca, and on floating platforms of vegetation. The reeds are harvested and bound together in bundles to make houses and fishing boats, called balsas.

○ ANDEAN STATION
Alausí, in Ecuador's Chimborazo province, is built on the Guayaquil–Quito railroad. The world's highest railroads are in the Andes, in Peru.

○ REED PIPES
Known as antaras or zampoñas, panpipes have been played since the days of the Incas.

silver and gold. However, many people, both in the cities and in the country, remain very poor. In the hot lowlands, farmers grow cotton, sugarcane, and bananas. Colombian coffee beans, grown on tropical slopes, are among the best in the world. On the cool plateaus, potatoes, corn, wheat, and a grain called quinoa are grown.

The forests produce valuable timber. Sardines, anchovies, and tuna are caught by the large Pacific fishing fleets. Shrimps are farmed along the coast. Fish are also processed to make fertilizers.

○ LOCAL TRANSPORT
A motorized rickshaw provides transportation in Chiclayo, the chief town of Peru's Lambayeque region. It lies on the Pan-American Highway, the road network that links North and South America.

☉ LIMA STADIUM

Peru's National Stadium is sited in Lima, the capital. Lima is home to nearly six million people.

☉ SILVER MOUNTAIN

When the Spanish conquered Bolivia, Cerro Rico, in Potosi, became the world's biggest silver mine. The riches were shipped back to Europe.

☉ COLOMBIAN CAPITAL

Mountains rise behind Bogotá's modern high-rise skyline. Colombia's chief city is home to some five million people.

The region is strongly Roman Catholic and there are many religious festivals and pilgrimages. Spanish is spoken in all four countries. There are many people of mestizo (mixed European and Indian) descent, as well as some of European, African, or Asian descent. Indigenous (native) peoples make up just one percent of the population in Colombia, but 25 percent in Ecuador, 45 percent in Peru, and 55 percent in Bolivia.

The two largest indigenous groups are the Aymara and Quechua. Most of these "Indians" are poor peasants and are largely ignored by those who hold power in the cities. In the mountains, life carries on as it has for centuries, with the local people weaving, going to market, and herding llamas. The haunting folk music of the Andes is played on guitars, panpipes, flutes, and drums.

☉ FARMING THE SLOPES

Farmers were already terracing the steep Andean slopes in ancient times, in order to conserve soil. The Incas were masters of irrigation techniques.

☉ MULE TRAIN

Surefooted but stubborn, mules have been used to transport goods in the Andes since the 1500s.

In prehistoric times, the northern Andes region was settled by waves of different tribes, and many advanced ancient civilizations developed there.

From about 1200 BC to 200 BC, the Chavín civilization produced stone carvings, pottery, and painted textiles. Strange lines and complex designs cut deep into the desert near Nazca in southern Peru may have been made to honor the gods. Farther north, the Moche valley was the center of a civilization that built pyramids in honor of the Sun, and engineered an irrigation system for crops in dry regions.

◊ INCA STONES
The Incas were master stone masons. Their stone buildings have withstood the strongest earthquakes.

◊ TEMPLE OF THE SUN
This pyramid dominated the Moche capital. Standing 131 feet high, it is believed to have been made of about 140 million mud bricks.

Over 1,000 years ago, the Chimú people of northern Peru were masters at working gold. They also produced pottery on a large scale.

Perhaps the most amazing civilization was that of the Incas, who defeated the Chimú in AD 1476. The Inca empire, with its capital at Cuzco in Peru, stretched from Ecuador to Chile, and ruled some 12 million people. The Incas built cities and towns with great temples, and they studied the stars.

Spain invaded Colombia in 1499. By 1532 a small force of Spanish soldiers, the conquistadors, had used treachery to overthrow the powerful Inca empire to the south. They were greedy for gold and silver, and the northern Andes offered wealth beyond their dreams.

◊ LA PAZ, BOLIVIA
A street vendor sells vegetables in La Paz, one of Bolivia's twin capitals. La Paz, at 11,913 feet above sea level, is the world's highest capital.

◊ LURE OF GOLD
The Spanish were first attracted to South America by rumors of a wealth of gold.

◊ INCA TRAIL
Across the empire, the Incas built mountain strongholds, towns, canals, forts, resthouses, and irrigation schemes, so more land could be farmed. Goods were carried by llama and messages by relays of runners.

MACHU PICCHU
The best-known of Peru's Inca cities was built high above the gorges of the Urubamba valley, probably in the 15th century. It was surrounded by terraced field strips for farming.

Spain's rule over the region lasted nearly 300 years. The Spanish built churches and cities, mined for silver, and used the indigenous people to work the land. In the 1820s a revolutionary named Simón Bolívar (1783–1830) led the struggle against continuing rule by Spain. His name was given to one of the territories he freed—Bolivia.

Liberated from Spanish rule, the newly independent countries soon fought each other. A few families of the ruling class became very wealthy, but most people remained poor into modern times.

QUITO, ECUADOR
The capital of Ecuador has old colonial buildings alongside modern offices and factories. The city is built at 9,350 feet above sea level, beneath the Pichincha volcano.

PILGRIMAGE
The Spanish conquerors brought Roman Catholicism to the Andes. This is the Sanctuary of Nuestra Señora de Acua Santa, in Ecuador.

CONQUEST
The Spanish reached Peru in 1532. They captured the emperor, Atahualpa, by treachery and soon conquered all the Inca lands, although resistance continued for 40 years.

TIMELINE

BC	
8500	Possible origins of farming in Peru
3000	Pottery made in Colombia and Ecuador
1500	Metalworking in Peru
900	Chavín civilization in Andes
200	Nazca civilization, Peru
AD	
1	Moche civilization, Peru
600	Tiahuanaco civilization, Bolivia
1200	Beginnings of Inca empire
1250	Chimu civilization, Peru
1400s	Inca empire at greatest extent
1531	Spanish land in Ecuador
1533	Incas defeated by Spanish
1538	Colombia conquered by Spanish
1545	Silver mining in Bolivia
1780	Indigenous uprising in Peru
1819	Colombia independent from Spain
1822	Ecuador joins Colombia
1824	Peru independent from Spain
1825	Bolivia independent from Spain
1830	Full independence for Colombia; Ecuador independent
1932	Chaco War (until 1935): Bolivia defeated by Paraguay
1941	Peru invades Ecuador
1948	Organization of American States signed, Colombia
1952	Bolivian National Revolution
1989	Drug gang violence in Colombia

133

BRAZIL
AND ITS NEIGHBORS

○ FLESH-EATERS
Shoals of flesh-eating piranha fish are found in the Amazon basin.

FACTS

BRAZIL
República Federativa do Brasil
AREA: 3,265,076 sq mi.
POPULATION: 172 million
CAPITAL: Brasília
OTHER CITIES: São Paulo, Rio de Janeiro, Salvador, Belo Horizonte, Pôrto Alegre
HIGHEST POINT: Neblina (9,888 ft)
OFFICIAL LANGUAGE: Portuguese
CURRENCY: Real

GUYANA
Co-operative Republic of Guyana
AREA: 83,000 sq mi.
POPULATION: 0.8 million
CAPITAL: Georgetown
OTHER CITIES: New Amsterdam, Linden
HIGHEST POINT: Roraima (9,094 ft)
OFFICIAL LANGUAGE: English
CURRENCY: Guyana dollar

SURINAM
Republic of Suriname
AREA: 63,251 sq mi.
POPULATION: 0.4 million
CAPITAL: Paramaribo
OTHER CITIES: Groningen, Nieuw Amsterdam
HIGHEST POINT: Juliana Top (4,035 ft)
OFFICIAL LANGUAGE: Dutch
CURRENCY: Surinam guilder

Venezuela ("Little Venice") was given its name because the vast, shallow inlet of Lake Maracaibo reminded early European explorers of the lagoons around Venice in Italy.

Venezuela is dominated by the Orinoco River, which forces its way between a northern spur of the Andes Mountains and the Guiana Highlands. It flows through the grassy plains of the llanos to form a wide, swampy delta on the Caribbean coast. In the central southeast, the Angel Falls—the world's highest waterfall—drop a spectacular 3,211 feet.

The low-lying Caribbean coast, with its hot, sticky climate, continues eastward through Guyana, Surinam, and French Guiana. In the south of these countries the land rises to the forested slopes of the Guiana Highlands.

Across the Brazilian border, the highlands descend to the great basin of the Amazon River. This mighty river is fed by thousands of waterways that seep through the tropical growth of the world's largest rainforest, which covers an area of over 815 million acres. Broad and muddy, the Amazon flows eastward to the Atlantic Ocean. Southern Brazil rises to the Brazilian Highlands and the tropical plateau of the Matto Grosso. This is drained in the south by the Paraná River.

○ GIANT SNAKE
The anaconda can grow to 30 feet long. It hunts in rivers and pools, and strangles or drowns its prey.

○ PALMS IN THE PANTANAL
In southwestern Brazil, the Pantanal wetlands are created by the seasonal flooding of the Paraguay River. The waters cover about 39,000 square miles of the Matto Grosso.

☼ ANTEATER
There are three South American anteater species. All have long, sticky tongues for eating ants and termites.

◑ IGUAÇU FALLS
The Iguaçu River plunges over rocks in hundreds of waterfalls before it joins the Paraná River on the Brazil–Argentina border.

GUYANA

SURINAM

FRENCH GUIANA

VENEZUELA

BRAZIL

PERU

Gulf of Venezuela
Netherlands Antilles
Port of Spain **TRINIDAD & TOBAGO**
Maracaibo **Caracas**
Barcelona
Lake Maracaibo
Pico Bolívar 5,002 m
ANDES MTS.
LLANOS
Orinoco
Orinoco Delta
VENEZUELA
Angel Falls
Georgetown
GUYANA
Paramaribo
SURINAM
Cayenne
FRENCH GUIANA
COLOMBIA
GUIANA HIGHLANDS
Orinoco
Branco
Pico da Neblina 3014 m
Negro
Japurá
Macapá
Marajó Bay
Marajó I.
São Marcos Bay
Belèm
Manaus
Amazon
Santarém
São Luis
S E L V A S
Madeira
Tapajós
Xingu
Tocantins
Teresina
Fortaleza
Natal
Juruá
Purus
Araguaia
Parnaiba
SERTÃO
Recife
São Francisco
Maceió
Rio Branco
Jiparaná
Aripuanã
Arinos
BRAZIL
SERRA DOS PARECIS
Guaporé
BOLIVIA
MATO GROSSO PLATEAU
Cuiabá
Sobradinho Reservoir
Salvador
Brasília
Goiânia
BRAZILIAN HIGHLANDS
Campo Grande
Uberlândia
Belo Horizonte
PARAGUAY
Paraná
Campos
São Paulo
Itaipu Res.
Santos
Rio de Janeiro
Cape Frio
Iguaçu Falls
Curitiba
SERRA DO MAR
ARGENTINA
Uruguay
Florianópolis
URUGUAY
Santa Maria
Pôrto Alegre
Patos Lagoon
Mirim Lake

◑ IN EASTERN BRAZIL
This sandstone pillar at Vila Velha, in Brazil's Espirito Sánto state, has been weathered by wind and rain from the South Atlantic.

☼ POISON-ARROW FROG

◑ TAPIR
Tapirs live in the dense tropical rainforests and swamps of South America. They use their flexible top lips to gather food.

◑ BIG RIVER
The Amazon, with a total length of about 4,000 miles, is the world's second-longest river after the Nile in North Africa.

135

The northern half of South America is divided up into four independent republics—Brazil, the largest country in the continent; Venezuela; and two small Caribbean countries, Surinam and Guyana. Neighboring French Guiana is still governed directly as a region of France.

◐ LAKE OF OIL
The Venezuelan economy depends on Lake Maracaibo's oil reserves.

FACTS

VENEZUELA
República de Venezuela
AREA: 352,144 sq mi.
POPULATION: 24.6 million
CAPITAL: Caracas
OTHER CITIES: Maracaibo, Valencia
HIGHEST POINT: Pico Bolívar (16,427 ft)
OFFICIAL LANGUAGE: Spanish
CURRENCY: Bolívar

FRENCH GUIANA
Guyane Française
Overseas region of France
AREA: 34,749 sq mi.
POPULATION: 0.2 million
CAPITAL: Cayenne
OFFICIAL LANGUAGE: French
CURRENCY: Euro

This part of the world has huge cities and busy ports, as well as remote forest and mountain areas that have never been explored. The region has great natural wealth in the form of Venezuelan oil, coal, iron ore, bauxite (for making aluminium), chrome, copper, gold, and silver. Brazilian factories make cars and computers.

The rainforests of the Amazon provide timber. Rapid clearance of the forests by farmers, miners, and loggers threatens to be a disaster not just for Brazil but for the planet as a whole. Beef cattle are raised on much of the cleared land.

Cattle are also reared on the wide llanos grasslands of Venezuela.

Brazil is the world's leading producer of coffee and sugarcane. Other crops include rice, corn, soya beans, cassava, and citrus fruits. Cayenne, in French Guiana, is famous for its red hot pepper, while Guyana is known for the sticky brown sugar first produced in the Demerara region.

◐ BRAZIL NUTS

◐ A VANISHING WORLD
The Amazon basin contains one-third of the world's surviving rainforest. This is one of the planet's most precious resources, but vast areas have already been destroyed.

◐ CASSAVA PLANTATION
The fleshy roots of the cassava plant are used to make flour; its leaves are eaten as a vegetable.

◐ CAYENNE PEPPER
This hot spice takes its name from the capital of French Guiana.

PARROT TRADE
Many wild parrots are collected from the rainforest to be sold as pets.

Despite its wealth of resources, the region has faced huge economic problems. There has been severe inflation, rising debt, and political corruption. Venezuela relies heavily on its oil, for which the price has fallen in recent years.

Although some people are wealthy, many are desperately poor. In big cities, such as Caracas and Rio de Janeiro, families with little chance of finding work crowd into makeshift shanty towns and slums. In remote areas, many of the indigenous peoples, referred to as "Indians," have been killed and had their land stolen. Their rivers have been poisoned and the forests where they hunt have been cut down.

SUGARCANE
Workers harvest the sugarcane crop. Next, the stalks are crushed and soaked in water to produce a sugary liquid. When this is heated, it separates into brown crystals of cane sugar and sticky molasses.

A SAFE ROAD
Cattle are herded along the Transpantaneira, the only route through Brazil's Pantanal wetlands.

SPACE AGE
The rocket launch site at Kourou in French Guiana is operated by the European Space Agency.

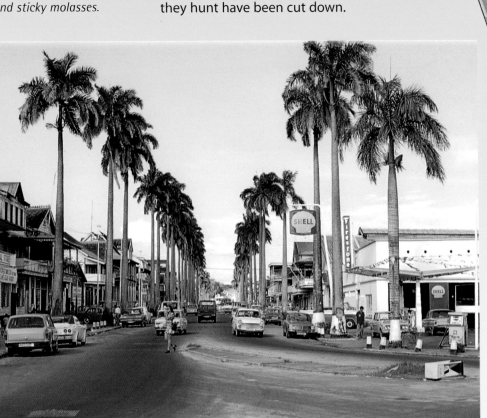

PARAMARIBO, SURINAM
Paramaribo, at the mouth of the Surinam River, is Surinam's capital and its biggest port. Nearly 50 percent of the population live there.

◐ SOCCER FANS
Soccer is popular all over South America, and nowhere more so than Brazil, five-times World Cup winners.

The first or indigenous peoples of northern South America now make up only a very small portion of the population—just five percent in Guyana and under two percent in Brazil. They mostly live in scattered communities, many in remote areas of rainforest where they hunt and fish. Groups include the Xingu, Yanomami, Shavanti, Kayapo, coastal Caribs, Warrau, and many others besides. More than 85 indigenous groups are known to have been wiped out over the last 100 years.

Many people of the region are mestizos, of mixed European and indigenous descent.

◐ MIXED DESCENT
Brazil is a multiracial society, with many people of mixed indigenous, European, or African descent.

◐ A RAINFOREST VILLAGE
The round huts of the Yanomami may be seen in Venezuela and Brazil. Yanomami lands have been steadily destroyed by mining since the 1970s.

European settlement of the region has been from Portugal, Spain, Italy, the Netherlands, France, Britain, and Germany. There are also sizeable black populations, of African descent. The Caribbean coast has a large Asian population, with many Javanese living in Surinam.

The region's official languages all date from its period of colonial rule—Portuguese in Brazil, Spanish in Venezuela, English in Guyana, Dutch in Surinam, and French in French Guiana.

◐ RIVER BORDERS
The Paraguay River flows past Corumba, a town on Brazil's border with Bolivia. The river goes on to form the Brazil–Paraguay, and Paraguay–Argentina borders.

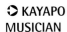

⟳ ON THE BEACH
Swimmers and sunbathers are attracted to Rio de Janeiro's beaches, on the South Atlantic coast. This one is at a wealthy southern suburb, Barra de Tijuca.

◑ KAYAPO MUSICIAN
The Kayapo people live in northeastern Brazil, between the Araguaia and Xingu rivers.

Brazil and Venezuela are largely Roman Catholic, but there are also Protestants, Hindus, and Muslims. Spirit religions such as Candomblé, influenced by both African and Roman Catholic traditions, are popular in Brazil.

As in most Latin American regions, soccer is by far the most popular sport. It is practiced on almost every beach, village clearing, or street corner. Brazil has the most successful World Cup record of any nation.

The fascinating mixture of cultures in the region has influenced festivals such as the five-day carnival in Rio de Janeiro, with its dazzling costume parades and dancing to Brazil's own rhythm, the samba. Ethnic variety has also contributed to regional cooking, which combines African, Asian, and European influences.

◑ SHANTY TOWN
São Paulo, home to over 15 million people, is Brazil's biggest city. Many desperately poor families live in makeshift housing and slums.

◑ CARACAS
The Venezuelan capital, Caracas, has spread out from its old colonial center to include city parks, high-rise offices and apartments, shopping malls, and factories.

⟳ CARNIVAL IN RIO
For five days each year the Brazilian city of Rio de Janeiro is taken over by carnival, with costumed revelers dancing the samba in the streets.

◑ JAVA COMES TO SURINAM
Many workers from Dutch colonies in Southeast Asia found work in Surinam after 1863. They brought their own culture, such as this ritual horse dance.

139

The early peoples of the rainforest left behind fewer reminders of their way of life than the peoples of the high Andes. They built with wood, creepers, and straw instead of stone—materials that do not survive long in humid, tropical climates. Even so, archeologists are beginning to learn more about the skill with which these peoples managed the forest, planting trees and seeds they could use for food, medicines, and shelter.

The Spanish arrived in Venezuela In 1498, and the Portuguese in Brazil two years later. Their arrival was a disaster for the indigenous peoples, many of whom died of European diseases. The French and Dutch occupied territory on the Caribbean coast during the 1600s and 1700s, with Britain capturing what is now Guyana in 1796. The Europeans planted sugarcane and other crops, and brought slaves from Africa to work the plantations. Later, many Asian laborers were hired to work along the Caribbean coast.

Venezuela broke away from Spanish rule between 1811 and 1821, after a war of independence led by freedom-fighter Simón Bolívar. Portugal became a kingdom in its own right in 1815, and was declared an independent empire seven years later.

⟳ PEDRO ALVARES CABRAL
This Portuguese navigator discovered Brazil by mistake, in 1500, when his fleet, bound for India, was carried west by ocean currents.

⟳ GEORGETOWN, GUYANA
The Caribbean port of Georgetown is Guyana's capital. City Hall, on the Avenue of the Republic, dates from the colonial period (1831–1970).

⟳ OPERA HOUSE, MANAUS
Manaus lies in the rainforest, on the Río Negro. Its ornate opera house dates from 1896, when the region was profiting from the rubber trade.

⟳ THE LIBERATOR
Simón Bolívar was born in Venezuela in 1783. In the 1820s, his armies helped to drive the Spanish out of South America.

⟳ FOREST HOME
The first Amazonians used forest products for building materials, foods, and medicines.

However, the rich landowners threw out the Portuguese royal family when it ordered an end to slavery.

In 1889, Brazil became a republic. In the 1960s it moved its capital from Rio de Janeiro, on the Atlantic coast, to Brasília, a new, specially built capital up in the Brazilian Highlands.

In 1946, French Guiana became ruled on an equal status with mainland France. Guyana gained independence from Britain in 1970, and Surinam from the Netherlands in 1975.

◯ BRASÍLIA
This purpose-built city, planned by architect Lucio Costa, became Brazil's capital in 1960. It was more centrally located than the previous capital, Río de Janeiro.

◯ THE OIL PRESIDENT
Carlos Andréas Perez was president of Venezuela 1974–79, during the country's oil boom.

◯ SPANISH CARACAS
Colonial buildings date back to the 1500s and 1600s, when Venezuela was ruled by Spain.

◯ LANDLESS PROTEST
Despite Brazil's vast natural resources, many millions of its citizens live below the poverty line. Here, landless farm laborers join a protest rally in São Paulo.

TIMELINE

AD
400	Marajoara culture, mouth of Amazon
1498	Spanish land in Venezuela
1500	Portuguese claim Brazil
1593	Spanish claim Surinam
1600s	Sugar plantations in Brazil: slave labor imported from Africa
1602	Dutch settle Surinam
1604	French settle Cayenne
1620s	Dutch settle Guyana
1667	Surinam becomes a Dutch colony
1749	Venezuelan revolt against Spain
1815	Brazil united with Portuguese kingdom
1821	Venezuela joins independent Colombia
1822	Brazil declares independence under Spanish prince, Pedro
1825	Pedro I recognized as emperor of Brazil
1829	Venezuela becomes independent state
1831	Guyana becomes colony of British Guiana
1834	Slavery abolished in British Guiana
1888	Slavery abolished in Brazil
1889	Brazil becomes a republic
1910	Oil discovered in Venezuela
1946	French Guiana becomes overseas department of France
1960	Brasília becomes capital of Brazil
1966	Guyana becomes independent
1975	Surinam becomes independent
1992	First Earth Summit (UN world environment conference), Río de Janeiro

141

ARGENTINA
AND ITS NEIGHBORS

Paraguay lies at the heart of South America. It is crossed by the Paraguay River, which flows into the Paraná. In the west is the tropical wilderness of the Gran Chaco, and in the east are both forests and grasslands, farms and ranches. Uruguay lies on the mouth of the River Plate, on the South Atlantic coast. It is a land of fertile plains and low hills.

In the northeast of Argentina is the rich farmland of the Mesopotamia region, lying between the Paraná and Uruguay rivers. The central north takes in part of the Gran Chaco, while the central eastern region is made up of open, rolling grassland. Known as the pampas, it is now used for ranching and agriculture. To the south again are the bleak, grassy plateaus and valleys of Patagonia.

The southern Andes form the border between Argentina and Chile, rising to the highest peaks in all the Americas. Chile lies between the western slopes and the South Pacific Ocean. This narrow coastal strip includes cool green regions, warm lands with a mild, Mediterranean climate, and the Atacama Desert—one of the driest spots on Earth, where rain may not fall for years at a time.

Across the Strait of Magellan, the continent breaks up into the islands of Tierra del Fuego and the cold, gray seas off Cape Horn.

◑ BROWN PELICAN

◑ GUANO ROCKS
This rock near Constitución in central Chile is covered in guanos (the droppings of seabirds). In parts of South America, guano is a valuable resource, collected to make fertilizers.

◑ VOLCANO
Volcanic peaks rise above Lake Chungara in Chile.

ARGENTINA
República Argentina
AREA: 1,073,399 sq mi.
POPULATION: 37.4 million
CAPITAL: Buenos Aires
OTHER CITIES: Córdoba, La Plata, San Miguel de Tucumán
HIGHEST POINT: Aconcagua (22,834 ft)
OFFICIAL LANGUAGE: Spanish
CURRENCY: Argentinean peso

CHILE
República de Chile
AREA: 292,135 sq mi.
POPULATION: 15.4 million
CAPITAL: Santiago
OTHER CITIES: Vina del Mar, Valparaíso, Concepción
HIGHEST POINT: Ojos del Salado (22,572 ft)
OFFICIAL LANGUAGE: Spanish
CURRENCY: Chilean peso

PARAGUAY
República del Paraguay
AREA: 157,048 sq mi.
POPULATION: 5.6 million
CAPITAL: Asunción
OTHER CITIES: Ciudad del Este, Pedro Juan Caballero
Highest point: Villarrica (2,230 ft)
OFFICIAL LANGUAGE: Spanish
CURRENCY: guaraní

URUGUAY
República Oriental del Uruguay
AREA: 67,574 sq mi.
POPULATION: 3.3 million
CAPITAL: Montevideo
OTHER CITIES: Salto, Rivera
HIGHEST POINT: Mirador Nacional (1,643 ft)
OFFICIAL LANGUAGE: Spanish
CURRENCY: Uruguayan peso

FALKLAND ISLANDS
Islas Malvinas
British Overseas Colony
AREA: 4,700 sq mi.
POPULATION: 2,000
CAPITAL: Stanley
OFFICIAL LANGUAGE: English
CURRENCY: Falkland Islands pound

⊙ CURTAIN OF SPRAY
Argentina borders Brazil along the Iguazú (Iguaçu) River. A long stretch of the river is broken by islands, rapids, and waterfalls.

⊙ IN PATAGONIA
South of the Río Negro, Argentina is a land of wind-swept plateaus and valleys.

⊙ PRICKLY PEAR

⊙ TIERRA DEL FUEGO
The southern tip of South America is a bleak peninsula occupied by both Argentina and Chile. The southernmost town in the world, Ushuaia, lies on the Beagle Channel.

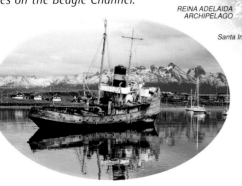

⊙ CANYON LANDS
Rivers have carved out canyons from the rocks of Patagonia. The Andes Mountains shield this vast, dry region of Argentina from the Pacific Ocean's rain-bearing winds.

PARAGUAY

⊙ ELEPHANT SEALS

⊙ IN THE SOUTHERN ANDES
The heavy ice of the Moreno Glacier grinds its way down to Lago Argentina, one of the most awesome sights in South America.

Arica
Iquique
ATACAMA DESERT
Calama
Antofagasta
BOLIVIA
Verde   Concepción
PARAGUAY
GRAN CHACO
Pilcomayo
Bermejo
Asunción   Ciudad del Este
Salta
Formosa
Ojos del Salado 6,880 m
San Miguel de Tucumán
Resistencia
Copiapó
Santiago del Estero
Corrientes   Posadas
Catamarca
Salado
Paraná
MESOPOTAMIA
Alto Paraná
La Rioja
Coquimbo
Pta. Lengua de Vaca
Mar Chiquito
Córdoba
Concordia   Salto
Uruguay
San Juan
SIERRA DE CORDOBA
Santa Fe
Paysandú
Aconcagua 6,959 m
Mendoza
Rosario
Paraná
Negro
Valparaiso
Santiago
San Luis
Río Cuarto
URUGUAY
Rancagua
San Rafael
Buenos Aires   La Plata   Montevideo
Talca
PAMPAS
Río de La Plata
Pta. Norte
Chillán
ARGENTINA
Cape San Antonio
Concepción
Pta. Lavapié
Bahía Blanca
Mar del Plata
CHILE
Neuquén
Bahía Blanca
Cape Corrientes
Temuco
Negro
Colorado
Valdivia
Pta. de la Galera
Limay
Viedma
Osorno
San Matías Gulf
Puerto Montt
PATAGONIA
Valdés Peninsula
Chiloé I.
Chubut
Rawson
C. Quilán
Chico
LOS CHONOS ARCHIPELAGO
Comodoro Rivadavia
URUGUAY
Lake Buenos Aires
San Jorge Gulf
Deseado
San Jorge Gulf
C. Tres Puntas
Penas Gulf
Puerto Deseado
PACIFIC OCEAN
Chico
Wellington I.
Santa Cruz
Puerto Santa Cruz
FALKLAND/MALVINAS ISLANDS
Bahía Grande
West Falkland
Stanley
East Falkland
Río Gallegos
REINA ADELAIDA ARCHIPELAGO
Strait of Magellan
Punta Arenas
Tierra del Fuego
C. San Diego
Santa Inés I.
Ushuaia
Cape Horn

URUGUAY

CHILE

ARGENTINA

SOUTH GEORGIA (U.K.)

⊙ ARMADILLO

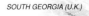

◔ JUICY FRUIT

The orchards of central Chile produce fruit for export, including oranges, lemons, apples, grapes, and pears.

The southern mainland of South America is divided into four independent republics—the small northern nations of Uruguay and Paraguay, the wide open spaces of Argentina, and the long, narrow territory of Chile. The region has experienced long years of rule by military regimes and there have also been wars over borders and territory. In 1982 Argentina went to war with the United Kingdom over ownership of the Falkland or Malvinas Islands, a small British colony in the South Atlantic Ocean. Today the region as a whole has moved to democratic systems of government, but faces many economic and political problems.

◔ CATTLE MARKET

A Chilean cowboy is called a huaso. Cattle are raised in the the central Chilean regions to the south of Santiago.

In Paraguay, cattle are raised and cotton is grown. The leaves of a plant called the Paraguay holly are used to make a bitter tea called yerba maté, which is also popular in Argentina. Uruguay, too, is a cattle country, with fruit grown on the coastal plains.

Argentina first became wealthy by exporting beef. Great herds of cattle are still raised on the pampas, and in Patagonia sheep are kept.

◔ ATLANTIC OUTPOST

Sheep are raised on the remote British colony of the Falkland Islands, or Islas Malvinas.

◔ SALT LAKE

The bone-dry air of Chile's Atacama Desert evaporates pools of water, leaving behind salt pans.

◔ SANTIAGO

Nine-out-of-ten Chileans live in towns or cities. The capital is the country's largest city. It is home to nearly five million people.

◔ COPPER KINGS

Chile is the world's biggest copper producer. The monster Chuquicamata open-cast mine is sited in the far north, in the Atacama Desert.

◑ ARGENTINIAN WINES
The sheltered region around Mendoza has a mild, dry climate. Rivers and irrigation schemes have allowed vines to be grown here since the 1600s.

◔ PLAZA DEL CONGRESO
At the heart of Buenos Aires, capital of Argentina, is the Palace of Congress. Congress is made up of two houses, the Senate and the Chamber of Deputies.

◔ VALDÉS WILDLIFE
Magellan penguins may be seen off Argentina's Valdés peninsula, along with elephant seals and whales.

The foothills of the Andes provide shelter for vineyards in the sunny region around Mendoza. Fisheries, oil, and natural gas are important industries of the far south—Ushuaia is the most southerly town in the world. Industry is centered around the capital of Buenos Aires and is based on food processing, leather goods, textiles, chemicals, and car manufacture.

Chile's industry is based around the port of Valparaiso, where iron, steel, chemicals, and textiles are produced, and the capital city of Santiago. The country has large reserves of copper in the north. The warm regions of central Chile produce wine and citrus fruits for export and the long coastline provides harbors for large fishing fleets.

◑ MILITARY RULE
The army held power in Argentina from 1976 to 1983, in Chile from 1973 to 1989, in Paraguay from 1954 to 1993, and in Uruguay from 1973 to 1984.

◑ CITY MEMORIAL
This obelisk rises above the Plaza de la República in central Buenos Aires. It commemorates the founding of the city in 1536.

◑ ITAIPÚ DAM
This is the world's biggest hydroelectric scheme, jointly run by Argentina and Paraguay. Building the dam created a 520 square mile reservoir, at a cost of US$25 billion.

145

Native American peoples migrated southward through the continent in prehistoric times. They had reached central South America by 14,000 BC and were in Patagonia by 12,000 BC.

While northern Chile came under the influence of the great civilizations of the northern Andes, the peoples of the far south lived by hunting on the grasslands or fishing along the coast in canoes.

◑ THE GAUCHOS
The tough, bragging cowboys of the Argentinean pampas were called gauchos. Today's cowboys still honor the gaucho tradition.

The Spanish invaded the region in the 1500s. They were fiercely resisted by indigenous groups such as the Querandí of the pampas and the Mapuche of Chile. The region broke away from Spanish rule in the 1800s, but generals fought out regional and civil wars. Native peoples were wiped out, and vast tracts of the pampas of Argentina were claimed as ranchland by wealthy landowners.

◑ ANDEAN CHURCH
A white church stands on the edge of the Andes at Tocanao, in Chile's Antofagasta region. It is built from volcanic stone.

◑ VIÑA DEL MAR
South American tourists flock to this resort, near Valparaíso in Chile, for the beaches and casino.

The ranches were worked by gauchos, wild-living cowboys of mixed Spanish–indigenous descent.

Immigrants poured into the region in the 1800s and 1900s: Spanish, Italians, Basques, Welsh, English, Germans, Swiss, Poles, Russians, Jews, and Syrians. More recently there were arrivals from Japan and Korea, and from other parts of South America.

Today the descendants of all these peoples dominate the region. Indigenous peoples now make up a tiny percentage of the population, but their cultures survive in some areas. The native Guaraní language is widely spoken in Paraguay. Spanish is spoken everywhere, but other European languages, from Italian to Welsh, may also be heard.

◑ DESERT MUMMY
Dead bodies from early South American civilizations have been preserved as mummies. This woman's skull was found in the Atacama Desert.

◑ POLO CHAMPIONS
European influence is evident in Argentina's passion (among the rich) for the game of polo. It has achieved international success in the sport.

GRAND PRIX
Motor racing has been a passion since the 1950s, when Argentinean Juan Fangio was five times Grand Prix champion.

EVITA
Eva Perón (1919–52), a former actress, married Argentinean politician Juan Perón in 1945. "Evita" became a popular and powerful figure.

LA BOCA
This district of Buenos Aires, along the polluted Riachuelo waterway, was founded by poor Basque and Italian immigrants. Today it is an artists' quarter, and the buildings are painted in bold, bright colors.

Far out in the South Atlantic, the Falkland Islanders remain English in their speech and customs. The mainland nations are mostly Roman Catholic, with Protestant and Jewish minorities.

The region has produced sporting champions in motor racing, soccer, and tennis, and the Andes Mountains are increasingly popular for skiing and outdoor pursuits. Both Chile and Argentina have produced great writers and poets in the last century, including the Argentinian Jorge Luis Borges (1899–1986) and the Chilean novelist Isabel Allende (b.1942).

TIMELINE

AD

1516	Río de la Plata discovered by the Spanish
1536	First founding of Buenos Aires by Spanish
1537	Spanish found Asunción
1541	Querandí people attack Buenos Aires; Spanish conquer Chile
1543	Rebuilding Buenos Aires (until 1580)
1726	Spanish build fort at Montevideo
1811	Paraguay becomes independent
1816	Argentina becomes independent
1818	Chile becomes independent
1825	Uruguay declares independence (recognized 1828)
1857	European settlement of the pampas
1865	Paraguay fights Uruguay, Argentina, and Brazil (until 1870)
1878	Wars against Native Americans in Argentina (until 1883)
1879	War of the Pacific (until 1884): Chile defeats Peru and Bolivia
1946	Juan Perón becomes president of Argentina
1954	Military coup in Paraguay
1973	Allende overthrown by General Augusto Pinochet in Chile
1976	Military rule in Argentina: imprisonment and murder of opponents
1982	Argentina invades the Falkland Islands, but is defeated by a British force
1991	Argentina, Brazil, Paraguay, and Uruguay form a trade grouping called Mercosur

147

N
W E
S

RUSSIA

KAZAKHSTAN

TURKEY
GEORGIA
ARMENIA
AZERBAIJAN
LEBANON
ISRAEL
SYRIA
JORDAN
IRAQ
TURKMENISTAN
UZBEKISTAN
MONGOLIA
NORTH
KOREA
JAPAN
SOUTH
KOREA
KYRGYZSTAN
TAJIKISTAN
IRAN
KUWAIT
AFGHANISTAN
CHINA
SAUDI
ARABIA
QATAR
UNITED
ARAB
EMIRATES
PAKISTAN
NEPAL
BHUTAN
TAIWAN
YEMEN
OMAN
INDIA
BANGLADESH
MYANMAR
(BURMA)
LAOS
THAILAND
VIETNAM
PHILIPPINES
SRI
LANKA
CAMBODIA
BRUNEI
BRUNEI
MALAYSIA
SINGAPORE
INDONESIA
EAST
TIMOR

KOMODO DRAGON,
INDONESIA

148

ASIA

⟲ Yangon,
MYANMAR

⟲ Hong Kong,
CHINA

⟲ Urgup Cones,
TURKEY

⟲ Space Monument,
RUSSIA

sia, the world's largest continent, covers about 30 percent of the world's land area. It is bordered by Europe and Africa to the west and by the Pacific Ocean to the east. There are chains of tiny volcanic islands in the east, an area known as "The Ring of Fire," because it is so prone to volcanoes.

Asia's northwestern limits are marked by the Ural and Caucasus mountains. Lands in the far north overlap the Arctic Circle and much of the region is tundra, frozen solid for most of the year. Farther south lies a swathe of evergreen forest and, beyond that, the steppes—open, fertile grasslands. Little rain reaches Central Asia, much of which is desert.

The world's highest mountain ranges, the Himalayas and the Karakorams, form a snowy barrier to the north of the Indian peninsula, and include the world's highest peak, Mount Everest. To the south, two of the world's greatest rivers, the Ganges and Brahmaputra,

run toward the warm Indian Ocean. They often flood, depositing rich, alluvial soil over the wide delta.

Asia's southwest coastline is cooled by breezes from the Red Sea and the Mediterranean, but the lands and islands of southern Asia have a tropical climate. There, the winters are hot and dry, while in summer stormy winds called monsoons bring heavy rains.

Asia's many ethnic groups include the Arabs of Southwest Asia, the Hindu people of India, and the Chinese in Eastern Asia. The continent was the home of major early civilizations and the birthplace of all the major world religions.

Many Asians are poor and about 60 percent live by farming. But in the last 50 years, some countries have developed quickly and raised their living standards. In parts of Southwest Asia, wealth has come from oil, while countries in Eastern and Southeast Asia have developed industries. Japan is Asia's most industrialized country, but some other countries in Eastern Asia have also developed quickly. Eastern Asia will dominate the world economy in the 21st century

RUSSIA
AND ITS NEIGHBORS

⊃ GRAY WOLF

⊙ **SNOW POWER**
A snowmobile makes it possible to travel across the ice of the Siberian winter.

Europe runs into Asia without any obvious borders, apart from mountain ranges and rivers. The Russian Federation and some of its neighbors straddle both continents.

Belarus lies on the great plain that stretches from Germany to Russia. To the south lie the steppes of Ukraine and Moldova, natural grasslands now harvested for wheat. Ukraine borders the Carpathian Mountains to the west and the warm Black Sea to the south. The Caucasus Mountains run southeastward through Georgia, Armenia, and Azerbaijan toward the Caspian Sea, the world's broadest inland sea. To the east of the Caspian Sea lie the Central Asian republics of Kazakhstan, Turkmenistan, Uzbekistan, and Kyrgyzstan. Here, dusty grasslands give way to deserts and soaring mountain peaks.

The Russian Federation is the biggest country in the world. The Ural Mountains are generally taken to be the dividing line between European Russia and Asian Russia, which extends as far as the Pacific Ocean. Russia's northern coast is mostly locked in Arctic ice. A vast, treeless plain—the tundra—gives way in the south to a great belt of forest, or taiga, made up of spruce and birch trees. In the southwest there are steppes (grassland) and in the southeast, deserts and mountains. Russia is drained by a number of great rivers including the Don, the Volga, the Ob, the Irtysh, and the Lena.

⊃ **TASHKENT MARKET**
The capital of Uzbekistan is an ancient center of trade and of textile manufacture.

ARMENIA
Haikakan Hanrapetoutioun
AREA: 11,500 sq mi.
POPULATION: 3.8 million
CAPITAL: Yerevan
OTHER CITIES: Gyumri, Ejmiadzin
HIGHEST POINT: Aragats (13,418 ft)
OFFICIAL LANGUAGE: Armenian
CURRENCY: Dram

AZERBAIJAN
Azerbaijchan Respublikasy
AREA: 33,400 sq mi.
POPULATION: 8 million
CAPITAL: Baku
OTHER CITIES: Ganka, Sumgait
HIGHEST POINT: Bazar Dyuzi (14,652 ft)
OFFICIAL LANGUAGE: Azeri
CURRENCY: Manat

BELARUS
Respublika Belarus
AREA: 80,200 sq mi.
POPULATION: 10 million
CAPITAL: Minsk
OTHER CITIES: Gomel, Pinsk
OFFICIAL LANGUAGE: Belarussian
CURRENCY: Rouble

GEORGIA
Sakartvelos Respublika
AREA: 26,900 sq mi.
POPULATION: 5 million
CAPITAL: Tbilisi
OTHER CITIES: Kutaisi, Rustavi
HIGHEST POINT: Shkhara (17,063 ft)
OFFICIAL LANGUAGE: Georgian
CURRENCY: Lari

KAZAKHSTAN
Qazaqstan Respublikasï
AREA: 1,049,200 sq mi.
POPULATION: 14.9 million
CAPITAL: Astana
OTHER CITIES: Qaraghandy, Shymkent
HIGHEST POINT: Tengri (20,991 ft)
OFFICIAL LANGUAGE: Kazakh
CURRENCY: Tenge

⟳ UKRAINIAN SUNSHINE
River shores on the Dnepr and Dnestr and warm coastlines on the Black Sea attract Eastern European holidaymakers to Ukraine.

⟳ ANANURI CASTLE, GEORGIA
Georgia became a powerful kingdom in the early Middle Ages. It was absorbed into the Russian empire in the 1800s.

GEORGIA

MOLDOVA

UKRAINE

BELARUS

RUSSIA

UZBEKISTAN

KAZAKHSTAN

TURKMENISTAN

KYRGYZSTAN

TAJIKISTAN

AZERBAIJAN

ARMENIA

⟳ ANCIENT RUINS
The kingdom of Sogdiana was conquered by Alexander the Great in 328 BC. Remains found here, at Pendzhikent in Uzbekistan, show that this was a crossroads of trade between India, China, and Persia (modern Iran).

⟳ ARAL SEA
Due to the over-irrigation of farmland and evaporation the Aral Sea is shrinking dramatically.

⟳ PLANT LIFE
Polar plants are low lying. This protects them from the bitter Arctic winds.

NUCLEAR DISASTER
A nuclear power plant at Chernobyl, in Ukraine (then part of the Soviet Union) melted down in 1986. Deadly radiation was blown across northern Europe.

SHOPPING IN MOSCOW
In the days of the Soviet Union, grand-looking state-owned stores offered little choice for consumers. Economic problems continue today.

Until 1991, all the countries of this region were part of a single country, the Soviet Union. This was formed in 1922, following the revolution in 1917 which brought Communists to power in Russia. Communist rule ended in 1991, and the country was renamed the Russian Federation.

At that time, many of the border regions broke away to become independent nations. Russian armed forces prevented some other bids for independence, as in the Chechenya region. A Commonwealth of Independent States (CIS) was formed to keep up economic links between the new nations.

The region as a whole is immensely rich in resources, including timber, oil, natural gas, gold, and diamonds. Transportation is a major problem in such a vast country, particularly in the remote wilderness of Siberia, where many resources are found. The Trans-Siberian rail network links Moscow, the Russian capital, with the Pacific port of Vladivostok.

SNOWY WINTERS
Most of the Russian Federation experiences long winters with heavy snowfall. Average January temperatures vary from 16°F in Moscow to 7°F in Vladivostok.

Cereal crops grow well in the fertile west and south, while warm southern lands such as Georgia produce fruits and wine. The Central Asian lands grow cotton. Industries are mostly based in the eastern European part of the region, and include iron and steel, truck manufacture, shipbuilding, and mining.

↻ THE SUMMER PALACE

The Summer Palace, built on one of the islands that make up the great city of St Petersburg, was built for Czar Peter the Great between 1710 and 1714.

☯ TRANS-SIBERIAN EXPRESS

The Trans-Siberian Railway runs between Moscow and Vladivostok. It was opened in 1905 and played an important part in Russian history. It remains the world's longest track, at 5,865 miles. The whole route takes eight days to travel. It now links up with services to Mongolia and China.

During the Communist era, the Soviet Union rapidly transformed from a largely undeveloped country into a great industrial power. By the 1980s, however, Russian industry was old-fashioned, inefficient, and polluting. In the post-Communist Russia of the 1990s, unemployment was high and many businesses were run by corrupt officials. Output fell disastrously and wages went unpaid. Even so, Russia remains powerful, and the poor countries around the Caspian and Aral Seas may soon be transformed by new oil wealth.

☯ JEWELED EGGS

Fabulous "eggs" were made as Easter gifts for the czars by jeweler Carl Fabergé (1846–1920).

☯ UZBEKI COTTON

Uzbekistan is the world's fourth-largest producer of cotton. This crop is being harvested and processed at Urgench.

☯ THE WINTER PALACE

The St Petersburg residence of the czars was built in 1762 and restored in 1839. With the adjoining Hermitage, it now houses one of the world's great art collections.

FACTS

MOLDOVA
Republica Moldova
AREA: 13,000 sq mi.
POPULATION: 4.3 million
CAPITAL: Chisinau
OTHER CITIES: Tiraspol, Beltsy
HIGHEST POINT: Balaneshty (1,409 ft)
OFFICIAL LANGUAGE: Moldovan
CURRENCY: Leu

RUSSIAN FEDERATION
Rossiskaya Federatsiya
AREA: 6,592,863 sq mi.
POPULATION: 144.4 million
CAPITAL: Moscow
OTHER CITIES: St Petersburg, Novosibirsk
HIGHEST POINT: Elbrus (18,510 ft)
OFFICIAL LANGUAGE: Russian
CURRENCY: Rouble

TAJIKISTAN
Repoblika i Tojikiston
AREA: 55,300 sq mi.
POPULATION: 6.2 million
CAPITAL: Dushanbe
OTHER CITIES: Kulyab, Khodzhent
HIGHEST POINT: Mt. Kommunizma (24, 590 ft)
OFFICIAL LANGUAGE: Tajik
CURRENCY: Somoni

153

○ ST BASIL'S CATHEDRAL
Dating back to 1555, the colorful onion-shaped domes of St Basil's rise above Red Square in the center of Moscow, the Russian capital.

The Russians are a Slavic people. They make up 80 percent or so of the population in the Russian Federation. The remaining 20 percent is made up of over 150 minority groups. Some of these peoples, including the Chukchee, Evenks, Nenets, and Saami, live in the sparsely populated Russian Arctic. Some of the Arctic peoples live by herding reindeer or by hunting. Among Russia's many other ethnic groups are the Cossacks of the steppes, the Kalmuk, Yakut, Tartars, Chechens, Cherkess, Dagestanis, Bashkir, Kets, Jews, Tuvinians, and Buryats.

To the west of the new Russian borders are the Slavic Belarussians and Ukrainians, and also the Moldovans, who are related to Romanians.

○ RUSSIAN BALLET
St Petersburg has a history of ballet dating back to 1738. Many great works were performed in the 1800s. The most famous company is the Maryinsky (formerly Kirov) Ballet.

South beyond the Caucasus are the Georgians, Osset, Armenians, and Azeris. To the east of the Caspian Sea are the Kazakhs, Turkmen, Uzbek, Kyrgyz, and Tajik.

Despite the Russian Federation's wide-open spaces, most people live to the west of the Urals, 75 percent of them in cities and towns.

○ ICE HOCKEY
Ice hockey is a popular sport in the Russian Federation. National (and earlier Soviet) teams are record-breaking winners of world-class and Olympic championships.

○ ORTHODOX PRIESTS
The Orthodox form of Christianity was brought to the Slavs by the Greek missionary St Cyril (AD 827–69).

○ THE TOMB OF A FAMOUS WARRIOR
The Gur-e Amir mausoleum in Samarkand, Uzbekistan, is decorated with mosaic tiles. It commemorates the Mongol emperor Timur the Lame, or Tamerlane (1336–1405), who conquered most of Central Asia. He died marching eastward to invade China.

○ THE COSSACKS
The Cossacks of the steppes were famed for their riding skills and wild dances. They were later recruited by the czars as soldiers.

⊙ LEO TOLSTOY

⊙ PETER TCHAIKOVSKY

⊙ THE ARTS
Russia has a rich history of writers and musicians. Notable among them were composer Peter Ilyich Tchaikovsky (1840–93) and writer Leo Tolstoy (1828–1910), author of War and Peace *and* Anna Karenina.

Christianity is the main religion in the west and southwest of the region; most people are Eastern Orthodox Christians. Onion-domed churches, some gilded, may be seen glittering in the sunshine in many towns. The Central Asian peoples are mostly Muslim, and there are also Jews and Buddhists. Many religions, including Christianity, were heavily suppressed in the early days of the Communist era.

⊙ MUSICAL TRADITION
Traditional folk music is popular throughout Russia. These musicians are performing in St Petersburg. The balalaika has a triangular body and a neck like a guitar.

During the Middle Ages, the Eastern Orthodox Church produced great works of art in the form of icons (holy pictures), and its worship is accompanied by fine choral singing. The arts have always been valued in Russia. St Petersburg and Moscow are centers of ballet. Great Russian composers included Dmitri Shostakovich (1906–75), and writers included the great playwright Anton Chekov (1860–1904).

⊙ ARCTIC TRAVEL
Dogs, reindeer, and horses were traditionally used to haul loads in the Russian Arctic. The rivers there freeze so hard that trucks are able to use them as highways.

⊙ RUSSIAN DOLLS
Hollow wooden dolls are a Russian tradition and a popular souvenir for any visitor to Russia. Each doll can be opened at the middle to reveal a smaller doll nesting inside.

FACTS

TURKMENISTAN
Turkmenistan
AREA: 188,500 sq mi.
POPULATION: 5.4 million
CAPITAL: Ashgabat
OTHER CITIES: Charjew, Dashkhovuz
HIGHEST POINT: Köpetdeg Range
OFFICIAL LANGUAGE: Oguz Turkic
CURRENCY: Manat

UKRAINE
Ukrayina
AREA: 233,100 sq mi.
POPULATION: 48.7 million
CAPITAL: Kiev
OTHER CITIES: Kharkiv, Odessa
HIGHEST POINT: Goverla (6,726 ft)
OFFICIAL LANGUAGE: Ukrainian
CURRENCY: Hryvnya

UZBEKISTAN
Uzbekiston Respublikasi
AREA: 172,700 sq mi.
POPULATION: 25.1 million
CAPITAL: Tashkent
OTHER CITIES: Samarkand, Bukhara
HIGHEST POINT: Beshtor Peak (14,104 ft)
OFFICIAL LANGUAGE: Uzbek
CURRENCY: Sum

◑ HOLY ICONS
Painting an icon was considered to be an act of worship in itself.

The steppes were settled in prehistoric times. About 2,500 years ago they were home to horseback warriors known as Scythians. In about AD 400 Slavs began to settle western Russia. Swedish Vikings known as Rus traded along the Volga and Dniepr rivers and as far east as the Aral Sea. They gave their name to Russia.

The first Russian states were based on trading posts at Kiev (in today's Ukraine) and Novgorod. Moscow was founded in 1147. In the 1200s the Slavs came under fierce attack by Mongol armies from Asia.

Russia was strong enough to resist the Mongols and built up its own empire. Its rulers were called czars. In the 1600s Czar Peter I, the "Great," modernized Russia and built the fine city of St Petersburg. Russian armies soon clashed with Turkey to the south. The empire spread eastward into Siberia and westward into Poland. It was invaded in turn by France in 1812.

A hundred years ago, the Russian people had few political rights. Their ruling class resisted calls for change.

◑ CUTTER OF BEARDS
Peter I abolished the special powers of Russia's old aristocratic families. Their long beards, symbols of privilege, were cut off.

◔ LENIN AND HIS TOMB
Vladimir Ilyich Ulyanov, known as Lenin (1870–1924), led the Bolsheviks in Russia's October Revolution. His tomb is in Moscow's Red Square (above left).

Revolution broke out in 1905 and again in 1917, when the czar and his family were killed. A socialist group called the Bolsheviks, led by a revolutionary known as Lenin, gained control of Russia and the old Russian empire during a civil war that lasted until 1920.

◔ RED ARMY LEADER
Leon Trotsky (1879–1940) was a Marxist revolutionary who led the Communist Red Army in Russia's civil war (1917–20). He was later exiled and murdered on the order of Joseph Stalin.

◔ PETER THE GREAT
Born in 1672, Czar Peter I traveled widely in Western Europe. By the time of his death in 1725, Russia had been transformed into a powerful modern state.

◑ OCTOBER REVOLUTION
Centuries of injustice under the rule of the czars came to an end in 1917, when revolutionary workers, students, and soldiers seized power in Russia.

☉ SPACE AGE
A monument to space exploration reaches skyward. The Soviet Union was the first nation to launch a satellite into the Earth's orbit.

☉ LAIKA, SPACE DOG

Lenin died in 1924. His successor was a ruthless politician named Joseph Stalin (1879–1953). Many thousands of Russians starved or died in labor camps under his rule. In 1941, Germany invaded. The Russian people resisted bravely and by 1945 the Germans had been pushed back into western Europe.

After the war, the Soviet Union controlled Eastern Europe. Its technology was advanced enough by 1961 to send the first person into space. The United States and its allies constantly challenged this power, during a "Cold War," which lasted until the 1980s. Then Soviet Communism collapsed and the Soviet Union broke up into separate states.

☉ IN MEMORY
Beneath the walls of the Kremlin, Moscow's medieval fortress, a flame burns in memory of the "unknown soldier." The Soviets suffered more casualties than any other nation during World War II.

☉ LOCAL WARS
As new states were created from the ruins of the Soviet Union, there were violent clashes over territory and borders. Between 1989 and 1994, Armenia fought with Azerbaijan over the territory of Nagorno-Karabakh.

☉ NEW RUSSIA
In 1990 Boris Yeltsin (on the right) became Russian president. He presided over the break-up of the old Soviet Union. Yeltsin's successor, the younger Vladimir Putin, faced severe problems in modernizing Russia.

TIMELINE

AD

900s	Vikings found states in Russia and Ukraine
988	Orthodox Christianity introduced
1223	Mongols invade steppes
1462	Ivan the Great frees Russia from Mongols (until 1505)
1547	Ivan the Terrible becomes czar
1881	Russian Czar Alexander I assassinated
1905	Russia defeated by Japan; revolution in Russia, democratic reform
1917	October Revolution in Russia
1922	Soviet Union (USSR) founded
1924	Death of Lenin
1936	Joseph Stalin terrorizes opponents
1939	Soviet pact with Nazi Germany
1940	USSR annexes Baltic states
1941	USSR joins Allies in "Great Patriotic War" against Nazi Germany (until 1945)
1946	USSR controls Eastern Europe; Cold War with West (until 1989)
1979	USSR invades Afghanistan
1985	Mikhail Gorbachev introduces reforms
1989	Central Europe breaks away from Soviet control
1991	Break-up of USSR; Russian Federation founded

SOUTHWEST ASIA

○ CEDAR TREE, LEBANON

BAHRAIN
Dawlat al Bahrayn – State of Bahrain
AREA: 267 sq mi.
POPULATION: 700,000
CAPITAL: Al Manamah
OTHER CITIES: Muharraq
HIGHEST POINT: Jabal ad Dukhan (440 ft)
OFFICIAL LANGUAGE: Arabic
CURRENCY: Bahraini dinar

CYPRUS
Kypriaki Dimokratia – Republic of Cyprus
AREA: 3,572 sq mi.
POPULATION: 873,000
CAPITAL: Nicosia
OTHER CITIES: Limassol, Larnaca
HIGHEST POINT: Mount Olympus (6,403 ft)
OFFICIAL LANGUAGES: Greek, Turkish
CURRENCY: Cyprus pound

IRAN
Jomhuri-e-Eslami-e-Iran – Islamic Republic of Iran
AREA: 634,440 sq mi.
POPULATION: 63.4 million
CAPITAL: Tehran
OTHER CITIES: Mashhad, Esfahan
HIGHEST POINT: Mount Damavand (18,385 ft)
OFFICIAL LANGUAGE: Farsi (Persian)
CURRENCY: Rial

IRAQ
Joumhouriya al 'Iraqia – Republic of Iraq
AREA: 169,235 sq mi.
POPULATION: 23.3 million
CAPITAL: Baghdad
OTHER CITIES: Mosul, Kirkuk
HIGHEST POINT: Haji Ebrahim (11,811 ft)
OFFICIAL LANGUAGE: Arabic
CURRENCY: Iraqi dinar

Southwest Asia—also known as the Middle East or the Near East—is a large region bordered by the Mediterranean and Black seas to the northwest and north, by the Red Sea to the southwest, and by the Indian Ocean to the southeast. Thinly populated deserts and dry grassland predominate. The most fertile regions are in the north, and include the Mediterranean island of Cyprus.

The northern part of Southwest Asia is mountainous, with high ranges extending through Turkey into Iran, where they include the Elburz Mountains in the north and the Zagros Mountains, which run southeast through western Iran. Mount Damavand in the Elburz Mountains is the region's highest peak. The Arabian peninsula also has mountain ranges, the longest of which borders the Red Sea and extends into southern Yemen. Inland are large plateau.

Most of Southwest Asia has a hot, desert climate. Part of the dry Arabian peninsula is covered by one of the world's bleakest sandy deserts—the Rub 'al Khali, or "Empty Quarter." Iran also has large deserts, some of which are covered by salt, created by evaporation following the occasional flood. Other dry areas include steppe grasslands, which also support low-growing shrubs.

Turkey has a wetter climate than most of the rest of the region. Its Mediterranean coastline has hot, dry summers and rainy, mild winters. But the dry, grassy interior plateaux have bitterly cold winters and frequent snowstorms.

Water is scarce in much of Southwest Asia. There are few major rivers—the two longest being the Euphrates and Tigris. These rise in the mountains of Turkey and flow across the dry country of Iraq. The fertile area between these two great rivers—the Fertile Crescent—saw the birth of some major early civilizations, including the Assyrians and Babylonians.

○ PALACE IN YEMEN
The Wadi Dahr Palace is perched on a steep rock in San'a, capital of Yemen.

○ JERBOA

◯ ESFAHAN, IRAN
The city of Esfahan in Iran is famous for its beautiful mosques.

N
W   E
S

IRAN

TURKEY

IRAQ

BAHRAIN

◯ SHIPS OF THE DESERT
Camels can survive for long periods without water. They are still used to carry goods across the deserts of Southwest Asia.

KUWAIT

CYPRUS

LEBANON

ISRAEL

SYRIA

JORDAN

Map labels
Istanbul
Gallipoli
Bursa
Eskisehir
Izmir
Ankara
Tuz Lake
Konya
Antalya
TAURUS MTS.
Kayseri
Gaziantep
Adana
Diyarbakir
BLACK SEA
Samsun
PONTIC MOUNTAINS
Sakarya
Kizil
T U R K E Y
Mt. Ararat 5,185m
Aras
Lake Van
CASPIAN SEA
Tabriz
Lake Urmia
Rasht
Babol
ELBURZ MTS.
Mt. Damavand 5,604m
TURKMENISTAN
Mashhad
AFGHANISTAN
Nicosia
CYPRUS
Limassol
Tripoli
Beirut
Haifa
Tel Aviv
Jerusalem
Elat
Aleppo
Homs
SYRIA
SYRIAN DESERT
Damascus
EGYPT
JORDAN
Al Jawf
Sakakah
Mosul
Euphrates
Tigris
As Sulaymaniyah
Kirkuk
I R A Q
Baghdad
Karbala
An Nasiriyah
Basra
Hamadan
Bakhtaran
ZAGROS MOUNTAINS
Tehran
Qom
Kashan
Esfahan
Dasht-e-Kavir
I R A N
Yazd
Ahvaz
Abadan
KUWAIT
Kuwait
Bushehr
Shiraz
Kerman
Dasht-e-Lut
Zahedan
AN NAFUD
Ad Dahna
Buraydah
Shaqra
Medina
HIJAZ
RED SEA
ASIR
Tihamah
Jiddah
Mecca
Jabal Sawda 3,133 m
SAUDI ARABIA
Riyadh
Ad Damman
Al Manamah
BAHRAIN
QATAR
Doha
Abu Dhabi
UNITED ARAB EMIRATES
Dubai
Bandar e Lengah
Bandar Abbas
Strait of Harmuz
Jask
Gulf of Oman
The Gulf
Muscat
Jabal Ash Sham 3,035m
O M A N
Sur
Masirah I.
Rub' al Khali (Empty Quarter)
Salalah
Kuria Muria Is.
Tarim
Hadramaut
San'a
Al Hudaydah
Y E M E N
Al Mukalla
Bab al Mandab
Aden
Gulf of Aden
Socotra (YEMEN)
'Abd al kuri
Jaza'ir Farasan
Amman

OMAN

QATAR

YEMEN

◯ FORT IN OMAN
Most Omani towns contain an old fort. Oman guards the entrance to The Gulf.

SAUDI ARABIA

◯ CITADEL, ALEPPO
This citadel in the ancient city of Aleppo, northern Syria, was built in the Middle Ages.

UNITED ARAB EMIRATES

◯ URGUP CONES
In the Goreme Valley in central Turkey, strange volcanic rock formations make a spectacular landscape.

⚬ ARABIAN SPICES
Many aromatic spices are used in Arab cooking.

FACTS

ISRAEL
Medinat Israel – State of Israel
AREA: 8,130 sq mi.
POPULATION: 6.2 million
CAPITAL: Jerusalem
OTHER CITIES: Tel Aviv-Jaffa, Haifa
HIGHEST POINT: Mount Meron (3,963 ft)
OFFICIAL LANGUAGES: Hebrew, Arabic
CURRENCY: Shekel

JORDAN
Al-Mamlaka Al-Urduniya Al-Hashemiyah – Hashemite Kingdom of Jordan
AREA: 37,737 sq mi.
POPULATION: 5.1 million
CAPITAL: Amman
OTHER CITIES: Zarqa, Irbid
HIGHEST POINT: Jabal Ramm (5,755 ft)
OFFICIAL LANGUAGE: Arabic
CURRENCY: Jordan dinar

KUWAIT
Dowlat al Kuwait – State of Kuwait
AREA: 6,879 sq mi.
POPULATION: 2.2 million
CAPITAL: Kuwait
OTHER CITIES: Al Jahra, Salimiya
HIGHEST POINT: 928 ft
OFFICIAL LANGUAGE: Arabic
CURRENCY: Kuwaiti dinar

LEBANON
Jumhouriya al-Lubnaniya – Republic of Lebanon
AREA: 4,015 sq mi.
POPULATION: 3.6 million
CAPITAL: Beirut
OTHER CITIES: Tripoli, Sidon
HIGHEST POINT: Qurnat as Sawda (10,115 ft)
OFFICIAL LANGUAGE: Arabic
CURRENCY: Lebanese pound

Southwest Asia contains 15 countries. The Arabs are the largest single group of people. Other large groups include the Iranians and the Turks. Smaller groups include the Greek and Turkish Cypriots, and the Jews in Israel.

Seven countries in the region are monarchies: Jordan and Saudi Arabia are headed by kings, while emirs rule Bahrain, Kuwait, Qatar, and United Arab Emirates. The head of state in Oman is the sultan. The other countries are republics. They include Iran, an Islamic republic, whose laws are based on the teachings of Islam.

Since 1974, Cyprus has been divided into the Greek Cypriot Republic in the south and the so-called Turkish Republic of Northern Cyprus, recognized only by Turkey.

⚬ TURKISH COPPERSMITH
Beautiful metal objects, carpets, and highly decorated dishes and bowls are made by Turkish craftworkers and sold in souks (markets).

⚬ GRAPEFRUITS, CYPRUS
Citrus fruits, such as grapefruits, oranges, and lemons, grow well in the sunny countries of Cyprus, Iran, and Israel.

⚬ OIL REFINERY, SAUDI ARABIA
Refineries process Saudi Arabia's valuable oil, producing fuels and chemicals that are used to make many products.

⚬ KUWAIT CITY
Kuwait City is capital of the oil-rich country of Kuwait. Iraq seized Kuwait in 1990, but Iraqi troops were forced out in 1991.

⚬ GATEWAY TO A SOUK
Damascus, Syria's capital, has a large souk (market). Inside, the maze of narrow streets is lined with traders.

The division of Cyprus followed fighting between the island's peoples. Conflict has also been a long-term problem between Israelis and their Arab neighbors.

Several Southwest Asian countries are rich in oil, the chief natural resource of the region. Exports of oil have helped several countries to raise their living standards. Saudi Arabia is the chief oil producer and has the world's largest reserves. Crude oil is refined to make many useful exports including petrol and petro-chemicals.

◯ DIAMOND POLISHING
Israeli craftsmen cut and polish diamonds, which are exported to many countries.

Two-thirds of the people of Southwest Asia live in cities. The largest cities include Istanbul and Ankara in Turkey, Tehran in Iran, Baghdad in Iraq, and Damascus in Syria. Many cities contain old quarters, with narrow roads and large, traditional markets—bazaars or souks—alongside modern skyscrapers.

◯ BEACH RESORT, TURKEY
Tourism is changing parts of Turkey, which has sunny beaches and many fascinating historic ruins.

About a third of the people live in villages and work as farmers. Others graze herds of camels, goats, and sheep. Major crops, often grown on irrigated land, include barley and wheat, while dates, olives, nuts, and citrus fruits are also important. The chief manufacturing countries are Iran and Turkey.

◯ YEMENI MARKET
Goods are piled high for sale at a market in San'a, Yemen.

◑ DESERT PATROL
Soldiers in Jordan are fiercely loyal to their king.

◯ OIL WELL IN IRAQ
Southwest Asia has about two-thirds of the world's known oil reserves—a valuable commodity to the West.

FACTS

OMAN
Sultanat 'Uman – Sultanate of Oman
AREA: 82,030 sq mi.
POPULATION: 2.5 million
CAPITAL: Muscat
OTHER CITIES: Salalah, Sur
Highest point: Jabal Ash Sham (9,957 ft)
OFFICIAL LANGUAGE: Arabic
CURRENCY: Omani rial

QATAR
Dawlat Qatar – State of Qatar
AREA: 4,247 sq mi.
POPULATION: 658,000
CAPITAL: Doha
OTHER CITIES: Dukhan, Umm Said
HIGHEST POINT: 338 ft
OFFICIAL LANGUAGE: Arabic
CURRENCY: Qatar riyal

SAUDI ARABIA
Mamlaka al-'Arabiya as Sa'udiya – Kingdom of Saudi Arabia
AREA: 829,996 sq mi.
POPULATION: 22.7 million
CAPITAL: Riyadh
OTHER CITIES: Jiddah, Mecca
HIGHEST POINT: Jabal Sawda (10,278 ft)
OFFICIAL LANGUAGE: Arabic
CURRENCY: Saudi riyal

SYRIA
Jumhuriya al-Arabya as-Suriya – Syrian Arab Republic
AREA: 71,498 sq mi.
POPULATION: 16.7 million
CAPITAL: Damascus
OTHER CITIES: Aleppo, Homs
HIGHEST POINT: Mount Hermon (9,232 ft)
OFFICIAL LANGUAGE: Arabic
CURRENCY: Syrian pound

WHIRLING DERVISHES
Some Muslim mystics, called dervishes, whirl and dance as part of their religious worship. The order of dancing dervishes was founded in 1273.

The most numerous people of Southwest Asia are the Arabs. Their language, Arabic, is the only official language in 11 of the 15 countries. Arabic is also an official language in Israel, together with Hebrew, which is spoken by the largest group of people, the Jews. The other main languages in Southwest Asia are Farsi (also called Persian) in Iran, Greek in Cyprus, and Turkish in Turkey and Cyprus.

Southwest Asia was the birthplace of three great religions: Judaism—the chief religion in Israel; Christianity, which is important in Cyprus and Lebanon; and Islam. About 86 percent of the people of Southwest Asia follow Islam, the religion of the Arabs.

Islamic art is highly decorative and adorns buildings and all kinds of artifacts. Arts and crafts practiced include

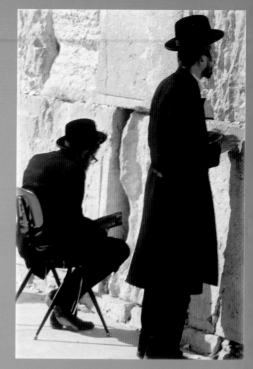

WAILING WALL
Jews visit the Western, or Wailing, Wall of an ancient temple in Jerusalem, Israel, to pray.

book binding and illustrations, calligraphy (beautiful hand-written lettering), carvings, ceramics, glassware, metalware, rugs, and textiles. Mosques (places of worship) throughout the region follow the elegant lines of Islamic architecture. The decorations use abstract patterns, often intertwining the shapes of leaves or winding plant stems. Unlike Christian churches, mosques do not show pictures of people or animals—such pictures in a religious setting are forbidden by Islamic teaching.

DONKEY RIDE
Donkeys and camels are used to carry people in many country areas in Southwest Asia.

BACKGAMMON BOARD
Backgammon is a board game for two players. It is especially popular in the countries bordering the eastern Mediterranean Sea.

MARSH ARABS
The marshy lower valleys of the Tigris and Euphrates rivers in southern Iraq are home to a people called the Marsh Arabs.

COVERED FACES
In this region, many Muslim women cover most of their bodies when outdoors. Some countries observe Islamic law strictly.

↻ LIVING TOGETHER
A kibbutz is the name for a type of Jewish community in Israel in which everyone shares the property, work, goods, and services.

↻ ISLAMIC ART
Abstract patterns and Arabic script are used to decorate mosques and other Islamic buildings. Islam forbids the depiction of people in art.

↻ RING-SHAPED BREAD ROLLS
Israelis enjoy bread rolls, called bagels. Other Israeli foods include chicken soup, chopped liver, and felafel (ground, fried chickpeas flavored with onion and spices).

↻ MOSQUE IN QOM
Qom is a holy city in Iran. Muslim traditions are strictly enforced in Iran. Its mosques are among the most beautiful in the world.

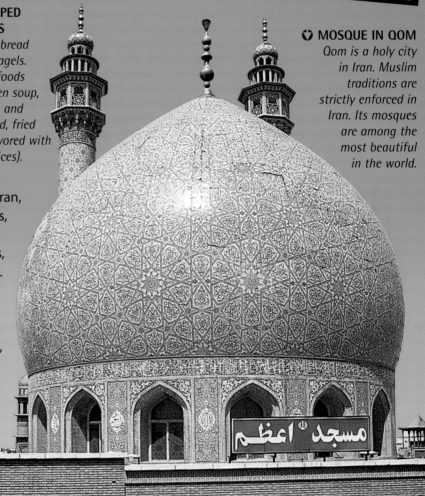

Islam plays a central part in daily life. In Iran, women wear full-length, black body veils, called *chadars*. They cover their ordinary clothes, concealing their head, shoulders, and, usually, the lower part of their faces. In some Muslim countries, women wear western clothes. Muslim women were once confined to their homes, but today many work in business, education, and government.

Basketball, soccer, weight-lifting, and wrestling are popular sports in many areas. Less energetic, but also popular, are the board games backgammon and chess. Skiing takes place in mountain areas, and camel-racing in the Arabian peninsula.

Flat bread and rice are basic foods in Southwest Asia, and dates are important in desert countries. Kebabs—pieces of meat and vegetables cooked on skewers—are popular, as are dairy products, such as cheese and yogurt.

163

ASIA

Southwest Asia played a leading role in the development of world civilization. It was there, about 11,000 years ago, that people first began to farm the land. The first towns and cities also grew up there, and people of the region invented writing and devised systems of laws.

The great civilizations developed in the lands around the Tigris and Euphrates rivers, a region called Mesopotamia, which means "between the rivers." The major civilizations were those of the Sumerians, Babylonians, and Assyrians. The Persians conquered Mesopotamia in 539 BC. Later, the Persian empire fell to the Greek general Alexander the Great in 331 BC.

☼ TROJAN HORSE, TURKEY
According to legend, during the Trojan War in the 12th century BC, Greek soldiers tricked their way into the city of Troy by hiding inside a huge, wooden horse.

☼ ANCIENT SUMERIAN
Sumer, in southeast Iraq, was the world's first major civilization (c. 3000–2000 BC). The Sumerians made fine cloth, jewelry, and pottery.

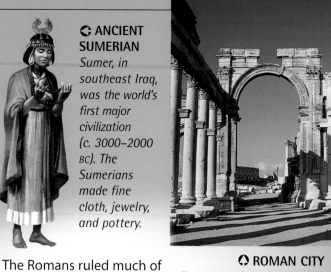

☼ ROMAN CITY
The ruins of the Roman city of Palmyra stand in the desert in central Syria.

The Romans ruled much of Southwest Asia at the time when Jesus Christ was born. Muhammad, the founder of Islam, was born in Mecca in the Arabian peninsula in about AD 570. His followers later built up a great Arab empire, which extended as far west as Spain. Later, the Turks ruled much of Southwest Asia.

☼ MUSLIM WARRIOR
Saladin (c. 1137–93) led the Muslims against the Crusaders. He captured Jerusalem in 1187.

FACTS

TURKEY
Türkiye Cumhuriyeti – Republic of Turkey
AREA: 299,156 sq mi.
POPULATION: 66.2 million
CAPITAL: Ankara
OTHER CITIES: Istanbul, Izmir
HIGHEST POINT: Mount Ararat (17,011 ft)
OFFICIAL LANGUAGE: Turkish
CURRENCY: Turkish lira

UNITED ARAB EMIRATES
Imarat al-Arabiya al-Muttahida – United Arab Emirates
AREA: 32,278 sq mi.
POPULATION: 3.1 million
CAPITAL: Abu Dhabi
OTHER CITIES: Dubai, Sharjah
HIGHEST POINT: Jabal Yibir (5,010 ft)
OFFICIAL LANGUAGE: Arabic
CURRENCY: Dirham

YEMEN
Jamhuriya al Yamaniya – Republic of Yemen
AREA: 203,849 sq mi.
POPULATION: 18 million
CAPITAL: San'a
OTHER CITIES: Aden, Ta'izz
HIGHEST POINT: Mount Hadur Shuayb (12,336 ft)
OFFICIAL LANGUAGE: Arabic
CURRENCY: Riyal

☼ CRUSADERS' CASTLES
The Krac des Chevaliers (Castle of the Knights) is the greatest medieval castle in Syria. It was an important base for the Christian Crusaders from 1142 to 1271.

☼ HITTITE SOLDIER
The Hittites of ancient Turkey conquered much of southwest Asia (c. 900–1200 BC).

T.E. Lawrence (1888–1935), a British soldier, helped to organize an Arab revolt against the Turks during World War I. He became known as Lawrence of Arabia.

◯ GOLDA MEIR
Meir (1898–1978) was Israel's prime minister in 1974 when Israel fought the Yom Kippur War against Arab forces.

However, after years of decline, the Turkish Ottoman empire collapsed at the end of World War I. After the war, several new Arab nations were created, and oil was discovered in some regions.

In the 1930s, many Jewish refugees settled in Palestine. The State of Israel was created in 1948—Israelis defeated Arab forces in a war that ended in 1949. Further Arab–Israeli wars occurred in 1956, 1967, and 1974. During the wars, Israel occupied the Sinai peninsula and the Gaza Strip from Egypt, the West Bank from Jordan, and the Golan Heights from Syria. In 1979, Israel and Egypt signed a peace treaty and Egypt regained the Sinai peninsula.

In the 1990s, Israel and the PLO (Palestine Liberation Organization) led by Yasir Arafat (b.1929) agreed on the creation of a new state for Palestinians, including the Gaza Strip and part of the West Bank.

The Kurds of northern Iraq fought unsuccessfully to found a Kurdish state, and Iran and Iraq fought a border war in the 1980s. In 1990, Iraq invaded Kuwait. But an international force led by the United States forced the Iraqi president Saddam Hussein (b.1937) to withdraw his troops in 1991. In 2003, Saddam's regime in Iraq was toppled from power by a US-led invasion force.

◯ PEACE TALKS
In 1993, Israel's prime minister Yitzhak Rabin (1922–95) and Palestinian leader Yasir Arafat were brought together by US President Bill Clinton. Peace in the Middle East remained elusive, however.

TIMELINE

BC

3500	Civilizations develop in the lower Tigris-Euphrates valleys (Mesopotamia)
539	Persians conquer Mesopotamia
331	Alexander the Great defeats the Persians
30	Most of Southwest Asia under Roman rule

AD

600s	Arabs found an Islamic empire
1095	Christian Crusades begin
1187	Saladin captures Jerusalem
1270	Christian Crusades end
1300s	Ottoman Turks begin to rule
1918	Collapse of the Ottoman empire
1948	State of Israel founded
1967	The Six-Day War: Israel seizes land from neighboring Arab countries
1979	Revolution in Iran: the shah (king) is overthrown and Ayatollah Khomeini heads an Islamic government
1980	Iran-Iraq War begins (until 1990)
1990	Iraq occupies Kuwait (until 1991)
1995	Assassination of Israeli prime minister Yitzhak Rabin
2003	US-led invasion of Iraq; Saddam Hussein is defeated

SOUTHERN
ASIA

⟳ YAK

The biggest country in Southern Asia is India, which covers an area about one-third the size of Europe. The northern part of the region is mountainous. It includes the great mountain ranges of the Hindu Kush in Afghanistan, the Karakoram Range between Pakistan and China, and the mighty Himalayas. Fertile plains extend from eastern Pakistan across northern India into Bangladesh. Some of the world's greatest rivers—the Indus, Ganges, and Brahmaputra—drain these plains. The lower parts of the Brahmaputra and Ganges in Bangladesh have created the world's largest delta.

Southern India consists mainly of a large plateau, the Deccan, which is bordered by two mountain ranges, the Western and Eastern Ghats. The large island of Sri Lanka, off the southern tip of India, has a mountainous central area surrounded by fertile plains. The Maldives are a chain of low coral islands to the southwest.

The northwest is mostly dry, especially in the Thar Desert on the border between Pakistan and India. The northern mountains have cold winters, but much of Southern Asia is warm and tropical.

The heavy rains that fall in summer are the main feature of the climate. The rains are brought by moist, monsoon winds that blow from the sea between May and October. Farmers eagerly await the rains, but the rains can make the rivers overflow, causing widespread flooding. The rivers in Bangladesh burst their banks in 1998 and flooded two-thirds of the country.

⟳ **THE GANGES: A HOLY RIVER**
In India, Hindu pilgrims visit the holy city of Varanasi to bathe in the sacred Ganges River.

◐ THE HIMALAYAS

The Himalayan mountain range is the highest in the world. Its highest peak, Mount Everest, rises to 29,028 feet above sea level.

◐ MOUNTAIN COUNTRY

Leh is capital of the region of Ladakh in northwestern India. It has a large Tibetan Buddhist monastery.

AFGHANISTAN

PAKISTAN

MALDIVES

NEPAL

BHUTAN

BANGLADESH

INDIA

SRI LANKA

◐ NEPALESE TEMPLE

Nyatapola temple, in Bhaktapur, is the highest temple in Nepal. The town is to the east of the capital, Katmandu.

◐ TRICKY TERRAIN

Travel is difficult in the mountains of northern Pakistan. Rope bridges span many of the fast-flowing rivers.

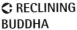

◐ RECLINING BUDDHA

The ancient Sri Lankan capital of Polonnaruwa has huge carvings of the Buddha. Buddhism is the chief religion in Sri Lanka.

◑ HINDU ARCHITECTURE

The Teli-ka-Mandir is an ancient Hindu temple in the city of Gwalior, central India.

167

⟲ ELEPHANT MAKE-UP
Painted elephants carry visitors up the steep slopes to the Indian fort of Amber, near Jaipur.

There are eight countries in Southern Asia. The largest is India, which makes up nearly two-thirds of the region and contains about three-fourths of the people. Pakistan, the second-largest country, makes up more than 15 percent of the region.

India is a federal state, made up of 25 states, each with its own government, and seven territories. Bangladesh, the Maldives, Pakistan, and Sri Lanka are also republics. So is Afghanistan, after a period of Islamic fundamentalist rule in the 1990s. Southern Asia also numbers two kingdoms: Bhutan and Nepal.

Since 1947, when modern India and Pakistan were born, some of their boundaries have been disputed. The chief problem concerns the region of Jammu and Kashmir in northwest India. India claims the entire area, but Pakistan occupies part of it.

Many people in Southern Asia are poor and live simply, from the land; more than 90 percent of the people in Bhutan and Nepal are poor farmers. Farming is the chief activity throughout the region.

⟲ BASKET-MAKING
Indian basket-makers use natural fibers, such as the leaves of palm trees.

⟲ PINK PALACE
The Hawa Mahal, or Palace of the Winds, is in the beautiful "pink" city of Jaipur. Jaipur was founded in 1728.

About 63 percent of the people work in farming. The chief crop is rice. India ranks second only to China in world production, while Bangladesh ranks fourth.

Other food crops include barley, millet, sorghum, and wheat, together with vegetables such as beans and peas, coconuts, a variety of fruits, and tea. Cotton, jute, rubber, and tobacco are also grown. Livestock farming is important in some countries, but Hindus do not eat meat—and cows are considered sacred.

⟲ INDIAN MARKET
Vegetables are cooked with spices and eaten with rice— the main food in India—or a flat bread called chapati.

⟲ SANDAL MAKER
Footwear and clothes are still made by hand in parts of Southern Asia. Huge factories also manufacture items for export.

Calcutta), and Chennai (formerly Madras). Other large cities include Karachi and Lahore in Pakistan. Many cities of Southern Asia contain old areas with slums, alongside modern high-rise buildings. The contrasts between the lives of rich and poor people are very great.

◐ FISHING IN BANGLADESH
Fish are caught in the Bay of Bengal and also in the many waterways that drain the flat parts of Bangladesh.

◐ COMPUTER INDUSTRY
Factories in Bangalore produce computers. High-tech industry is increasing in India, although most people still live by farming.

◐ TEA LEAVES
The leaves of tea plants are so delicate they must be hand-picked. India and Sri Lanka are among the world's leading tea producers.

◑ CHILLI PEPPERS

◑ PEDAL POWER
One kind of rickshaw, also called a pedicab, is driven by a man or boy on a bicycle. Another kind is a two-wheeled carriage pulled by a person on foot. Simple forms of transportation compete for passengers with taxis in many towns and cities.

◐ GROWING RICE
Paddy fields, enclosed by low banks of soil, are plowed and flooded before rice shoots are planted.

FACTS

MALDIVES
Divehi Raajjeyge Jumhooriyya – Republic of the Maldives
AREA: 115 sq mi.
POPULATION: 275,000
CAPITAL: Malé
OTHER CITIES: none
HIGHEST POINT: Wilingili Island (79 ft)
OFFICIAL LANGUAGE: Divehi
CURRENCY: Rufiyaa

NEPAL
Nepal Adhirajya – Kingdom of Nepal
AREA: 56,827 sq mi.
POPULATION: 25.2 million
CAPITAL: Katmandu
OTHER CITIES: Lalitpur, Biratnagar
HIGHEST POINT: Mount Everest (29,028 ft)
OFFICIAL LANGUAGE: Nepali
CURRENCY: Nepalese rupee

PAKISTAN
Islami Jamhuriya e Pakistan – Islamic Republic of Pakistan
AREA: 307,373 sq mi.
POPULATION: 144.6 million
CAPITAL: Islamabad
OTHER CITIES: Karachi, Lahore, Faisalabad
HIGHEST POINT: K2 (28,251 ft)
OFFICIAL LANGUAGE: Urdu
CURRENCY: Pakistan rupee

SRI LANKA
Sri Lanka Prajathanthrika Samajavadi Janarajaya – Democratic Socialist Republic of Sri Lanka
AREA: 25,332 sq mi.
POPULATION: 19.4 million
CAPITAL: Colombo
OTHER CITIES: Dehiwela-Mt Lavinia, Moratuwa
HIGHEST POINT: Pidurutalagala (8,280 ft)
OFFICIAL LANGUAGES: Sinhala, Tamil
CURRENCY: Sri Lanka rupee

◯ SHERPAS IN NEPAL

The tough Sherpa people of northeastern Nepal are known for their mountaineering and military skills. Some work as mountain guides.

◯ PAINTED VEHICLES

Long-distance drivers in India and Pakistan often decorate their trucks. Road transportation is important because distances in Southern Asia are so great.

◯ DIWALI

Held each fall, Diwali is the Hindu festival of light. To mark the new year and to honor Lakshmi, the goddess of good fortune, people light oil lamps or candles and exchange cards and gifts.

India's people are divided into two main groups: the lighter-skinned Indo-Aryans in the north and the darker-skinned Dravidians in the south. There are 16 major languages and more than 1,000 minor languages and dialects. The main official language is Hindi. English is an "associate" national language.

The people in the northwestern part of Southern Asia include Afghans, Indo-Aryans, and Persians. The Sinhalese of Sri Lanka and the people in the Maldives are descendants of people from northern India, while the ancestors of Sri Lankan Tamils came from southern India.

Southern Asians excel in the decorative arts and in architecture and sculpture—across the region can be seen superb Hindu temples, Muslim mosques, and huge statues of the Buddha. Traditional music and dance are popular, and movie-making is another Indian art-form.

◯ JAIN BUILDING

Jainism is an Indian religion dating back 2,500 years. This Jain temple is in the Great Indian (Thar) Desert region in northwest India.

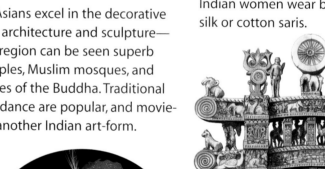

◯ HOUSEBOATS

In India's troubled region of Jammu and Kashmir, some people live on houseboats on the lakes. Their handicrafts include making beautiful hand-painted papier mâché boxes, which are sold to tourists in Delhi.

Many people in the cities of Southern Asia wear Western clothes, but traditional dhotis—white cloths wrapped around the body and tucked between the legs—are also worn by men. Many Indian women wear brightly colored silk or cotton saris.

◯ BUDDHIST GATEWAY

Buddhism is the chief religion in Bhutan and Sri Lanka. This is the gateway to a Buddhist shrine.

◯ HINDU WEDDING

Wealthy Indians have elaborate wedding ceremonies. These days, many weddings take place at hotels.

Hinduism, one of the world's oldest religions, dates back about 4,000 years. It is followed by 63 percent of the people of Southern Asia. Hindus worship many gods—Shiva, Krishna, and Vishnu are the most well-known—who are forms of one universal spirit. Hindus believe that the soul never dies. Instead, it is reincarnated (reborn) in the body of a human or animal. One of the many religious festivals celebrated is Diwali, the Hindu festival of light. Another is the spring festival of Holi.

⊙ LAMAS
Lamas are monks who practice Lamaism, or Tibetan Buddhism.

⊙ SNAKE CHARMER
An Indian snake charmer sways to-and-fro as he plays his music. The cobra rises up, mesmerized by the movement of the instrument.

Hindus make up 80 percent of India's population. India also has about 100 million Muslims, 36 million Christians, and nearly seven million Buddhists. Hinduism is the main religion in Nepal, while Islam is the religion of Afghanistan, Bangladesh, the Maldives, and Pakistan. Buddhism is the leading faith in Bhutan and Sri Lanka.

⊙ VILLAGE GODS
Eight-out-of-ten Indians are Hindus. Many villages have their own statues of gods.

⊙ TEMPLE AT KHAJURAHO
In the Hindu temple-complex at Khajuraho, in north-central India, there are 22 great temples, each decorated with elaborate carvings.

⊙ PRAYER BELLS
Buddhists shake bells during worship to frighten away evil spirits and attract good ones.

⊙ SPRING FESTIVAL
Holi is an ancient Hindu spring festival, when people throw colored water and powders over each other. Differences of age, caste, and sex are disregarded on this day.

◑ DEMOCRATIC ELECTIONS
India is the world's biggest democracy, with more voters than any other country. It has held regular elections since it won independence.

◑ INDUS CIVILIZATION

The ancient citadel of Mohenjo-daro had wide streets, large houses, good sewers, grain stores, and a Great Bath, used for religious rituals.

◑ CLAY STATUE

Beautiful statues were found among the ruins of the ancient city of Mohenjo-daro. This one is thought to be of a priest or king.

Between 2500 BC and 1700 BC, the Indus Valley civilization flourished in what is now Pakistan and northwestern India. Their two great cities were Harappa and Mohenjo-daro. About 1500 BC, Aryan people from the northwest invaded India and developed the Hindu cultures of the region. After Alexander the Great reached the Indus Valley region about 320 BC, a major Buddhist culture grew up in the north. Following other invasions, Mongol invaders took northern India in the AD1400s. By 1526, India was part of a large Mongol empire.

◑ TAJ MAHAL

The white marble Taj Mahal, in Agra, India, was built as a tomb for Mumtaz Mahal, favorite wife of Shah Jahan (1592–1666). It is one of the world's most famous and beautiful buildings.

◑ INDEPENDENCE DAY PARADE
Soldiers march to celebrate India's independence from Britain. Military service in India is voluntary.

◔ MASS MIGRATION

When India and Pakistan became independent in 1947, millions of Muslims and Hindus moved country. Attacks on refugee columns resulted in many deaths.

◑ EMPEROR ASOKA

Emperor Asoka ruled over the Maurya empire (272–232 BC). He conquered large areas and converted from Hinduism to Buddhism.

From the 16th century, European traders began to visit Southern Asia. As the Mongol empire declined, the British East India Company gradually gained control of large areas. An unsuccessful rebellion against the East India Company took place in 1857 and, in 1858, Britain took control of the region. Britain helped to develop the region with railroads, a telephone system, and irrigation works.

But many Indians wanted independence. From 1920, they were led by a lawyer, Mohandas K. Gandhi (1869–1948), also known as Mahatma Gandhi, who led campaigns of non-violent resistance. After World War II, Britain agreed to make India independent. Following violence between Hindus and Muslims, the country's leaders agreed to partition British India into Muslim Pakistan and a mainly Hindu India. Millions of people became refugees and many were killed.

Fighting also occurred in the northwest, where India and Pakistan fought over Kashmir. Pakistan was divided into two separate areas: West and East Pakistan. In 1971, civil war broke out and East Pakistan became a separate country, Bangladesh. In Afghanistan, Russian troops invaded to prop up the Communist government, but pulled out in 1988, after which Islamic Taliban forces imposed a strict regime. In 2001 a coalition of US and allied forces, backing Afghan rebels, drove out the Taliban, and set up a new government.

In Sri Lanka, some Hindu Tamils supported a guerrilla group, the Tamil Tigers, who want their own country. Relations between India and Pakistan are strained over Kashmir. Both countries have nuclear weapons.

◑ GOLDEN TEMPLE, AMRITSAR

The Golden Temple, the most sacred Sikh temple, is in Amritsar, in northwest India. Sikhs make up two percent of India's population.

◑ NATIONAL LEADERS

In 1947, Muslim Pakistan came into being, led by Muhammad Ali Jinnah (1876–1948, on the right). India's first prime minister was Jawaharlal Nehru (1889–1964, on the left).

173

EASTERN ASIA

○ BUDDHIST MONK, LHASA

Lhasa is the capital of Tibet—now a region of China. Many Tibetans would like Tibet to become an independent country.

By area, Eastern Asia is dominated by China, the world's third-largest country after Russia and Canada. China claims the island of Taiwan, although Taiwan is a separate territory with its own government. Eastern Asia also includes North Korea, South Korea, and Mongolia. Japan is also part of Eastern Asia, but is covered separately (see page 182).

In the western part of Eastern Asia are high plateaus, mountain ranges, and deserts. On the border between Tibet and Nepal rises Mount Everest, the world's highest mountain. The inland deserts are hot in summer, but are bitterly cold in winter. The Gobi Desert, which lies partly in northern China and partly in Mongolia, is one of the bleakest deserts on Earth.

By contrast, the eastern part of this region has fertile plains, uplands, and densely populated river valleys. Three great rivers cross eastern China—the Huang He (formerly named the Yellow River), the Chang Jiang (Yangtze), and the Xi Jiang in the southeast. North and South Korea occupy a rugged peninsula that juts out from northeastern China. Most Koreans live on the plains and around the coast.

CHINA
Zhonghua Renmin Gonghe Guo – People's Republic of China
AREA: 3,676,300 sq mi.
POPULATION: 1,275 million
CAPITAL: Beijing
OTHER CITIES: Shanghai, Tianjin, Shenyang, Wuhan
HIGHEST POINT: Mount Everest (29,028 ft)
OFFICIAL LANGUAGE: Mandarin Chinese
CURRENCY: Yuan

MONGOLIA
Mongol Uls – Mongolia
AREA: 604,800 sq mi.
POPULATION: 2.5 million
CAPITAL: Ulan Bator
OTHER CITIES: Darhan, Erdenet
HIGHEST POINT: Altai Mountains (14,350 ft)
OFFICIAL LANGUAGE: Khalka Mongolian
CURRENCY: Tugrik

NORTH KOREA
Chosun Minchu-chui Inmin Konghwa-guk – People's Democratic Republic of Korea
AREA: 46,536 sq mi.
POPULATION: 22 million
CAPITAL: Pyongang
OTHER CITIES: Hamhung, Cho'ngjin
HIGHEST POINT: Paektu-san (Paektu Mountain) 9,003 ft
OFFICIAL LANGUAGE: Korean
CURRENCY: Won

Tibet is a high, windswept plateau, with bitterly cold winters and short, cool summers. The north and northwest is mainly dry, with bare desert or areas of dry grassland, called steppe. Summers in southeast China range from warm to hot, while winters are cool. The northeast, including most of Korea, has cold winters.

○ FOREST OF STONE
Worn limestone rocks resembling giant tree trunks form the Yunnan stone forest in southern China. The area lies southeast of Kunming.

○ GIANT PANDA
Giant pandas are rare. They live in the bamboo forests of west and southwest China, and are threatened by loss of their habitat.

NORTH KOREA

MONGOLIA

◑ HONG KONG
Formerly a British colony, Hong Kong was returned to Chinese rule as a Special Administrative Region in 1997.

◑ SEOUL, KOREA
Seoul is the capital of South Korea. It is one of the world's largest cities and has many high-rise buildings and industries.

CHINA

◑ GREAT WALL OF CHINA
The 4,600-mile-long Great Wall of China was built to keep out invaders from the north.

◑ PEKINESE DOG

SOUTH KOREA

TAIWAN

◑ SHANGHAI
Shanghai is China's largest city. It is also the country's chief port and industrial city.

KOWLOON, HONG KONG

Hong Kong consists of 235 islands and an area on the mainland of China. Kowloon is on the mainland. It is a busy place, with many shops and industries.

PICKING TEA

Tea is one of the main crops in southern China. China ranks second only to India in the production of tea.

In recent years, Eastern Asia has suffered from many disputes. One issue concerns Taiwan and other offshore islands. Since 1949, when the Chinese Communists took over the mainland, Taiwan has been the home of the Nationalists, who founded a rival "Republic of China." China still claims Taiwan, but the Taiwanese oppose union with Communist China. Some old colonial problems have been solved. First, in 1997, Britain returned Hong Kong to China. Then, in 1999, Portugal returned Macao, a small territory in southwestern China. China and Russia ended long-running border disputes in 1998.

No solution appears in sight concerning Tibet in the southwest. Tibet has been part of China since the early 1950s, but many Tibetans want to regain their independence and see the return of their exiled religious leader, the Dalai Lama.

FISHING WITH BIRDS

Chinese fishermen train birds called cormorants to catch fish for them in inland waters.

STOCK EXCHANGE, HONG KONG

Hong Kong is one of the world's leading financial centers.

The border between North and South Korea is disputed. After World War II, North Korea became a Communist country, while South Korea, aided by the United States, allied itself with Western countries. From 1950 to 1953, the Korean War caused great destruction, and North and South Korea remain divided. South Korea is a multi-party democracy, as is Mongolia, which was a Communist country until 1990. Communist governments still rule North Korea and China.

FACTS

SOUTH KOREA
Daehan Min-Kuk – Republic of Korea
AREA: 38,330 sq mi.
POPULATION: 47.6 million
CAPITAL: Seoul
OTHER CITIES: Pusan, Taegu
HIGHEST POINT: Halla San (Halla Mountain, 6,398 ft)
OFFICIAL LANGUAGE: Korean
CURRENCY: Won

TAIWAN
Chung-hua Min-kuo – Republic of China
AREA: 13,968 sq mi.
POPULATION: 22.3 million
CAPITAL: Taipei
OTHER CITIES: Kao-hsiung, T'ai-chung
HIGHEST POINT: Yü Shan (Mount Morrison, 13,113 ft)
OFFICIAL LANGUAGE: Mandarin Chinese
CURRENCY: New Taiwan dollar

GOLDEN LION

This golden lion is one of the many statues found in Beijing's Forbidden City, the large palace-complex of the former emperors.

MARKET, BEIJING

Chinese people from the countryside travel to the cities to sell their produce at markets. As well as vegetables, many live birds and other animals are sold, to be cooked and eaten with rice or noodles.

RICE PLANT

JADE CAMEL

Since ancient times, the Chinese have mined jade and used it to make beautiful carvings. This jade camel is more than 1,000 years old.

Nearly 70 percent of the people of Eastern Asia, excluding Japan, work on farms. Only ten percent of the land in China is farmed, but the country is a major producer of farm products, including rice, sweet potatoes, tea, and wheat. China also raises more than a third of the world's pigs.

Only 29 percent of China's people live in cities and towns, yet over 30 Chinese cities have populations of more than a million people. China's resources include coal and oil. Although many people are poor, China is a rapidly developing country.

"Special economic zones" in the east have many industries, which are partly financed by foreign companies.

South Korea and Taiwan are also important manufacturing nations. Communist North Korea also has industries, but living standards are lower there.

PRINTING IN SOUTH KOREA

The printing of books, newspapers, and magazines is important in the drive to educate people. Most Asians believe that education is vital if their countries are to make economic progress.

CHINESE JUNK

Junks are wooden vessels with two or more sails. They were traditionally used by Chinese and other sailors in Eastern Asia. Some people live on junks.

◑ CHINESE FOOD
Rice is eaten in southern China, but most northerners prefer wheat. Vegetables, pork, and poultry are also popular.

China contains more than one-fifth of the world's population. The birth-rate was so high that the government made laws to slow down the rate of population growth. For example, couples are encouraged to have one child only; women may not marry until the age of 20; and men may not marry until they are 22.

About 92 percent of the people of China belong to the Han group. Their language, Chinese, is always written in the same way, but spoken Chinese has many dialects. People from one part of the country often cannot understand people from elsewhere. The dialect called Northern or Mandarin Chinese is the official language.

◑ UNARMED COMBAT
Chinese karate is called kung fu. It employs circular movements that differ from the powerful movements of other forms of karate.

◑ LIFE ON THE WATER
Most Chinese cities have housing shortages. Some people live on boats moored along the coast or rivers. China contains some of the world's most densely populated areas.

Besides the Han, China also has 55 minority groups. Some speak Chinese dialects, others have their own languages. Important minorities include Kazaks and Uigurs in the northwest, Mongols in the north, Koreans in the northeast, and Tibetans in the southeast.

The Communist governments in Eastern Asia have discouraged religious worship. However, many people follow Buddhism, Confucianism, or Taoism, and sometimes a mixture of all three. Some Muslims live in western China and in Mongolia. Christians make up about one-fourth of the population of South Korea.

◑ TALENTED CHILDREN
Chinese children with special talents receive extra schooling at the weekend. Some learn to play the piba, a stringed instrument.

◐ MONGOLIAN YURT
The traditional homes of Mongolian herders are felt tents, called yurts. They can be easily taken down and moved to a new site.

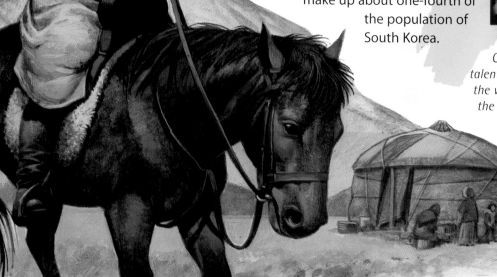

BUDDHIST MONK

Forms of Buddhism are followed in China (including Tibet), South Korea and Mongolia.

Eastern Asia has long artistic traditions. Early Chinese art includes beautiful pottery and carved jade statues. China also has much great literature, delicate watercolor painting, sculpture, embroidery, music, and theater.

People enjoy many kinds of recreation. Many Chinese get up early every morning to engage in an ancient and graceful form of exercise called taijiquan. Sports include baseball, basketball, soccer, table tennis, and volleyball.

Rice is the chief food in the warm, southern parts of the region, while wheat is important in the cooler north. Pork and poultry are the main meats, while bamboo shoots, cabbages, and tofu (soya bean curd)

SUMMER FESTIVAL

Every May, dragon boat races are held in Hong Kong. After the races, there are displays of martial arts and street theater to enjoy. The revelers snack on dragon boat dumplings and roasted pinenuts, and firecrackers are let off well into the night.

are popular vegetables. Beijing duck is a special treat in China. It consists of slices of crisp roast duck wrapped in thin pancakes. Koreans enjoy kimchi, a spicy mixture of cabbage, radishes, and other vegetables. Tea is the chief drink.

CHINESE WRITING

Chinese writing consists of characters that stand for words or parts of words.

TIANANMEN SQUARE, BEIJING

Firework displays and parades are held in Tiananmen Square in central Beijing. The Forbidden City and parliament buildings border the square.

CHINESE OPERA

Beijing opera combines drama with songs and dances. The actors wear elaborate costumes and make-up.

QING VASE

Chinese artists have made pottery for thousands of years. The early part of the Qing dynasty, which began in 1614, produced superb vases like this highly decorated example.

⟳ BEIJING

In the Ming dynasty, a wall and moat were built around Beijing. In the Qing dynasty, more palaces, temples, and other buildings were added outside the city wall.

Early civilizations developed in the fertile valleys of eastern China about 3,500 years ago. China's history from the 1700s BC until 1912 is divided into dynasties—rule by members of a family or group.

The Qin dynasty (221 BC–206 BC) was the first to set up a strong central government to rule eastern China. The Han dynasty that followed founded a strong empire, ruling an area as large as the Roman empire. China came under foreign rule when the Mongols conquered the country in the 13th century and set up the Yuan dynasty. The Mongols conquered a vast area extending westward from Korea to eastern Europe.

Chinese rule was restored in 1368, but in the 17th century, the Manchu from Manchuria set up the Qin dynasty. Manchu rule was weakened in 1895 when China was defeated by Japan, which occupied Korea in 1910. Dynastic rule came to an end in 1912, when China became a republic. Japan seized Manchuria in 1931 and China fought against Japanese invaders between 1937 and 1945.

At the end of World War II, civil war in China continued between the Communists and the Nationalists. In 1949, the Communists, under Mao Zedong (1893–1976), took over mainland China, while the Nationalists under Chiang Kai-shek (1887–1975) retreated to Taiwan.

Under Communist rule, the governments of China, North Korea, and Mongolia took over all land and industry. Although they improved the lives of many poor peasants, they also suppressed all opponents of Communism.

⟳ TERRACOTTA ARMY, XI'AN

In the vast burial chamber of Emperor Shi Huangdi, who lived in the 3rd century BC, thousands of lifesized clay soldiers were found.

⟳ SILK ROAD TRADERS

The Silk Road was the long, arduous trade route between China and Syria, used in Roman and later times. It crossed mountains and deserts.

⟳ MANCHU EMPEROR

The Manchus set up the Qing dynasty. Only the emperor was allowed to wear a silk gown embroidered with a five-clawed dragon.

⟳ CANTON HARBOR

Guangzhou (formerly Canton) is a Chinese port to the northwest of Hong Kong. During the 1800s, it was the only Chinese port open to Westerners.

LAST EMPEROR
Pu Yi was China's last emperor. He was two when he became emperor in 1908.

Some Communist policies caused severe economic problems. From the 1980s, China introduced economic reforms, especially in the east, where foreign companies were welcomed. But the Communists kept control of China's government.

In 1990 Mongolia held free elections, which led to the establishment of democratic government. South Korea, Taiwan, and the British territory of Hong Kong set up high-tech and other industries, rapidly developing their economies. In 1997, Hong Kong, which Britain had controlled since 1842, was returned to China. It became a "Special Administrative Region," but retained many of the laws introduced by Britain.

CHAIRMAN MAO
Mao Zedong (or Mao Tse-tung) became China's leader when the Communists took power in 1949. He died in 1976.

THE LONG MARCH
In the 1930s, under Nationalist attack, the Chinese Communists undertook the Long March to northern China. On the march, Mao Zedong emerged as the Communist leader.

MING TOMB
Many Chinese and foreigners visit the Ming tombs. The Ming dynasty lasted from 1368 until 1644.

DENG XIAOPING
From 1976, Deng Xiaoping made many economic changes in China.

TIMELINE

BC

1700s Eastern Asia's first major civilization founded in the Huang He valley

214 Under Emperor Shi Huangdi, China is united; Great Wall of China is fortified and sections joined

202 BC–AD 220 Chinese culture flourishes under Han dynasty (until 220 AD)

AD

1279 Mongols begin to rule Mongolia, Korea, and all of China

1368 Chinese culture develops under the Ming dynasty (until 1644)

1644 Manchus rule China, Mongolia, and Korea (until 1910, when Japan occupies the peninsula)

1912 Republic of China founded

1937 China at war with Japan (until 1945)

1949 Communists establish the People's Republic of China

1950 Korean War (until 1953)

1989 Tiananmen Square massacre of student demonstrators, Beijing

1997 Britain hands Hong Kong to China

1999 Portugal hands Macao to China

JAPAN

FACTS

JAPAN
Nihon, or Nippon Koku –
Land of the Rising Sun
AREA: 145,869 sq mi.
POPULATION: 127 million
CAPITAL: Tokyo
OTHER CITIES: Osaka,
Yokohama, Nagoya
HIGHEST POINT: Mount Fuji
(12,388 ft)
OFFICIAL LANGUAGE:
Japanese
CURRENCY: Yen

↻ SPRING FLOWERS
*Each spring, the cherry trees blossom
first in the warm south, then in the
north. This is marked by spring festivals.*

↻ BUDDHIST STATUE, KYOTO
*Many Japanese follow a
mixture of Shintoism and
Buddhism, the country's two
main religions.*

Japan is part of Eastern Asia. It consists of four main islands and thousands of small ones. The main islands, in order of size, are Honshu, Hokkaido, Kyushu, and Shikoku. These islands make up more than 98 percent of Japan.

South of Shikoku lies the Ryukyu island chain, and south of Tokyo are the Bonin Islands. The land is mainly mountainous, with some small, fertile, and thickly populated plains around the coast. Mount Fuji, a dormant volcano, is Japan's highest peak. Most of the country's rivers are short and fast-flowing.

The climate varies from north to south. Hokkaido in the north has cold, snowy winters, while Kyushu and Shikoku have mild winters and long, hot summers. The rainfall is generally abundant and forests cover about two-thirds of the land. Evergreens, such as fir and spruce, grow in the north, with deciduous trees, such as maple and oak, in the warmer center and south. Wild animals include bears, wild boar, and deer. Japan is the world's northern limit for monkeys, including the Japanese macaque.

Whales, dolphins, and many kinds of fish live in the seas around Japan. The country is rich in waterbirds, including the cormorant, which can be trained to catch fish.

Japan lies on a part of the Earth called "the Pacific ring of fire." Along this zone, the Earth's plates are on the move. Under much of Japan, the Pacific plate is sinking under the Eurasian plate. Every time the Pacific plate moves downward, it makes the ground shake. An earthquake in 1923 struck the Tokyo-Yokohama area, killing 100,000 people. Earthquakes off the coast can trigger huge waves, called tsunamis. When these waves hit the shore, they do tremendous damage. The 1923 earthquake generated a 36-foot-high tsunami.

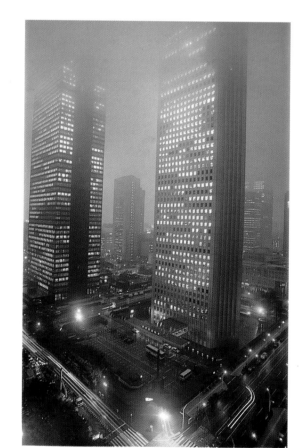

↻ THE LIGHTS OF TOKYO
*Badly damaged by an earthquake in 1923, and by bombing
in World War II, Tokyo is now a huge, thriving, densely
populated modern city and a major center for industry.*

○ WARM BATHS

Japanese macaques are large monkeys that live on the island of Hokkaido in the far north of Japan. In cold weather, they sometimes bathe in warm springs, known as onsen.

○ EARTHQUAKE DAMAGE

A powerful earthquake struck Kobe in 1995, killing more than 5,000 people.

JAPAN

SEA OF JAPAN

J A P A N

Tokyo

PACIFIC OCEAN

○ BONSAI TREE

Japanese gardeners have perfected the art of growing miniature trees, known as bonsai.

○ KYUSHU ISLAND

Kyushu is the most southerly of Japan's four main islands. Its climate is much warmer than that of northern Japan.

○ PUFFER FISH

The poisonous puffer fish, or fugu, is found in the Pacific Ocean. Its flesh is a delicacy in Japan. Chefs must train for at least three years to learn how to cut off the poisonous parts of the fish.

○ MOUNT FUJI

Volcanic Mount Fuji, also called Fujiyama or Fuji-san, is Japan's highest peak, at 12,388 feet. It last erupted in 1708.

183

○ PAPER LANTERNS
Wood, wood pulp, and paper are made in Japan. Paper products range from lanterns to sliding walls used in homes.

○ ROBOTS AT WORK
Automation has helped Japan become the world's leading car producer. Japan also exports trucks and motorcycles. Using modern technology to make Japanese goods keeps down the prices in world markets.

For long periods in the past, Japan was ruled by emperors, who held great power. Before and during World War II, Emperor Hirohito was regarded as a god. After World War II, Japan became a constitutional monarchy and the emperor a symbol of the state confined to ceremonial duties. The country has an elected two-chamber Diet (parliament), whose members choose the prime minister.

○ TEA PLANTATION
Japan is one of the world's top ten producers of tea. Green tea is drunk with every meal.

By population, Japan ranks eighth among the countries of the world. Although the forested mountains are thinly populated, the coastal plains are among the world's most densely populated areas. About 78 percent of the people live in cities and towns. There are 11 cities with a population of more than a million.

Japan lacks natural resources and has to import food and many of the materials needed by its industries. But it ranks second only to the United States in its production of goods and services. Only 15 percent of the land is farmed, but Japanese farmers use intensive, scientific methods to achieve some of the world's highest yields, and Japan produces about 70 percent of the food it needs. Rice is the main crop, but eggs, fruit, meat, milk, and vegetables are also important. Japan is the world's fourth-largest fishing nation, judged by the volume of its catch. Fish, rice, and vegetables are the main ingredients for many meals, such as the ever-popular sushi.

○ SUSHI
Sushi, a delicious and popular dish, consists of rice "rolls" flavored with vinegar, raw fish, shellfish, and pickles.

○ WHALING
Whales are an important source of meat and oil in Japan, and festivals are held to celebrate them. But international laws have forced Japanese fleets to restrict their catches.

○ CRASH BANDICOOT
Japan's top quality electronic goods, including big-name computer games, are sold around the world.

AKASHI KAIKYO ROAD BRIDGE
Completed in 1998, the bridge linking the island of Awaji to Honshu is the world's longest cable suspension bridge.

MAGLEV TRAIN
Maglev (magnetic levitation) trains float above a fixed track without touching it. High-speed maglev trains can reach 311 mph. Japan has an extensive rail system for city commuters.

The country is one of the world's great industrial and trading nations. It leads the world in producing cars, ships, and steel. It is also a major producer of commercial vehicles, computers and other electronic goods, home appliances such as refrigerators, freezers, and washing machines, and radios and television sets. Japan also has a large chemical industry and silk is a traditional product.

DECORATED FAN
The folding fan was probably invented in Japan about 1,300 years ago. Fans are used by entertainers.

DIGITAL CAMERAS
Japan produces many of the world's finest cameras, lenses, video cameras and recorders, and precision instruments.

Japan imports coal and oil to fuel power plants, and also has nuclear power plants. Many of its rivers are harnessed to produce electricity at hydroelectric plants. The country has one of the world's best transportation services and one of the world's largest merchant fleets.

OYSTER BEDS
The Japanese cultivate oyster beds, which provide delicious seafood and precious pearls.

TEA CEREMONY
Geisha women conduct traditional tea ceremonies. They learn from childhood how to entertain guests with conversation, music, and dance.

Almost 99 percent of the people of Japan are Japanese. The chief minorities are the Ainu—most of whom live on Hokkaido—Koreans, and Chinese. Some scholars think that the Ainu may have been the first people in Japan. Japanese is the official language, but it has many dialects. The Tokyo dialect is the standard form used on radio and television.

Shinto and Buddhism are the chief religions, and many people follow elements from both of these faiths.

Baseball and sumo (a kind of wrestling) are leading sports, together with martial arts such as judo, karate, and kendo (a type of fencing). The Japanese also enjoy golf, skiing, tennis, and volleyball. Calligraphy (beautiful lettering, often painted with a soft brush), music, and dance are art forms in Japan.

Theater is popular. The ancient No plays are performed by actors in masks, while kabuki plays are melodramas, usually with spectacular sets. Since World War II, Japanese movies have become popular around the world. Many films tell stories about samurai (warriors) or the shoguns (generals who ruled in the name of the emperors). Other art forms include architecture, especially Buddhist temples, literature (including poems called haiku), painting, and sculpture.

WEALTHY WOMAN
In the Tokugawa period, rich women had very elaborate hair styles held together with giant pins.

JAPANESE SAMURAI
The samurai were professional knights or warriors in the Middle Ages.

KOI CARP
Beautiful koi carp are bred to decorate the tranquil ponds in Japanese ornamental gardens.

TEMPLE OF THE GOLDEN PAVILION, KYOTO
Kyoto was the capital of Japan from 794 to 1868. It has many beautiful old buildings, including this magnificent temple, which was rebuilt in 1955 after a devastating fire.

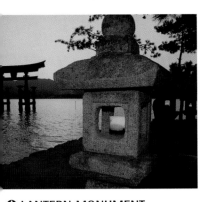

Japan's modern history began when Portuguese sailors reached the islands in 1543. However, the Japanese feared that the introduction of Christianity by missionaries would lead to domination by European powers. During the 1630s, Japan cut itself off from the world and by 1640 Christianity had almost disappeared from Japan.

◑ LANTERN MONUMENT
In 1945, the United States dropped atomic bombs on Hiroshima and Nagasaki. The terrible destruction led to Japan's surrender.

In 1853, the United States forced the Tokugawa shogunate to open ports to US trade. After the restoration of the emperor's powers in 1867, Japan began to modernize its economy and set up many industries. This gave Japan increasing military power, leading to wars with China and Russia.

◑ ARMORED CAR
Japan began a war with China in 1937. This war became part of World War II (1939–45).

Japan supported the Allies in World War I (1914–18). In 1931 it occupied Manchuria. From 1937, it conquered much of China, and during World War II (1939–45), it conquered Southeast Asia and the western Pacific. Japan was finally defeated in 1945. From the 1950s, it rebuilt its industries with great determination and has become one of the world's leading economic powers.

◑ SUMO WRESTLERS
A form of wrestling called sumo is the leading spectator sport in Japan.

◑ WIND-BLOWN WAVES AT SHICHI-RI BY HIROSHIGE
Hiroshige (1797–1858) was one of the greatest Japanese artists of the 19th century.

◑ KABUKI
In traditional Japanese kabuki plays, actors use exaggerated gestures and wear elaborate costumes.

TIMELINE

BC

660 According to legend, Jimmu Tenno becomes Japan's first emperor

AD

300 Yamato kingdom unifies Japan

c.600 Prince Shotoku makes Buddhism state religion and sets up constitution

710 Nara becomes Japanese capital

785 Heian (modern-day Kyoto) becomes capital (until 1868)

1192 First shogun (general) appointed

1274 Mongol invasion thwarted by typhoon (known as kamikaze, "divine wind")

1600 Tokugawa Period of national seclusion, called sakoku (until 1867)

1854 US Commander Matthew C. Perry opens two Japanese ports to US trade

1867 Shogun rule ends

1904 Russo–Japanese War (until 1905): Japan defeats Russia

1914 World War I (until 1918): Japan sides with the Allies

1937 Japan begins a war against China

1939 World War II (until 1945): Japan sides with Germany; US drops atomic bombs on Hiroshima and Nagasaki

1947 Japan adopts democratic constitution

1989 Emperor Hirohito dies; his son Akihito becomes emperor

187

SOUTHEAST ASIA

↻ RETICULATED PYTHON
The reticulated python of Southeast Asia may grow to 30 feet in length.

↻ FOREST APE
Orangutans are apes found in Borneo and Sumatra. Rainforest destruction has made them rare.

↻ YANGON, MYANMAR
Pagodas are towers belonging to Buddhist temples. The shape is based on the Indian stupa, which covered the remains of a king or holy man.

Southeast Asia consists of a large peninsula attached to India and China, together with thousands of islands to the east and south of the peninsula. Like Eastern Asia, Southeast Asia contains several fast-developing countries, notably Singapore, Thailand, and Malaysia.

The peninsula has fertile plains, where most of the people live, and some rugged mountains. The area is drained by several major rivers. The longest is the Mekong, which rises in Tibet and flows through Laos, Thailand, and Cambodia before reaching its large delta in Vietnam. Myanmar (named Burma until 1989), has the Ayeyarwady (formerly Irrawaddy) River. Its delta is one of the world's great rice-growing areas.

Malaysia lies partly on the peninsula and partly on the island of Borneo. The small state of Singapore consists of about 50 islands; the Philippines has about 7,100 islands; and Indonesia about 13,600. The Philippines and Indonesia are largely mountainous. Both countries are liable to earthquakes, and many of the highest peaks are active volcanoes. Some of the biggest volcanic eruptions in modern times have occurred in this region. They include Tambora (1815), Krakatoa (1883), and Mount Merapi (1931), all in Indonesia, and Mount Pinatubo in the Philippines (1991).

Southeast Asia has high temperatures throughout the year and abundant rainfall. But while much of the peninsula has a wet and dry monsoon climate, the southern islands are rainy throughout the year. The wettest areas have evergreen rainforests rich in plant and animal species. Mangrove swamps thrive along many coasts.

BRUNEI
Negara Brunei Darussalam –
State of Brunei Darussalam
AREA: 2,226 sq mi.
POPULATION: 344,000
CAPITAL: Bandar Seri Begawan
OTHER CITIES: Seria, Kuala Belait
HIGHEST POINT: Bukit Betalong (2,995 ft)
OFFICIAL LANGUAGE: Malay, English
CURRENCY: Brunei dollar

CAMBODIA
Preah Reach Ana Pak
Kampuchea –
Kingdom of Cambodia
AREA: 69,898 sq mi.
POPULATION: 12.7 million
CAPITAL: Phnom Penh
OTHER CITIES: Kompong Cham, Battambang
HIGHEST POINT: Phnum Aôral (5,948 ft)
OFFICIAL LANGUAGE: Khmer
CURRENCY: Riel

INDONESIA
Republik Indonesia –
Republic of Indonesia
AREA: 735,354 sq mi.
POPULATION: 212 million
CAPITAL: Jakarta
OTHER CITIES: Bandung, Surabaya, Medan
HIGHEST POINT: Puncak Jaya (16,503 ft)
OFFICIAL LANGUAGE: Bahasa Indonesian
CURRENCY: Indonesian rupiah

LAOS
Saathiaranarath Prachhathipatay
Prachhachhon Lao – Lao
People's Democratic Republic
AREA: 91,429 sq mi.
POPULATION: 5.6 million
CAPITAL: Vientiane
OTHER CITIES: Savannakhet, Luang Prabang
HIGHEST POINT: Mount Bia (9,242 ft)
OFFICIAL LANGUAGE: Lao
CURRENCY: Kip

❂ CRATER LAKE
The craters of some of Indonesia's many volcanoes are filled with brightly colored mineral-rich water.

❂ MOSQUE, BRUNEI
Two-thirds of the people of Brunei are Muslim. Islam is also the chief religion of Indonesia.

MYANMAR

LAOS

N
W   E
S

CAMBODIA

MALAYSIA

VIETNAM

PHILIPPINES

INDONESIA

THAILAND

SINGAPORE

❂ MOUNTAINOUS VIETNAM
Scenic mountains rise along Vietnam's borders with China, Laos, and Cambodia. But most people live on the lowlands.

BRUNEI

EAST TIMOR

Map labels:
MYANMAR (BURMA), CHINA, Mandalay, Hanoi, Haiphong, Akyab, ARAKAN YOMA, PEGU YOMA, TANEN R., Luang Prabang, LAOS, Chiang Mai, Yangon (Rangoon), Vientiane, Pathen (Bassein), Mawlamyine (Moulmein), THAILAND, Nakhon Ratchasima, Da Nang, Bangkok, Tavoy, CAMBODIA, TONLE SAP, Nha Trang, Merqui, Phnom Penh, VIETNAM, Gulf of Thailand, Ho Chi Minh City, Phuket, George Town, Kuala Terengganu, Ipoh, Kelang, Medan, Natuna Is., MALAYSIA, Strait of Malacca, Kuala Lumpur, BRUNEI, Johor Baharu, SINGAPORE, Sumatra, SARAWAK, Kapuas, Pontianak, BORNEO, Balikpapan, Padang, Hari, Bangka, Jambi, Belitung, Barito, Banjarmasin, INDONESIA, Palembang, PEG BARISAN, JAVA SEA, Jakarta, Semarang, Java, Bandung, Surabaya, Bali, Lombok, Malang, Sumbawa, Sumba, Laoag, Luzon, Mt. Pinatubo, Manila, Mindoro, PHILIPPINES, Panay, Tacloban, Iloilo, Cebu City, Palawan, Negros, Bohol, SULU SEA, Mindanao, Davao, Mt. Kinabalu 4,094 m, Zamboanga, Mt. Apo 2,954 m, Bandar Seri Begawan, Sandakan, SABAH, CELEBES SEA, Manado, MOLUCCA SEA, Halmahere, Palu, Sulawesi, Moluccas, Sorong, CERAM SEA, Jayapura, WEST PAPUA, Seram, Biru, Ambon, Puncak Jaya 5,030m, NEW GUINEA, PAPUA NEW GUINEA, Ujung Pandang, BANDA SEA, Aru Is., FLORES SEA, Baubau, Wetar, Tanimbar Islands, Flores, Dili, EAST TIMOR, Ende, Kupang

❂ PENANG, MALAYSIA
Penang Island lies off the northwest coast of Malaysia. During the 1800s its chief port, George Town, was an important shipping center. Today the island is a popular tourist resort.

❂ KOMODO DRAGON
The 10-foot-long Komodo dragon is the largest living lizard.

☉ RUBY PANNING
The world's finest rubies are found in river gravels in Myanmar. Thailand also produces beautiful rubies.

☉ COCONUT HARVEST
In Thailand, monkeys are trained to collect coconuts, the fruit of the coconut palm.

☉ PALACE STATUE
Many statues stand in the Royal Palace in Bangkok, Thailand. The statues reveal the natural grace of the Thai people.

☉ TOURISM
Tourism is a major industry employing many people in Thailand. Bali (in Indonesia), Malaysia, and the Philippines also attract many tourists.

There are ten countries in the Southeast Asia region. Cambodia, Malaysia, and Thailand are monarchies, with elected parliaments. Brunei is also a monarchy, ruled by a sultan. Because of the country's large oil exports, the sultan has become one of the world's richest men.

Most of the countries of Southeast Asia are republics, though not all are truly democratic. Vietnam had a Communist government after its reunification in 1975, but later moved toward a more free-market economy. The Philippines and Singapore are multi-party republics with flourishing export-based economies. Myanmar has a military government.

The largest nation in the region is Indonesia, the world's most populous Muslim country. Its ethnic and religious minorities, such as the Aceh (in Sumatra), Christians in Maluku, and the people of East Timor have faced repression and there have been outbreaks of rebellion and violence. East Timor, occupied by Indonesia after Portuguese colonial rule ended in 1975, gained independence in 2002. By then Indonesia had abandoned its authoritarian president Suharto (in power 1967–88). In such a diverse nation, with some 200 ethnic groups, achieving national unity is difficult.

About half of the people in Southeast Asia are farmers or farm workers, many of them poor. The chief crop is rice. Indonesia, Myanmar, the Philippines, Thailand, and Vietnam rank among the world's top ten rice producers.

☉ BASKETS OF FRUIT
Many tropical fruits grow on the hot island of Bali, a tourist island in Indonesia.

◯ ROYAL PALACE, BANGKOK
Thailand is an ancient monarchy. Unlike the other countries of Southeast Asia, it was never colonized by a European country.

Other major products include coffee, tropical fruits such as pineapples, corn, rubber, tea, and timber. Brunei, Indonesia, Malaysia, and Vietnam produce oil and natural gas. Other resources include coal in Indonesia and Vietnam, precious stones in Myanmar, and tin in Indonesia, Malaysia, Thailand, and Vietnam.

Nearly a third of the people live in cities or towns. The largest cities are Jakarta in Indonesia, Manila in the Philippines, Bangkok in Thailand, Ho Chi Minh City and Hanoi in Vietnam, and Singapore City. Singapore is a small country, but it is the region's richest. Its highly skilled workers have made it a major center of manufacturing, producing chemicals, electronic products, scientific instruments, ships, and textiles. Indonesia, Malaysia, and Thailand have also developed industries. In contrast, neighboring Vietnam, Cambodia, and Laos are poor countries, whose economies have been badly damaged by wars.

◯ OYSTER AND PEARL
The waters off the strangely shaped island of Sulawesi, Indonesia, are the source of oysters that yield top-quality pearls.

◯ FLOATING MARKETS
Canals criss-cross Bangkok, Thailand. In places, boats loaded with produce form floating markets.

◯ WATER BUFFALO
Farmers use water buffalo to pull plows in paddy fields. The animals like to wallow in mud and water.

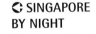

◯ SINGAPORE BY NIGHT
Singapore City is a bustling center of industry, finance, and trade.

◯ TERRACED RICE FIELDS,
Terraced fields, used mainly for growing rice, have been cut like giant steps into the steep hillsides in the Philippines.

◯ BALINESE PROCESSION
Processions are held on the mainly Hindu island of Bali.

◯ BUDDHIST MONKS, MYANMAR
About nine-out-of-ten people in Myanmar are Buddhist. Buddhism is also the chief religion in Cambodia, Laos, and Thailand.

◯ THAI CHILDREN
Primary education is free in Thailand, and 94 percent of the people over 15 years old can read and write.

Southeast Asia has about 490 million people. Most are of Chinese, Indian, or Malay descent. Many languages are spoken, especially in Indonesia, which has about 250 languages of its own.

Buddhism is the chief religion of much of the mainland peninsula of Southeast Asia. But Islam is important in Malaysia and Brunei. About 87 percent of Indonesians are Muslim, although Indonesia also has Christian and Hindu minorities. In the Philippines, about 90 percent of the people are Christian. The Philippines is the only large country in Asia with a Christian majority. The Communist governments in Laos and Vietnam have discouraged any kind of religious worship.

Ancient and modern architecture is one of the region's finest art forms. Visitors may admire the beautiful Buddhist and Hindu temples and the Muslim mosques. Music and dance are popular, especially at festivals, such as harvest celebrations and village fairs. In Indonesia, gamelan bands play drums, flutes, metal gongs, stringed, and xylophonelike instruments.

◯ TRIBAL WARRIOR
The peoples living in remote areas in the Philippines include the pygmy Negritos, descendants of people who settled there 30,000 years ago.

○ STATUE OF BUDDHA, VIETNAM

The government in Vietnam has discouraged religious worship, but many people follow Buddhist teachings.

Puppet dramas are popular in Indonesia and Malaysia. The person who operates the puppets tells the story and speaks the parts of the characters. The Philippines and Vietnam also have long literary traditions.

Leading sports include soccer, badminton, and basketball.

Traditional ox-races and bullfights are held at festivals in Indonesia. In Thailand, a version of boxing allows the boxers to use both their hands and their feet to strike their opponents.

Many people in the cities wear Western clothes. Traditional garments such as sarongs are also worn. Sarongs are long pieces of cloth that men and women wrap around their bodies. Muslim men usually wear hats, and women also cover their heads, but seldom wear veils.

Rice is the main food in Southeast Asia. It is eaten with meat, fish, and vegetables. One popular dish in Malaysia is satay. It consists of pieces of meat cooked on a skewer and dipped in a hot sauce. Adobo in the Philippines is a dish of chicken and pork cooked in soya sauce and vinegar.

○ DAYAK WOMAN

Small tribal groups live in isolated parts of Southeast Asia. They include the Dayaks of Borneo.

○ HOOKED ON PAIN

Devotees undergo pain to prove their strong religious faith at the Taipsu festival, George Town, Malaysia.

○ DANCERS IN BALI

In Bali, dance is used as a way of telling Hindu stories. The dancers use graceful movements—particularly of the hands and feet—which take years of training.

◔ LONGHOUSE

Dayak family groups in Borneo live in longhouses. Up to a hundred people may live together in one house.

○ JAVANESE SHADOW PUPPET

Puppeteers in Java, Indonesia, enact a story by casting shadows of puppets onto a screen.

193

ASIA

From about 3000 BC, people from Central Asia and southern China began to settle in Southeast Asia. The original, darker-skinned peoples were forced to live in remote areas. From about AD 100, a series of great kingdoms developed in the region, including the Funan kingdom in Cambodia. From the AD 600s, the Srivajaya kingdom arose in Sumatra and became a major sea power. But perhaps the best-known kingdom belonged to the Angkor civilization, which flourished in Cambodia between the 800s and the 1400s. It was named for its capital, the ruins of which, with its superb temples, still stand today.

RAMA IV
King Mongut (Rama IV) ruled Thailand from 1851 to 1868. He allowed many Western ideas to be introduced.

BRITISH BURMA
Britain gradually conquered Burma (now Myanmar) through wars in 1824–26, 1852, and 1885. Burma finally became a province of British India.

In the 19th century, Britain gradually took over Singapore, Malaysia, and Burma (now Myanmar), while France took over Indochina (now Cambodia, Laos, and Vietnam). By the early 20th century, only Thailand remained free of foreign rule. But European power in the region collapsed when Japan conquered Southeast Asia during World War II (1939–45). Following the defeat of Japan in 1945, the countries of Southeast Asia gradually won their independence from the European colonizers.

Communism attracted many people in the region and Communist guerrillas fought for independence in Indochina and elsewhere.

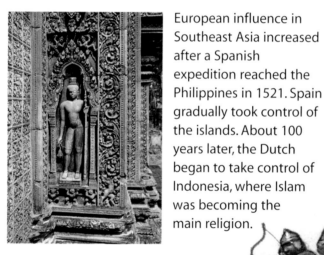

European influence in Southeast Asia increased after a Spanish expedition reached the Philippines in 1521. Spain gradually took control of the islands. About 100 years later, the Dutch began to take control of Indonesia, where Islam was becoming the main religion.

RELIC FROM ANGKOR
Angkor was the ancient capital of a civilization that flourished in Cambodia between the 9th and 15th centuries. This guardian figure was found there.

KHMER WARRIORS
In the 12th century, the Khmer rulers of Angkor conquered areas that are now in Laos, Thailand, and Vietnam.

⟳ POL POT
Communist leader Pol Pot (c.1925–98) seized control of Cambodia in the 1970s. His forces killed thousands of Cambodians.

In 1954, France withdrew from Indochina, which was divided into Cambodia, Laos, North Vietnam, and South Vietnam. Communist North Vietnam aided Communists in other parts of Indochina and, in the early 1960s, the United States sent troops to stop South Vietnam falling to the Communists. The war ended in 1975, when Vietnam became one nation.

Although disturbed by civil war in Cambodia and military rule in Myanmar, several countries by 2000 had made great strides in developing their economies. The Association of Southeast Asian Nations (ASEAN) was set up in 1967 to help its members trade together. By 2003, all the countries of Southeast Asia were members of ASEAN.

⟳ RAFFLES HOTEL
Sir Stamford Raffles (1781–1826), the founder of Singapore City, played an important part in establishing British footholds in Southeast Asia. His name is remembered in the Raffles Hotel.

⟳ ANGKOR WAT
The temple of Angkor Wat was the finest building in the ancient capital of Angkor. The city ruins were rediscovered in 1860.

TIMELINE

AD

800s	Powerful Hindu-Buddhist kingdom rules Cambodia with Angkor as its capital (until 1400s)
1431	Forces from the Thai Ayutthaya kingdom conquer Angkor
1525	Spain claims the Philippines (until 1898)
1898	Spain gives the Philippines to the United States
1620s	Dutch begin to control Indonesia
1800s	Britain and France take over most of the Southeast Asian peninsula
1941	Japan conquers Southeast Asia (until 1945)
1946	Laos independent from France; Philippines declared a republic
1953	Cambodia independent from France
1957	The Vietnam War (until 1975)
1963	Malaysia is formed
1965	Singapore breaks away from Malaysia
1984	Sultanate of Brunei fully independent
1986	Revolution in the Philippines
1998	Fall of Suharto regime in Indonesia
2002	East Timor, former province of Indonesia, becomes an independent nation

⟳ IMELDA'S SHOES
President Marcos (1917–89) fell from power in the Philippines in 1986. He was accused of corruption. His wife, Imelda, was criticized for her extravagance, after the people discovered her vast collection of clothes and shoes.

⟳ HO CHI MINH
Communist leader Ho Chi Minh (1890–1969) led North Vietnam during the Vietnamese War (1957–75).

195

N
W   E
S

MOROCCO
TUNISIA
ALGERIA
LIBYA
EGYPT
Western
Sahara
MAURITANIA
NIGER
CHAD
SUDAN
ERITREA
SENEGAL
GAMBIA
DJIBOUTI
GUINEA
BISSAU
GUINEA
BURKINO
FASO
NIGERIA
SOMALIA
SIERRA
LEONE
BENIN
GHANA
CÔTE
D'IVOIRE
TOGO
ETHIOPIA
LIBERIA
CENTRAL
AFRICAN
REPUBLIC
CAMEROON
EQUATORIAL GUINEA
UGANDA
KENYA
GABON
REPUBLIC
OF
CONGO
DEMOCRATIC
REPUBLIC
OF THE
CONGO
RWANDA
BURUNDI
SEYCHELLES
TANZANIA
COMOROS
ANGOLA
ZAMBIA
MALAWI
MOZAMBIQUE
MADAGASCAR
MAURITIUS
ZIMBABWE
Réunion
(France)
NAMIBIA
BOTSWANA
SWAZILAND
SOUTH
AFRICA
LESOTHO

196

⟳ AFRICAN DOG

AFRICA

◊ Sand dune,
NAMIBIA

◊ Niger valley,
MALI

◊ Painted house,
GHANA

◊ Elephant,
TANZANIA

Africa is the world's second-largest continent after Asia, covering about 20 percent of the world's land area. Most of Africa is a plateau, surrounded by narrow coastal plains. The highest peak is Kilimanjaro, a dormant (sleeping) volcano in northern Tanzania. Africa is drained by some major rivers, including the Nile, Congo, and Niger.

Northwest and southwest Africa have mild Mediterranean-type climates. Between these regions lie vast, hot deserts, tropical grassland called savanna, and dense rainforests around the Equator. The savanna is home to antelopes, elephants, lions, and zebras. Many other animals, such as gorillas and chimpanzees, are found in the rainforests. The number of animals in Africa has steadily decreased because of over-hunting and because their habitats have been cleared to create farms. Many governments have created national parks to protect their wildlife.

The continent has two main groups of people. North of the Sahara Desert, the Arab and Berber people speak Arabic and follow Islam. The black Africans to the south of the Sahara are divided into more than 1,000 ethnic groups. Some are Muslim and others are Christian, but many still follow ancient, local religions, in which spirit worship is important.

Africa contains many of the world's poorest countries. Many people are farmers, using simple farm tools. They produce little more than they need to feed their families and, when droughts occur, many starve. Agriculture employs nearly 60 percent of the people. Africa has valuable resources, such as oil and many metals, which are exported. But, apart from South Africa and Egypt, few countries have many manufacturing industries.

About 50 years ago, European countries ruled most of the continent. Today, most Africans run their own countries. But in some regions progress has been hampered by economic problems and instability.

NORTH AFRICA

⊙ FENNEC FOX

⊙ OLD VOLCANOES

The Ahaggar Mountains in southern Algeria contain jagged peaks formed from the necks of ancient, extinct (dead) volcanoes. These rock formations are called plugs.

North Africa, as shown on the map, makes up nearly half of Africa. It consists largely of a low plateau, between 500 and 1,970 feet above sea level. The highest peaks are in the Ethiopian Highlands in the southeast and the Atlas Mountains in the northwest. Smaller highlands made of jagged volcanic rocks rise above the plateau.

Northwestern Morocco, together with the plains along the Mediterranean Sea coast, have dry, hot summers and mild, rainy winters. The Sahara, the world's largest desert, covers more than three-fifths of North Africa. With an area of about 5.8 million square miles, it is nearly as big as the United States.

The world's highest air temperature in the shade, 136°F, was recorded in the Sahara. However, nights can be cold, and people wear thick cloaks to keep themselves warm. Several years may pass in the Sahara with hardly any rain. Then a sudden, freak storm may cause floods. But the desert contains green oases, where water from beneath the ground reaches the surface. The region with the most water is the Nile valley. South of the Sahara, the desert merges into a dry grassland region called the Sahel. South of the Sahel lie areas of savanna, with scattered trees. Some rainforests grow in the far southwest.

In the Mediterranean region, trees such as oaks and olives grow. Elsewhere, the the palm tree is common. The most important desert animal for humans is the camel, which can travel long distances without water. Other notable animals include the Barbary ape in the northeast and the gelada baboon in Ethiopia.

⊙ DESERT, MOROCCO
The Sahara in North Africa stretches from the Atlantic Ocean to the Red Sea.

ALGERIA
Jamhuriya al Jazairiya ad-Dimuqratiya ash-Shabiya – People's Democratic Republic of Algeria
AREA: 919,591 sq mi.
POPULATION: 30.8 million
CAPITAL: Algiers
OTHER CITIES: Oran, Constantine, Annaba
HIGHEST POINT: Mount Tahat (9,574 ft)
OFFICIAL LANGUAGE: Arabic
CURRENCY: Algerian dinar

CAPE VERDE
República de Cabo Verde – Republic of Cape Verde
AREA: 1,557 sq mi.
POPULATION: 446,000
CAPITAL: Praia
OTHER CITIES: Mindelo, São Filipe
HIGHEST POINT: Pico (9,281 ft)
OFFICIAL LANGUAGE: Portuguese
CURRENCY: Cape Verde escudo

CHAD
République du Tchad – Republic of Chad
AREA: 495,753 sq mi.
POPULATION: 8.7 million
CAPITAL: N'Djamena
OTHER CITIES: Moundou, Bongor
HIGHEST POINT: Emi Koussi (11,204 ft)
OFFICIAL LANGUAGES: Arabic, French
CURRENCY: CFA franc

DJIBOUTI
Jumhouriyya Djibouti – Republic of Djibouti
AREA: 8,957 sq mi.
POPULATION: 619,000
CAPITAL: Djibouti
OTHER CITIES: none
HIGHEST POINT: Mousaalli (6,768 ft)
OFFICIAL LANGUAGE: Arabic, French
CURRENCY: Djibouti franc

✪ LIVING BY THE NILE
The River Nile provides essential water for crop irrigation. Egypt's Nile valley is North Africa's most populated region.

EGYPT

✪ NIGER VALLEY, MALI
The Niger is the third-longest river in Africa. It brings water to dry areas south of the Sahara.

ALGERIA

TUNISIA

LIBYA

ERITREA

DJIBOUTI

MOROCCO

CAPE VERDE ISLANDS

MAURITANIA

✪ ASNI, MOROCCO
Asni is a market town in the foothills of the Atlas Mountains, south of the city of Marrakech.

MALI

CHAD

NIGER

SUDAN

ETHIOPIA

✪ DESERT LANDMARK
The pyramids near Cairo, Egypt, were built by the rulers of ancient Egypt, about 3000 BC.

⟳ **PEANUTS**
Peanuts are also called groundnuts. Sudan is a leading producer.

There are 14 independent countries in North Africa. Twelve are republics, while Morocco is ruled by a king. The government of Eritrea, which was part of Ethiopia from 1952 to 1993, is transitional—that is, its constitution has not been finalized.

The region also includes the disputed territory of Western Sahara, which was ruled by Spain until 1976. When Spain withdrew, Morocco occupied the northern two-thirds, while Mauritania took the rest. The local Saharan people demanded independence and attacked the Moroccans and Mauritanians. Mauritania withdrew from Western Sahara in 1979, leaving Morocco in charge. Fighting continued, with the rebels claiming that their territory was an independent republic. The United Nations is trying to keep the peace and solve the dispute.

Ethnic and religious differences have caused problems in North Africa, too. In Sudan, for example, Muslim government forces have fought civil wars with the people in the south, many of whom either practice traditional religions or are Christian.

⟳ **TANNERIES, FEZ**
Fez is an ancient royal capital city in Morocco. Its tanneries prepare leather, which is made into a wide range of products.

⟳ **EMPERORS' CROWNS**
Axum, a historic city in northern Ethiopia, was a royal capital from 500 BC. It has many ancient treasures.

FACTS

EGYPT
Jamhuriyat Misr al-Arabiya – Arab Republic of Egypt
AREA: 386,660 sq mi.
POPULATION: 65.2 million
CAPITAL: Cairo
OTHER CITIES: Alexandria, El Giza
HIGHEST POINT: Jabal Katrinah (8,652 ft)
OFFICIAL LANGUAGE: Arabic
CURRENCY: Egyptian pound

ERITREA
State of Eritrea
AREA: 45,405 sq mi.
POPULATION: 4.3 million
Capital: Asmara
Other cities: Asseb, Keren
HIGHEST POINT: Mount Soira (10,180 ft)
OFFICIAL LANGUAGE: None
CURRENCY: Nakfa

ETHIOPIA
Federal Democratic Republic of Ethiopia
AREA: 426,370 sq mi.
POPULATION: 66 million
CAPITAL: Addis Ababa
OTHER CITIES: Dire Dawa, Harar
HIGHEST POINT: Ras Dashen (13,976 ft)
OFFICIAL LANGUAGE: None
CURRENCY: Birr

LIBYA
Jamahiriya Al-Arabiya Al-Libiya Al Shabiya Al-Ishtirakiya Al-Uzma – Great Socialist People's Libyan Arab Republic
AREA: 679,370 sq mi.
POPULATION: 5.2 million
CAPITAL: Tripoli
OTHER CITIES: Benghazi, Misurata
HIGHEST POINT: Bette Peak (7,500 ft)
OFFICIAL LANGUAGE: Arabic
CURRENCY: Libyan dinar

⟳ **MOROCCAN CARPETS**
Highly decorated carpets are among the products made by skilled Arab and Berber craftspeople in North Africa.

⟳ **DECORATED CAMEL**
Tourists enjoy camel rides in North Africa. The camels here have one hump. They kneel to let riders climb on and off them.

SUEZ CANAL
The Suez Canal, which opened in 1869, provides a valuable and significant short cut for shipping passing between the Indian Ocean and the Mediterranean Sea.

ORANGES, TUNISIA
Oranges and other citrus fruits grow well in the sunny climate of North Africa.

Poverty is widespread in North Africa; the United Nations classifies most countries as poor, developing areas. The wealthier countries include Algeria and Libya, which both have reserves of oil and natural gas, and Morocco, where phosphate rock is mined and made into fertilizer. Niger, one of the poorest countries, is a major producer of uranium.

Overall, agriculture employs more than 50 percent of North Africans. Important crops include barley, citrus fruits, and olives in the Mediterranean countries; cotton and sugar cane in the Nile valley; and dates at desert oases. South of the Sahara, millet and sorghum are leading food crops, while coffee is Ethiopia's main export.

Manufacturing is unimportant in most North African countries. The chief industrial region is the Nile delta north of Cairo, the capital of Egypt. With more than ten million people, Cairo is the largest city in North Africa. About 37 percent of North Africans live in cities and towns. Other cities with populations of more than two million are Alexandria and El Giza, Egypt; Casablanca, Morocco; and Addis Ababa, Ethiopia.

MARKET, ALGERIA
On market days, people buy and sell produce, meet friends, and catch up on local news.

ASWAN HIGH DAM
The Aswan High Dam on the River Nile in Egypt produces hydroelectricity. The dam began operating in 1968. It holds back Lake Nasser.

SNAKE CHARMER
Snake charmers and other entertainers perform at the Djemaa El Fna, a market in central Marrakech, Morocco.

FACTS

MALI
République du Mali – Republic of Mali
AREA: 478,839 sq mi.
POPULATION: 11 million
CAPITAL: Bamako
OTHER CITIES: Ségou, Mopti
HIGHEST POINT: Homboro Tondo (3,789 ft)
OFFICIAL LANGUAGE: French
CURRENCY: CFA franc

MAURITANIA
République Islamique Arabe et Africaine de Mauritanie – Islamic Republic of Mauritania
AREA: 395,954 sq mi.
POPULATION: 2.6 million
CAPITAL: Nouakchott
OTHER CITIES: Nouadhibou, Kaédi
HIGHEST POINT: Kediet Ijill (3,002 ft)
OFFICIAL LANGUAGE: Arabic
CURRENCY: Ouguiya

MOROCCO
Mamlaka al Maghrebia – Kingdom of Morocco
AREA: 172,394 sq mi.
POPULATION: 29 million
CAPITAL: Rabat
OTHER CITIES: Casablanca, Marrakech
HIGHEST POINT: Jebel Toubkal (13,665 ft)
OFFICIAL LANGUAGE: Arabic
CURRENCY: Moroccan dirham

NIGER
République du Niger – Republic of Niger
AREA: 489,189 sq mi.
POPULATION: 10.3 million
CAPITAL: Niamey
OTHER CITIES: Zinder, Maradi
HIGHEST POINT: Mount Gréboun (6,378 ft)
OFFICIAL LANGUAGE: French
CURRENCY: CFA franc

○ MARKET DAY

A woman carries her baby through the market in Bamako, capital of Mali. Bamako is a major economic center on the Niger River.

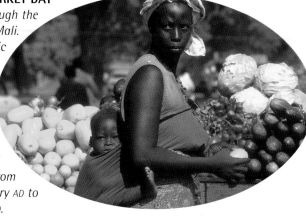

○ OBELISK, AXUM

Obelisks up to 100-feet tall still stand in Axum, Ethiopia. The kingdom of Axum lasted from the 2nd century AD to about 1000 AD.

Most people in Africa north of the Sahara speak Arabic and are Muslim. The countries share a common culture, with similar kinds of buildings, literature, and other art forms. Some Muslims dislike Western ideas and support groups who call for the return of fundamentalist Islamic laws and practices. In Algeria, the conflict between the government and Muslim fundamentalists led to fighting in the 1990s.

○ SULTAN'S MOSQUE, CAIRO

Rising above the huge city of Cairo— the largest city in Africa—are the tall minarets (prayer towers) of the Sultan's mosque.

Many languages are spoken in the countries south of the Sahara, and the customs of the people vary from group to group. For example, more than 70 languages and 200 dialects are spoken in Ethiopia, which has no single official language. Several other countries use a European language for official purposes. Soccer is the leading sport throughout the region.

A food dish called ful, or fool, which consists of broad beans cooked in oil, is a favorite in Egypt and Sudan.

○ MUAMMAR GADDAFI

Colonel Gaddafi (b.1942) became Libya's leader in 1969. He encouraged a return to the fundamental principles of Islam.

SUDAN
Jamhuryat es-Sudan – Republic of Sudan
AREA: 967,495 sq mi.
POPULATION: 36 million
CAPITAL: Khartoum
OTHER CITIES: Omdurman, Khartoum North, Port Sudan
HIGHEST POINT: Mount Kinyeti (10,456 ft)
OFFICIAL LANGUAGE: Arabic
CURRENCY: Sudanese dinar

TUNISIA
Jumhuriya at Tunisiya – Republic of Tunisia
AREA: 63,169 sq mi.
POPULATION: 9.8 million
CAPITAL: Tunis
OTHER CITIES: Sfax, Aryanah
HIGHEST POINT: Mount Chambi (5,066 ft)
OFFICIAL LANGUAGE: Arabic
CURRENCY: Tunisian dinar

WESTERN SAHARA
Western Sahara (disputed territory largely occupied by Morocco) – local nationalists have named it the Saharan Arab Democratic Republic
AREA: 102,702 sq mi.
POPULATION: 228,000
CAPITAL: El-Aaiún
OTHER CITIES: Dakhla
HIGHEST POINT: 2,700 ft
OFFICIAL LANGUAGE: Arabic
CURRENCY: Moroccan dirham

○ HANNIBAL

In 218 BC, the great general, Hannibal—born in Carthage, Tunisia—led a surprise attack on the Romans using war elephants.

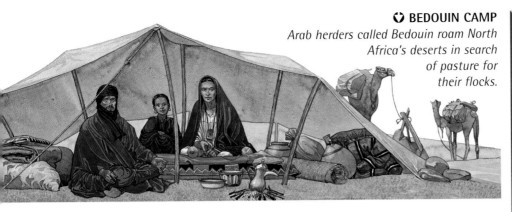

⟳ BEDOUIN CAMP
Arab herders called Bedouin roam North Africa's deserts in search of pasture for their flocks.

◐ SAND OVEN, TIMBUKTU
Timbuktu, Mali, was once a great trading city. Many ancient traditions still survive there.

Couscous (steamed wheat) served with fish, meat, and vegetables is popular in northwest Africa. Ethiopians enjoy wat, a spicy stew eaten with injera, a flat bread.

About 5000 BC, North Africa was wetter than it is today and the Sahara was a grassland. By 4000 BC the climate had become drier and people moved into areas with water, notably the fertile Nile valley. Here, from about 3100 BC, ancient Egypt developed into a major civilization. Other early cultures developed to the south in Sudan and Ethiopia, which became a Christian empire in the 4th century AD.

In the Middle Ages, Arab and Berber traders regularly crossed the desert in camel caravans. These traders recorded several major medieval empires ruled by Africans. They included ancient Ghana and Mali, which were based in the upper Niger River region, in what is now just Mali.

↻ TUAREG
The Tuareg are a nomadic people. The men wear clothes of a distinctive blue color.

By the early 20th century, most of the North African countries, apart from Ethiopia, were under European rule. They won independence in the 1950s and 1960s. Political and economic problems have slowed development.

◐ SPHINX, LUXOR
Statues of imaginary creatures called sphinxes lined avenues to temples in ancient Egyptian cities, including Karnak at Luxor.

⟳ WASHING DAY, EGYPT
Egyptians in the Nile valley still use the river as they did in ancient times.

TIMELINE

BC

5000	Sahara is a grassland
4000	Sahara begins to dry up as climate warms
3100	Upper and Lower Egypt unite to form one of the world's greatest early civilizations
1400	Ancient Egypt reaches its peak
264–146	The Punic Wars between Rome and Carthage
30	Egypt and the Mediterranean coasts of North Africa come under Roman rule

AD

639	Arabs from Arabia introduce Arabic and Islam into North Africa (by 710)
1000	Large kingdoms arise in southwestern North Africa
1800s	Europeans begin to claim parts of North Africa
1882	British troops occupy Egypt
1922	Egypt becomes a partly independent monarchy
1950s	Independence won by Libya (1951), Sudan (1952), Morocco and Tunisia (1956)
1960	Chad, Mali, Mauritania, and Niger become independent from France
1962	Algeria becomes independent
1978	Egypt reaches a peace agreement with Israel, after 30 years of hostility
1991	Algeria cancels elections won by a Muslim party; civil war until 2000
1993	Eritrea breaks away from Ethiopia after a long war

WEST AFRICA

⟳ PARROT
Parrots live in West African forests.

FACTS

BENIN
République du Bénin
AREA: 5,632,000 sq mi.
POPULATION: 6.6 million
CAPITAL: Porto-Novo
OTHER CITIES: Cotonou, Djougou, Abomey-Calavi
HIGHEST POINT: Atacora Mountains (about 2,000 ft)
OFFICIAL LANGUAGE: French
CURRENCY: CFA franc

BURKINA FASO
République Démocratique du Burkina Faso – Democratic Republic of Burkina Faso
AREA: 105,795 sq mi.
POPULATION: 12.3 million
CAPITAL: Ouagadougou
OTHER CITIES: Bobo-Dioulasso, Koudougou
HIGHEST POINT: Aiguille de Sindou (2,352 ft)
OFFICIAL LANGUAGE: French
CURRENCY: CFA franc

CAMEROON
République du Cameroun – Republic of Cameroon
AREA: 295,434 sq mi.
POPULATION: 15.8 million
CAPITAL: Yaoundé
OTHER CITIES: Douala, Bafoussam, Garoua
HIGHEST POINT: Mount Cameroon (13,353 ft)
OFFICIAL LANGUAGES: French, English
CURRENCY: CFA franc

West Africa covers about 12 percent of Africa. It extends from Senegal and Gambia in the west to Cameroon in the east. The largest country, Nigeria, covers about a fourth of West Africa and is home to more than half of the people of West Africa. With a population of more than 126 million, Nigeria has more people than any other African country.

The landscape consists of coastal plains and a large inland plateau. The highest peak is Mount Cameroon, an active volcano. Moist winds blow from the sea up the slopes of Mount Cameroon, bringing heavy rain. With an average of 395 inches a year, the slopes of this mountain are one of the wettest places in the world.

West Africa has high temperatures throughout the year, and the southern coasts have rain all year round. Dense rainforests once covered the region, but much of the original forest has been cut down to make way for farmland. The northern part of West Africa has heavy summer rains, but winters are dry. Here, the forest merges into savanna with scattered trees, although leafy forests line the rivers.

The chief river is the Niger, which rises not far from the Atlantic Ocean, follows a huge arc through Mali and Niger, and then finally empties into the Gulf of Guinea in Nigeria. Part of Lake Chad lies in northeastern Nigeria, but the largest inland body of water entirely in West Africa is Lake Volta in Ghana. It is a reservoir, formed behind a huge dam.

⟳ STILT HOUSES
Heavy rains in West Africa often cause rivers to overflow, so many houses are built on stilts to keep them above the flood water.

○ MERCHANT, BURKINA FASO

Farming employs 90 percent of the people of Burkina Faso. About 70 percent of the people cannot read or write.

○ BEAUTIFUL BEACHES

West Africa has fine beaches and beautiful scenery. The Gambia has the most developed tourist industry in West Africa.

GUINEA

SENEGAL

GAMBIA

CÔTE D'IVOIRE

BURKINA FASO

○ WIDE-EYED

Bushbabies are active at night. They dart through the forest trees.

NIGERIA

○ WATERFALL, NIGERIA

Waterfalls and rapids are common features on the Niger River in Nigeria— long stretches of the river are unnavigable.

GUINEA-BISSAU

SIERRA LEONE

LIBERIA

CAMEROON

EQUATORIAL GUINEA

BENIN

GHANA

TOGO

○ ROCKY OUTCROP

Behind West Africa's narrow coastal plains, the land rises to tablelands broken by occasional mountains.

○ ACACIA TREE

Acacias are typical of tropical Africa. Many grow on the drier savanna grasslands of West Africa.

205

⟳ LAGOS, NIGERIA

Lagos, formerly Nigeria's capital, is the largest city in West Africa. When it became too gridlocked, a new capital was built at Abuja.

There are 14 countries in West Africa. Most of them are republics, although military groups have ruled several countries for long periods. The military leaders claimed that civilian governments were inefficient or corrupt, but they, too, were often accused of the same things.

Nigeria became independent from Britain in 1960. In 1966 a military group overthrew the civilian government. Since then there has been much conflict. In 1967, the Ibo people in the southeast tried to break away from Nigeria and establish a separate country named Biafra, causing a civil war that ended in 1970. Military leaders again took over in 1983. Elections held in 1993 were cancelled by the military leaders, and Nigeria was ruled by the army until elections in 1999 brought a return to democratic government.

Military take-overs have occurred in most West African countries, and two—Equatorial Guinea and Central African Republic—suffered periods of brutal military dictatorship. Even countries that have enjoyed relatively stable government, like Cameroon and Senegal, have had spells of violence.

The World Bank classifies the 14 countries of West Africa as "low-income economies." Agriculture employs about 55 percent of the people, but many farmers are poor, producing little more than they need to provide for their families.

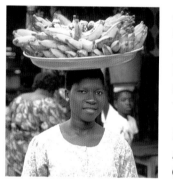

⟳ BANANA SELLER, GHANA

Bananas are grown throughout West Africa. But Ghana's most valuable crop and export is cocoa.

⟳ CHILLIES, NIGERIA

Chilli peppers are used to make food spicy hot.

⟳ RUBBER, LIBERIA

Rubber trees are grown on plantations in Côte d'Ivoire, Liberia, and Nigeria. Workers tap the trees to collect a fluid called latex, which is made into rubber.

EQUATORIAL GUINEA
República de Guinea Ecuatorial – Republic of Equatorial Guinea
AREA: 10,830 sq mi.
POPULATION: 486,000
CAPITAL: Malabo
OTHER CITIES: Bata, Ela-Nguema
HIGHEST POINT: Pico de Basilé (9,869 ft)
OFFICIAL LANGUAGES: Spanish, French
CURRENCY: CFA franc

THE GAMBIA
Republic of The Gambia
AREA: 4,361 sq mi.
POPULATION: 1.4 million
CAPITAL: Banjul
OTHER CITIES: Serekunda, Brikama
HIGHEST POINT: about 240 ft
OFFICIAL LANGUAGE: English
CURRENCY: Dalasi

GHANA
Republic of Ghana
AREA: 92,098 sq mi.
POPULATION: 19.9 million
CAPITAL: Accra
OTHER CITIES: Kumasi, Tamale, Tema, Sekondi-Takoradi
HIGHEST POINT: Afadjato (2,904 ft)
OFFICIAL LANGUAGE: English
CURRENCY: Cedi

GUINEA
République de Guinée – Republic of Guinea
AREA: 94,925 sq mi.
POPULATION: 7.6 million
CAPITAL: Conakry
OTHER CITIES: Kankan, Nzérékoré
HIGHEST POINT: Mount Nimba (5,748 ft)
OFFICIAL LANGUAGE: French
CURRENCY: Guinean franc

FACTS

GUINEA-BISSAU
República da Guiné-Bissau –
Republic of Guinea-Bissau
AREA: 13,948 sq mi.
POPULATION: 1.3 million
CAPITAL: Bissau
OTHER CITIES: Bafatá, Gabú
HIGHEST POINT: Pico de
Basilé (9,869 ft)
OFFICIAL LANGUAGE:
Portuguese
CURRENCY: CFA franc

CÔTE D'IVOIRE (IVORY COAST)
République de la Côte d'Ivoire –
Republic of the Ivory Coast
AREA: 124,503 sq mi.
POPULATION: 16.4 million
CAPITAL: Yamoussoukro
OTHER CITIES: Abidjan,
Bouaké, Daloa
HIGHEST POINT: Mount
Nimba (5,748 ft)
OFFICIAL LANGUAGE: French
CURRENCY: CFA franc

LIBERIA
Republic of Liberia
AREA: 43,000 sq mi.
POPULATION: 3.2 million
CAPITAL: Monrovia
OTHER CITIES: Harbel,
Gbarnga, Buchanan
HIGHEST POINT: Nimba
Mountains (4,527 ft)
OFFICIAL LANGUAGE: English
CURRENCY: Liberian dollar

NIGERIA
Federal Republic of Nigeria
AREA: 356,667 sq mi.
POPULATION: 126.6 million
CAPITAL: Abuja
OTHER CITIES: Lagos, Ibadan,
Kano, Ogbomosho
HIGHEST POINT: Dimlang
Peak (6,700 ft)
OFFICIAL LANGUAGE: English
CURRENCY: Naira

◔ TIMBER RAFTS
In West Africa, rainforest trees are cut down so that valuable tropical hardwoods such as ebony and teak can be exported.

◑ DIAMOND MINE, GHANA
Ghana produces diamonds, bauxite (used to make aluminium), gold, and manganese. But most Ghanaians are farmers.

In the hot, wet south, important crops include bananas, cassava, cocoa, coffee, palm oil and other palm products, rubber, and yams. To the north, crops such as groundnuts, corn, millet, and sorghum are important. Livestock is raised on the savanna.

Mineral resources in West Africa include oil in Nigeria and Cameroon, bauxite (aluminium ore) in Guinea and Ghana, gold in Ghana, and iron ore in Liberia. Manufacturing has grown, especially around Abidjan in Côte d'Ivoire, Dakar in Senegal, and in Nigeria, but elsewhere it is generally on a small scale.

◑ TOURISM, THE GAMBIA
Tourists in The Gambia are able to go on organized trips, called safaris, to see wildlife in the forests.

About 38 percent of the people live in cities and towns. The largest city is Lagos, former capital of Nigeria, with a population of about 13 million. Other cities include Abidjan, Côte d'Ivoire (2.5 million); Accra, Ghana (1.8 million); Dakar, Senegal (1.7 million); and Conakry, Guinea (1.5 million).

◑ SALT SACKS, THE GAMBIA
Salt is obtained from seawater that is trapped in ponds and left to evaporate in the open air.

◐ FISHING, NIGERIA
Fish is an important food. Fishermen operate in inland waters, coastal lagoons, and on the open sea.

NIGERIAN FAMILY
Nigerians wear traditional clothes made of brightly colored fabrics, or Western clothes more usually in towns.

SENEGAL
République du Sénégal – Republic of Senegal
AREA: 75,950 sq mi.
POPULATION: 10.3 million
CAPITAL: Dakar
OTHER CITIES: Thiès, Kaolack, Zinguinchor
HIGHEST POINT: 1,634 ft
OFFICIAL LANGUAGE: French
CURRENCY: CFA franc

SIERRA LEONE
Republic of Sierra Leone
AREA: 27,700 sq mi.
POPULATION: 5.4 million
CAPITAL: Freetown
OTHER CITIES: Koidu-New Sembehun, Bo
HIGHEST POINT: Loma Mansa (6,381 ft)
OFFICIAL LANGUAGE: English
CURRENCY: Leone

TOGO
République Togolaise – Republic of Togo
AREA: 21,925 sq mi.
POPULATION: 5.1 million
CAPITAL: Lomé
OTHER CITIES: Sokodé, Kpalimé
HIGHEST POINT: Agou (3,235 ft)
OFFICIAL LANGUAGE: French
CURRENCY: CFA franc

With some 210 million people, West Africa is the most densely populated part of the continent. Many different ethnic groups make up the population—there are about 250 in Nigeria alone—each with its own language. Islam is the chief religion in Gambia, Guinea, Nigeria, Senegal, and Sierra Leone, and also in the northern parts of the other countries. Around a third of the people are Christian and nearly a fifth practice traditional religions.

YORUBA SCULPTURE FROM NIGERIA
Yoruba sculpture is among Africa's finest. Some sculpture was made to decorate courts. Other pieces were made for religious purposes.

LION COFFIN, GHANA
To honor the dead, some Ghanaians buy impressive carved and elaborately painted coffins, resembling lions, other animals, or even Cadillac cars.

Music and dance are popular pastimes in West Africa, and soccer is the leading sport. Storytelling is another important part of the culture, with folk tales being passed from one generation to the next.

Important foods are cassava, corn, millet, plantains (a kind of banana), and yams, often eaten with spicy sauces.

One of the best known early African cultures flourished in central Nigeria between 2,200 and 1,800 years ago. There, the Nok people made beautiful, large terracotta sculptures of heads. These sculptures are the oldest known in Africa south of the Sahara.

NOK POTTERY, NIGERIA
Pottery is still made at Nok, where magnificent clay sculptures were made about 2,000 years ago. The pottery was fired in clay ovens.

TIMELINE

BC

500 Nok civilization flourishes in central Nigeria (until AD 200)

AD

1100s Kano, in northern Nigeria, is the chief trading city for Saharan camel caravans; Islam spreads through West Africa

1440s Portuguese reach West Africa; the slave trade begins soon afterward

1600s Ashanti unite into a nation, which, at its peak, includes western Togo, much of Ghana, and eastern Côte d'Ivoire

1822 The American Colonization buys land in Liberia for freed slaves

1847 Liberia becomes independent

1880s European colonization of Africa

1957 Ghana becomes independent

1958 Guinea becomes independent

1960 Benin, Burkina Faso, French Cameroon, Central African Republic, Côte d'Ivoire, Nigeria, Senegal, and Togo become independent

1961 British Cameroon becomes independent, with part joining Nigeria and part Cameroon

1965 The Gambia gains independence

1968 Equatorial Guinea and Sierra Leone become independent

1999 Civilian rule is restored in Nigeria; civil war in Sierra Leone

⟳ PAINTED HOMES, GHANA
Most village homes have thick mud walls and small windows, or none at all. This keeps the insides cool by day. Many are highly decorated.

⟳ AFRICAN DRUMS
Drumming plays a major part in West African music. Competing rhythms are played by several drummers.

In about AD 1000, another Nigerian culture, the Ife, produced superb bronze sculptures. But the best-known bronzes were made in the kingdom of Benin, between 1450 and 1750. Today sculpture remains important in the region—wooden masks and carvings are made for use in traditional religious ceremonies.

During the Middle Ages, northern West Africa was in contact with North Africa through Muslim traders who crossed the Sahara on camel caravans to exchange goods. Europeans explored the West African coast in the mid-15th century, and by about 1530 the trans-Atlantic slave trade from Africa to the Americas had begun. The Portuguese and later the Dutch, British, French, Swedish, Danes, and others all traded in slaves. The British abolished the slave trade in 1807, although it continued until the mid 19th century. In the late 19th century, most of West Africa came under European rule. The colonized countries gained independence in the 1950s and 1960s.

◑ MUSICAL INSTRUMENT
The kora is a kind of harp-lute often used to accompany storytellers.

⟳ CHIEFS GO DEMOCRATIC
In 1957, Ghana became the first black African country to win independence. Power passed from Britain to an elected parliament. But democracy proved fragile. Ghana, like many other African countries, suffered periods of dictatorship.

CENTRAL, EASTERN, AND SOUTHERN AFRICA

Central Africa forms the basin of Africa's second-longest river, the Congo. East Africa, by contrast, is a high plateau. Above this rise Africa's two highest peaks: Kilimanjaro in Tanzania and Mount Kenya in Kenya. Southern Africa also consists of a plateau, marked with some saucerlike depressions, such as the Okavango Delta in northern Botswana. Here, the Okavango River flows into an inland depression. The coastal plains are narrow, except in Mozambique and Somalia.

The region also includes Madagascar, the world's fourth-largest island, and the small island nations of the Comoros, Mauritius, and the Seychelles.

Central Africa has a hot and mostly rainy climate. Rainforests cover much of the northern part of the Congo basin, with savanna in the south. Savanna covers most of East Africa, where temperatures are lower. Much of Southern Africa is also covered by savanna, but some areas are dry. The Namib Desert in the southwest is one of the world's driest places, while the Kalahari in Namibia, Botswana, and South Africa is semi-desert. The southern parts of South Africa have a temperate climate. The area around Cape Town in the southwest has hot, dry summers and mild, rainy winters.

The Congo basin contains many rainforest animals. Some, such as the mountain gorilla of eastern Congo and Rwanda, are rare because of hunting. Other endangered animals include monkeys and the okapi, a relative of the giraffe.

ISALO MASSIF, MADAGASCAR
Madagascar is home to many unique plants and animals that are found nowhere else.

MOUNT KILIMANJARO, TANZANIA

NAMIB DESERT
Huge sand dunes build up and shift across the Namib Desert on Namibia's coast. Few living things can survive there.

KENYA

BURUNDI

CHIMPANZEE
Chimpanzees live in Central Africa's forests.

THE VICTORIA FALLS
These falls thunder down the Zambezi River between Zambia and Zimbabwe.

CENTRAL AFRICAN REPUBLIC

UGANDA

RWANDA

SOMALIA

GABON

CONGO, REP. OF

CONGO, DEM. REP. OF

ANGOLA

NAMIBIA

BOTSWANA

SOUTH AFRICA

LESOTHO

SWAZILAND

ZIMBABWE

TANZANIA

SEYCHELLES

MALAWI

MAURITIUS

MADAGASCAR

Map labels

CHAD
CENTRAL AFRICAN REPUBLIC
Bozoum
Bangassou
Bomu
SUDAN
Uele
ETHIOPIA
Cape Caseyr
Berbera
SOMALIA
Bangui
CAMEROON
Congo
UGANDA
Lake Turkana
Juba
REP. OF CONGO
Mbandaka
Kisangani
Margherita Peak 5,709m
Kampala
Kisumu
Mt. Kenya ▲ 5,199m
KENYA
Mogadishu
Libreville
SÃO TOMÉ & PRÍNCIPE
GABON
Cape Lopez
Brazzaville
Kinshasa
DEMOCRATIC REP. OF CONGO
RWANDA
Kigali
Lake Victoria
Nairobi
Tana
Kismayu
INDIAN OCEAN
Bukavu
BURUNDI
Bujumbura
Mwanza
Mombasa
Matadi
Cabinda (ANGOLA)
Kananga
Kasai
Sankuru
Lake Tanganyika
Rufiji
Dodoma
Kilimanjaro 5,895m
Zanzibar
Dar-es-Salaam
SEYCHELLES
Luanda
ANGOLA PLATEAU
Likasi
Lake Mweru
TANZANIA
Aldabra Is.
ZAMBIA
Lubumbashi
Lake Nyasa
C. Delgado
COMOROS
C. d'Ambre
ANGOLA
Lobito
Huambo
Ndola
MALAWI
Lilongwe
Antisiranana
Namibe
Cunene
Cubango
Cuito
ZAMBIA
Lusaka
Zambezi
Blantyre
Moçambique
Mahajanga
Etosha Pan
Okavango Delta
Livingstone
Harare
ZIMBABWE
MOZAMBIQUE
Mozambique Channel
Toamasina
NAMIBIA
Windhoek
BOTSWANA
Bulawayo
Limpopo
Beira
Antananarivo
MAURITIUS
Réunion (France)
KALAHARI DESERT
Gaborone
MADAGASCAR
Fianarantsoa
NAMIB DESERT
Pretoria
Maputo
C. Ste. Marie
Johannesburg
High Veld
Mbabane
SWAZILAND
Orange
Kimberley
Maseru
LESOTHO
Durban
SOUTH AFRICA
Great Karoo
DRAKENSBERG
Cape Town
East London
Cape of Good Hope
Cape Agulhas
Port Elizabeth

MOZAMBIQUE

MADAGASCAR

GIRAFFE
Giraffes stride across the African savanna—a rich habitat for wildlife, including lions, elephants, zebras, and warthogs.

THE BAOBAB
Africa's baobab trees—recognizable by their swollen trunks, which store water—can live more than 1,000 years.

RURAL ZIMBABWE
Rolling tablelands broken by rocky mountains like these in Zimbabwe are typical of the southern African landscape.

FACTS

COMOROS
République Féderale Islamique
des Comores – Federal Islamic
Republic of the Comoros
AREA: 836 sq mi.
POPULATION: 560,000
CAPITAL: Moroni
OTHER CITIES: Mutsamudu
HIGHEST POINT: Mount
Kartala (7,746 ft)
OFFICIAL LANGUAGES:
Comorian, Arabic, French
CURRENCY: Comorian franc

**CONGO,
DEMOCRATIC
REPUBLIC OF THE**
République Démocratique du
Congo – Democratic Republic of
the Congo
AREA: 905,350 sq mi.
POPULATION: 53 million
CAPITAL: Kinshasa
OTHER CITIES: Lubumbashi,
Mbuji-Mayi, Kisangani
HIGHEST POINT: Mount
Ruwenzori (16,762 ft)
OFFICIAL LANGUAGE: French
CURRENCY: Congolese franc

**CONGO,
REPUBLIC OF**
République du Congo –
Republic of Congo
AREA: 132,046 sq mi.
POPULATION: 2.9 million
CAPITAL: Brazzaville
OTHER CITIES: Pointe-Noire,
Loubomo
HIGHEST POINT: Létéki
(16,762 ft)
OFFICIAL LANGUAGE: French
CURRENCY: CFA franc

GABON
République Gabonaise –
Gabonese Republic
AREA: 103,346 sq mi.
POPULATION: 1.2 million
CAPITAL: Libreville
OTHER CITIES: Port-Gentil,
Franceville
HIGHEST POINT: Mount
Iboundji (3,904 ft)
OFFICIAL LANGUAGE: French
CURRENCY: CFA franc

KENYA
Jamhuri ya Kenya –
Republic of Kenya
AREA: 220,625 sq mi.
POPULATION: 30.7 million
CAPITAL: Nairobi
OTHER CITIES: Mombasa,
Kisumu, Nakuru
HIGHEST POINT: Mount
Kenya (17,060 ft)
OFFICIAL LANGUAGES: Swahili,
English
CURRENCY: Kenya shilling

⟳ FISHING, LUANDA
*Fishing is important
along Angola's coast.*

**⟳ SOUTH AFRICAN
APPLES**

**⟳ CAPE TOWN,
SOUTH AFRICA**
*Flat-topped Table Mountain
overlooks Cape Town, South
Africa's legislative capital.
Cape Town is also a major
port and industrial city.*

In Central, Eastern, and
Southern Africa there
are 24 independent
countries and one French
island territory named
Réunion. The countries
are all republics, except
for Lesotho and
Swaziland in the south,
which have kings as their
heads of state.

The boundaries between
the countries were drawn
in colonial times, when the region was ruled by
European powers. Some boundaries divide people
belonging to the same ethnic group. Somali people,
for example, live not only in Somalia, but also in
Djibouti, Ethiopia, and northern Kenya. This has
created problems along Somalia's borders.

Many countries have a
large number of ethnic
groups, and this has led to violent clashes. In Burundi
and Rwanda, for example, fighting broke out between
the two main groups, the Tutsi and the Hutu, resulting
in thousands of deaths. Other countries to have
suffered from ethnic civil wars in recent years include
Angola, the Democratic Republic of the Congo
(formerly Zaire), and Uganda.

In South Africa, European colonizers introduced a
policy called apartheid, under which white people
ruled, while non-whites had little or no power.

⟳ MOMBASA, KENYA
*Sunshine and beaches
attract tourists to tropical
Africa. Camel rides and boat
trips are added attractions.*

⟡ GOLD MINE
Gauteng province in South Africa is famous for its gold mines.

This led to a civil war. But, in 1994, a government with a black majority took power. Nelson Mandela, the leading black opponent of apartheid, was president from 1994 until 1999.

Agriculture employs about two-thirds of the people in this part of Africa. However, many farmers produce barely enough to support their families. Different crops are grown depending on the climate. Corn is a major food crop, while coffee, tobacco, tea, and various fruits are important exports.

⟡ CIVIL UNREST
Conflict between Hutus and Tutsis in Rwanda and Burundi has shattered the countries' economies.

Natural resources include oil in Gabon and Congo; copper in Zambia; diamonds in Botswana, the Democratic Republic of the Congo, South Africa, and Namibia; gold in South Africa; and uranium in Namibia and South Africa. However, apart from South Africa, the region lacks large-scale manufacturing centers. South Africa is the most developed country in this part of Africa, but many of its black Africans are poor.

In 2001, the Organization of African Unity met for the last time in Zambia. After 38 years, this organization of African states was transforming itself into the African Union, with its own parliament, court, currency, and laws.

⟡ HYDROELECTRIC DAM, ZIMBABWE
Hydroelectric plants at dams on Africa's great rivers produce large amounts of cheap electricity.

⟲ OSTRICH CHICKS, SOUTH AFRICA
Ostriches were once prized for their feathers, but today farmers rear them mainly for their hides.

FACTS

LESOTHO
Kingdom of Lesotho
AREA: 11,720 sq mi.
POPULATION: 2.2 million
CAPITAL: Maseru
OTHER CITIES: Maputsoe, Teyateyaneng
HIGHEST POINT: Thabana Ntlenyana (11,425 ft)
OFFICIAL LANGUAGES: Sotho, English
CURRENCY: Loti

MADAGASCAR
Repobikan'i Madagasikara, République de Madagascar – Republic of Madagascar
AREA: 226,658 sq mi.
POPULATION: 16 million
CAPITAL: Antananarivo
OTHER CITIES: Toamasina, Antsirabe, Mahajanga
HIGHEST POINT: Maromotro (9,436 ft)
OFFICIAL LANGUAGES: Malagasy, French, English
CURRENCY: Malagasy franc

MALAWI
Dkiko la Malawi – Republic of Malawi
AREA: 45,747 sq mi.
POPULATION: 10.5 million
CAPITAL: Lilongwe
OTHER CITIES: Blantyre, Mzuzu
HIGHEST POINT: Sapitwe (9,843 ft)
OFFICIAL LANGUAGE: English
CURRENCY: Malawi kwacha

MAURITIUS
Republic of Mauritius
AREA: 788 sq mi.
POPULATION: 1.2 million
CAPITAL: Port Louis
OTHER CITIES: Beau Bassin-Rose Hill, Vacoas-Phoenix
HIGHEST POINT: Piton de la Rivière Noire (2,711 ft)
OFFICIAL LANGUAGE: English
CURRENCY: Mauritian rupee

MOZAMBIQUE
República de Moçambique – Republic of Mozambique
AREA: 309,496 sq mi.
POPULATION: 19.4 million
CAPITAL: Maputo
OTHER CITIES: Beira, Nampula
HIGHEST POINT: Mount Binga (7,992 ft)
OFFICIAL LANGUAGE: Portuguese
CURRENCY: Metical

◑ MBUTI DANCER
The Mbuti are a pygmy people who live in the northeastern part of the Democratic Republic of the Congo.

Most people in Central, Eastern, and Southern Africa speak a Bantu-related language—Kongo in Central Africa; Swahili in East Africa; and Xhosa and Zulu in South Africa, for example.

The ancestors of the Bantu-speaking people originated in an area around the Cameroon–Nigeria border. They were farmers, who used iron tools. More than 2,000 years ago they began to spread east and south, taking over the land from earlier peoples, including pygmies, who were forest hunters, and the Khoikhoi and San (also called Hottentots and Bushmen) in the southwest. A few of these people survive, mainly in remote areas. But the main minority groups today are people of European and Asian origin.

Christianity was introduced to the region by European missionaries, and today more than three-fifths of the people are Christian. About 22 percent follow ancient religions, most of which include the worship of ancestors and spirits. Muslims, who make up 12 percent of the population, are found mostly in Eastern Africa.

Music, especially drumming, is a major traditional art form.

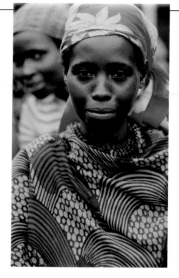

◑ HUTU WOMAN
Rwanda and Burundi have three ethnic groups: the majority Hutu, the Tutsis, and a few pygmies.

◑ ZULU WOMAN
Many Zulu men work in mines and industries. Their wives stay at home and bring up the children.

◐ A SAMBURU MAN FROM KENYA
Kenya has about 40 ethnic groups. The Samburu are related to the Masai.

◑ CONGO MASK
Masks are used in ceremonies by people who follow traditional religions.

◑ TOWNSHIP
Huge "townships," where shelters are made from whatever people can find, have grown up near South African towns. Poverty and crime are major problems.

In recent years, several kinds of African jazz have developed. Dance is another popular pastime. Soccer is the leading sport, but cricket and rugby football are also widely played in South Africa, Zimbabwe, and other countries.

The carving of wooden statues and masks is an art form in the region, especially in Central Africa. Many beautiful carvings are made for use in traditional religious ceremonies, and are then thrown away. Pottery, baskets decorated with beads and shells, and shields used in ritual dances are other items of great beauty made throughout the region.

The most common food dishes are simple—most people cannot afford luxury food items. Corn is the principal food in savanna regions. It is pounded into a flour, which is cooked to form a kind of porridge. The porridge is eaten with beans or some other vegetable, often cooked in a spicy sauce. Fish and meat are eaten when people can afford them.

◐ CATHEDRAL, GABON
Christianity is the leading religion in Central, Eastern, and Southern Africa. It was introduced by European missionaries, including the explorer David Livingstone.

◐ KENYAN ATHLETE
East Africa has produced many fine athletes. They excel at long-distance running, especially at high altitudes.

◑ XHOSA VILLAGE
Most Xhosa live in villages in southeastern South Africa. Many depend on money sent from relatives working in the cities.

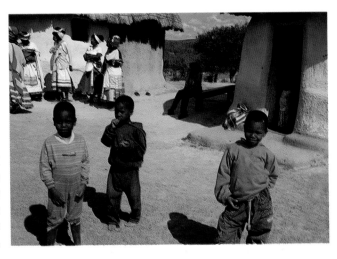

FACTS

SOMALIA
Jamhuriyadda Dimugradiga ee Soomaaliya – Somali Democratic Republic
AREA: 246,200 sq mi.
POPULATION: 7.5 million
CAPITAL: Mogadishu
OTHER CITIES: Hargeisa, Kismayu, Berbera
HIGHEST POINT: Surud Ad (2,969 ft)
OFFICIAL LANGUAGES: Somali, Arabic
CURRENCY: Somali shilling

SOUTH AFRICA
Republic of South Africa
AREA: 471,443 sq mi.
POPULATION: 43.5 million
CAPITAL: Pretoria (executive), Cape Town (legislative), Bloemfontein (judicial)
OTHER CITIES: Johannesburg, Durban, Port Elizabeth
HIGHEST POINT: Mount aux Sources (10,768 ft)
OFFICIAL LANGUAGES: Afrikaans, English, Ndebele, North Sotho, South Sotho, Swazi, Tsonga, Tswana, Venda, Xhosa, Zulu
CURRENCY: Rand

SWAZILAND
Umboso weSwatini – Kingdom of Swaziland
AREA: 6,704 sq mi.
POPULATION: 1.1 million
CAPITAL: Mbabane
OTHER CITIES: Manzini, Nhlangano
HIGHEST POINT: Mount Emlembe (6,109 ft)
OFFICIAL LANGUAGES: Swazi, English
CURRENCY: Lilangeni

TANZANIA
Jamhuri ya Muungano wa Tanzania – United Republic of Tanzania
AREA: 341,216 sq mi.
POPULATION: 36.2 million
CAPITAL: Dodoma
OTHER CITIES: Dar es Salaam, Mwanza, Tanga
HIGHEST POINT: Kilimanjaro (19,340 ft)
OFFICIAL LANGUAGES: Swahili, English
CURRENCY: Tanzania shilling

215

○ THE GREAT TREK
In 1836, Boer (Afrikaner) settlers moved inland from the Cape to escape British rule.

Scientists have found fossils of humanlike creatures that lived in East Africa over two million years ago. Some experts think that this was the place where the first modern human beings appeared.

In prehistoric times, people in Central, Eastern, and Southern Africa lived by hunting animals and gathering nuts and berries. From about 2,000 years ago, Bantu-speaking farmers entered the region from the northwest. They intermarried with the original people, although some small groups of hunter-gatherers survived in remote areas.

The Bantu-speaking people developed large and powerful kingdoms. From the 15th century, however, most of these kingdoms were weakened by the demand for slaves made by Europeans. The Europeans themselves rarely ventured inland, but Africans from the coast attacked the inland kingdoms and took captives, who they sold as slaves to the European traders on the coasts. Large areas were devastated by these slave wars.

○ FORT JESUS, KENYA
Fort Jesus, built by the Portuguese in the 1590s, helped them win control over the East African coast.

○ GREAT ZIMBABWE
This great walled citadel, now in ruins, was built by the Shona in Zimbabwe in the 1300s.

○ AUSTRALOPITHECUS
Remains of early humans have been found in Eastern and Southern Africa.

○ ZULU WARS
The Zulus of South Africa clashed with white settlers, called Boers, in 1836. Zulu resistance to European rule continued until 1879, when British troops finally defeated the Zulu army.

FACTS

UGANDA
Republic of Uganda
AREA: 93,065 sq mi.
POPULATION: 24 million
CAPITAL: Kampala
OTHER CITIES: Jinja, Mbale, Masaka
HIGHEST POINT: Mount Ruwenzori (16,762 ft)
OFFICIAL LANGUAGE: English
CURRENCY: Uganda shilling

ZAMBIA
Republic of Zambia
AREA: 290,586 sq mi.
POPULATION: 9.7 million
CAPITAL: Lusaka
OTHER CITIES: Ndola, Kitwe, Mufulira
HIGHEST POINT: 6,781 ft
OFFICIAL LANGUAGE: English
CURRENCY: Zambian kwacha

ZIMBABWE
Republic of Zimbabwe
AREA: 150,871 sq mi.
POPULATION: 11.3 million
CAPITAL: Harare
OTHER CITIES: Bulawayo, Chitungwiza, Mutare
HIGHEST POINT: Mount Inyangani (8,507 ft)
OFFICIAL LANGUAGE: English
CURRENCY: Zimbabwe dollar

REUNION (FRANCE)
Département de la Réunion –
Department of Réunion
AREA: 969 sq mi.
POPULATION: 664,000
CAPITAL: Saint-Denis
OTHER CITIES: Le Port, Le Tampon
HIGHEST POINT: Piton des Neiges (10,070 ft)
OFFICIAL LANGUAGE: French
CURRENCY: Euro

One important European settlement was made by the Dutch in 1652—Cape Town. It served as a supply station for Dutch ships sailing between Europe and Southeast Asia, and became the nucleus of what is now South Africa.

During the 19th century, explorers mapped the African interior. In the late 1800s, European countries divided the region among themselves, in what became known as the "Scramble for Africa." Most of these colonies won their independence in the 1960s and 1970s. Zimbabwe (formerly Rhodesia) did not get majority rule until 1980, and Namibia, formerly ruled by South Africa, became independent in 1990.

In 1948, South Africa's white's-only government began a policy known as apartheid. Whites controlled the government and the economy. Blacks had no right to vote and their lives were strictly controlled. From the 1960s, most other countries condemned South Africa's policies, while opposition from black groups in South Africa gradually increased.

Apartheid was ended in the early 1990s and, in 1994, all the people of South Africa voted in elections that resulted in a black majority government. However, the new South Africa faces huge problems, including poverty and the threat of HIV/AIDS infection

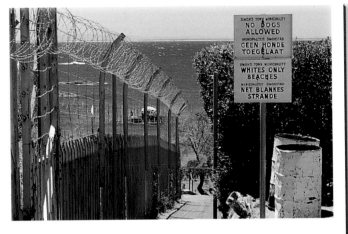

◑ RACIAL DISCRIMINATION
From 1948, life in South Africa was dominated by racial restrictions. Non-whites were forced to use separate basic facilities from whites, and had to use separate beaches.

✪ BARTOLOMEU DIAS MEMORIAL
Dias (1450–1500) was the first European to reach the southern tip of Africa.

✪ NELSON MANDELA
Nelson Mandela led the African National Congress to victory in South Africa's first non-racial elections in 1994. Mandela had been imprisoned from 1962 to 1990 for his opposition to apartheid.

TIMELINE

AD

1100	Arab traders settle East Africa
1250	Great Zimbabwe develops
1487	Bartolomeu Dias rounds the southern tip of Africa
1652	Dutch find Cape Town
1800s	European colonization
1958	Central African Republic becomes independent
1960	Democratic Republic of the Congo, Republic of the Congo, Gabon, and Somalia gain independence
1962	Burundi, Rwanda, and Uganda become independent
1963	Kenya becomes independent
1964	Lesotho, Malawi, Tanzania, and Zambia become independent
1966	Botswana becomes independent
1968	Swaziland becomes independent
1975	Angola and Mozambique become independent
1990	South Africa grants independence to Namibia
1994	South Africa's first fully democratic elections
2002	The Organization of African Unity renamed itself the African Union

217

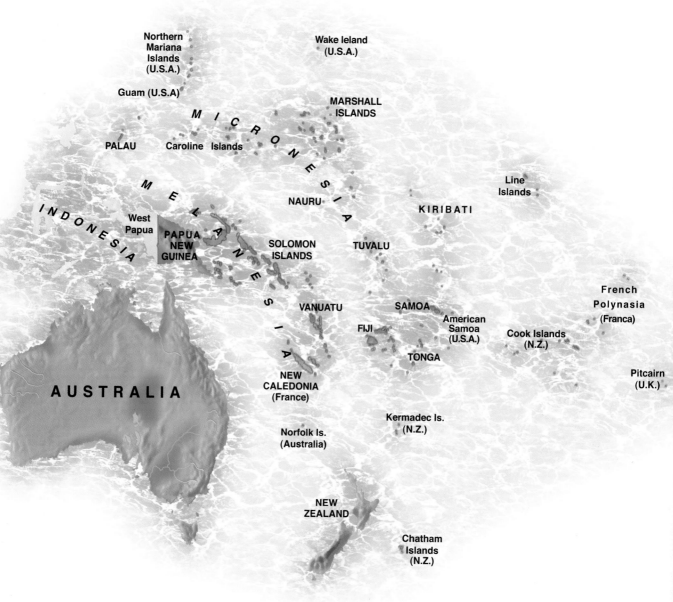

Northern
Mariana
Islands
(U.S.A.)

Guam (U.S.A)

Wake Ieland
(U.S.A.)

M I C R O N E S I A

PALAU   Caroline Islands

MARSHALL
ISLANDS

Line
Islands

I N D O N E S I A

M E L A N E S I A

West
Papua

PAPUA
NEW
GUINEA

NAURU

KIRIBATI

SOLOMON
ISLANDS

TUVALU

VANUATU

SAMOA

FIJI

American
Samoa
(U.S.A.)

French
Polynasia
(Franca)

TONGA

Cook Islands
(N.Z.)

AUSTRALIA

NEW
CALEDONIA
(France)

Pitcairn
(U.K.)

Kermadec Is.
(N.Z.)

Norfolk Is.
(Australia)

NEW
ZEALAND

Chatham
Islands
(N.Z.)

KANGAROO

OCEANIA

⟡ Great Barrier Reef,
AUSTRALIA

⟡ Sydney Opera House,
AUSTRALIA

⟡ Uluru (Ayers Rock),
AUSTRALIA

⟡ Beach houses,
FIJI

The continent of Oceania is also known as Australasia. It takes in a vast swathe of the Pacific Ocean, stretching from the Tropic of Cancer in the north to Stewart Island (New Zealand) in the south.

Australia takes up 90 percent of the land area. Too large to be called an island, it is normally rated as the smallest of the world's major landmasses. Australia is a land of empty deserts, ringed by temperate grassland and rainforest, scrub, and tropical rainforest.

To its north lies the island of New Guinea. The western part of the island (West Papua) is ruled by the Asian nation of Indonesia, while the eastern part forms the independent state of Papua New Guinea. To the southeast lies the island chain of New Zealand, dominated by North and South Island. These are beautiful, cooler lands with volcanic mountains, deep sea inlets, forests, and grassy plains.

Strung out across the open Pacific Ocean are thousands of tiny coral and volcanic islands, grouped into nations and dependent territories. They are sometimes divided into ethnic regions. Micronesia includes Guam, Kiribati (pronounced Kiribass), and the Mariana, Marshall, and Caroline islands. Melanesia includes Papua New Guinea, Vanuatu, New Caledonia, Fiji, and the Solomon Islands. Polynesia includes Tonga, Samoa, the Line Islands, Tuvalu, French Polynesia, and Pitcairn Island.

219

AUSTRALIA

◐ THORNY
DEVIL

◐ PHILLIP ISLAND
Collapsing rock has formed stacks and pinnacles off Phillip Island, near Melbourne. Bordered by Western Port and the Bass Strait, the island is famous for its fairy penguins.

◐ GREAT BARRIER REEF
Divers explore this magical world of corals, brilliantly colored fish, giant clams, and starfish.

Australia lies between the Indian and Pacific Oceans. Its northern shores are washed by warm, tropical seas, while the island of Tasmania to the south lies in cooler, stormier waters. Its northeastern coast is protected by the world's longest coral reef, the Great Barrier Reef, which extends for 1,260 miles from north to south.

Running parallel to the east coast are the mountains of the Great Dividing Range. At the southern end of this range are the Australian Alps. Australia's longest river, the Murray, whose chief tributary is the Darling, rises near Mount Kosciusko.

The interior of Australia is mostly wilderness, made up of the Great Victoria Desert, the Gibson, and the Great Sandy Desert. There are rocky outcrops, salt pans, dried-out lakes, and, along the Great Australian Bight, the flatlands of the Nullarbor Plain. Surrounding the deserts are regions of dry scrub, savanna grassland, tropical rainforest, temperate grassland, and eucalyptus forest. Australia's habitats are home to many species of animal and bird found nowhere else on Earth, such as koalas, kangaroos, Tasmanian devils, and duck-billed platypuses.

The great majority of Australians live in the big cities along the east, south, and southwest coasts, where the temperature is pleasant and the ground fertile. Where conditions permit in the interior, or "outback," there are huge cattle and sheep stations, and also mines.

◐ BYRON BAY
Unspoilt sands and rolling breakers extend for huge distances along the northern coast of New South Wales.

○ THE OLGAS
Known to the Aborigines as Kata Tjuta (meaning "many heads"), these strange, rounded domes of rock rise 30 miles to the west of Uluru (Ayers Rock) in central Australia.

Torres Strait
C. York
Melville I.
Bathurst I.
C. Arnhem
Darwin
CAPE YORK PENINSULA
Gulf of Carpentaria
Joseph Bonaparte Gulf
Daly
Arnhem Land
Groote Eylandt
Great Barrier Reef
Bonaparte Archipelago
Drysdale
Victoria
Roper
Wellesley Is.
Mitchell
Cairns
KIMBERLEY PLATEAU
Broome
Fitzroy
Gilbert
Norman
Townsville
GREAT DIVIDING RANGE
Eighty Mile Beach
NORTHERN TERRITORY
Mount Isa
Flinders
Port Hedland
De Grey
Barrow I.
Fortescue
Mt. Bruce ▲
GREAT SANDY DESERT
Georgina
Proserpine
Mackay
C. Townsend
Ashburton
QUEENSLAND
Rockhampton
GIBSON DESERT
MACDONNELL RANGES
Alice Springs
Diamantina
Thomson
Bundaberg
Lake Macleod
Carnarvon
Uluru (Ayers Rock) 867m ▲
Finke
SIMPSON DESERT
Barcoo
Balyando
Dirk Hartog I.
Murchison
WESTERN AUSTRALIA
MUSGRAVE RANGES
Alberga
L. Eyre
Cooper Creek
Warrego
Culgoa
Brisbane
Toowoomba
Gold Coast
GREAT VICTORIA DESERT
SOUTH AUSTRALIA
Barwon
Grafton
Geraldton
Laverton
Broken Hill
Coffs Harbour
NULLARBOR PLAIN
L. Everard
L. Torrens
Kalgoorlie-Boulder
Darling
NEW SOUTH WALES
Maitland
Perth
Great Australian Bight
L. Gairdner
FLINDERS RANGE
Milgura
Lachlan
Newcastle
Fremantle
Sydney
C. Naturaliste
Bunbury
Port Lincoln
Spencer Gulf
Adelaide
Wagga Wagga
Wollongong
C. Leeuwin
Albany
Archipelago of the Recherche
Murray
Canberra
AUSTRALIAN CAPITAL TERRITORY
Kangaroo I.
VICTORIA
Bendigo
Mt. Kosciusko 2,228m ▲
C. Howe
Ballarat
Melbourne
Mount Gambier
Geelong
Wilson's Promontory
TASMAN SEA
C. Otway
King I.
Bass Strait
Flinders I.
Cape Barren I.
Burnie
Davenport
Launceston
TASMANIA
Queenstown
Hobart
South East C.

○ WAVE ROCK
Like a wave frozen in stone, this rock in Western Australia has been shaped by wind and rain.

○ MURRAY RIVER TURTLE

AUSTRALIA

○ UP A GUM TREE
The furry, gray koala spends most of its time in eucalyptus trees. Babies remain in a pouch on their mother's body for six months after birth.

○ LAKE EYRE
This vast salt lake lies below sea level in South Australia. It is normally dry, as the river waters that feed it soon evaporate, leaving the ground encrusted with mineral salts.

◐ PINEAPPLE PLANTATION
Queensland's hot, moist climate produces tropical crops such as pineapples, bananas, and sugarcane.

Australia is an independent nation organized on federal lines. Canberra is its purpose-built center of government, located in Australian Capital Territory (ACT) in the southeast of the country. The most populous states are New South Wales and Victoria in the southeast, followed by Queensland in the northwest, Western Australia, South Australia, and the island of Tasmania. The wilderness of Northern Territory is very sparsely populated.

◐ CAMELS IN THE DESERT
Dromedaries (single-humped camels) were first brought to Australia in the 1860s. They were used by the explorer Robert O'Hara Burke (1820–61) and may still be seen in the deserts today.

Australia also governs some outlying ocean territories, including Norfolk Island, Christmas Island, Cocos (Keeling) Islands, the Ashmore and Cartier Islands, the Coral Sea Islands, Heard Island, and Macdonald Island.

Originally a group of British colonies, the Commonwealth of Australia still has the British monarch as its head of state. However, republicanism has widespread political support. Although cultural links with the British Isles are still strong, Australia now sees itself as a Pacific nation and part of the Pacific regional economy.

◐ WIND POWER
A windmill stands as a landmark in the empty outback. In these dry and dusty lands, wind may be used to raise precious underground reserves of water, for storage in tanks.

◐ CHRISTMAS ISLAND
A territory of Australia, tiny Christmas Island lies in the Indian Ocean about 185 miles south of Java. Its population is mostly made up of Malays and Chinese, who mine phosphates or work in tourism.

◑ WILDFIRE!
When the bush is as dry as tinder, one stray spark can set off a blaze. Vast bushfires are all too common, threatening property and life.

⟳ ROAD TRAIN

With no other vehicles in sight, thundering long-distance truck-trains kick up clouds of dust as they haul multiple trailers across the wilderness.

Cattle and sheep were traditional strengths of the Australian economy. A ranch, known as a "station," may still occupy over 3,860 square miles, and light aircraft may be needed to travel from one end of a farm to another. Agriculture produces wheat, sugarcane, and tropical and temperate fruits. Australia's many excellent red and white wines are now famous around the world.

⟳ SHEEP SHEARING

Part of Australian folklore, the sheep shearer was once the mainstay of the Australian economy. He is still kept busy today.

⟳ A BIRDS-EYE VIEW

A helicopter carries tourists over blue seas and reefs off Cairns, in northern Queensland. Australia is becoming a major world tourist destination.

⟳ AUSTRALIAN WINES

Vineyards were planted in South Australia's Barossa Valley in the 1840s. Quality has steadily improved and today Australia produces a wide variety of excellent wines, which are exported around the world.

The gold rush of the 1850s opened up Australia to mining, and today the country is a major exporter of iron ore, nickel, bauxite, gold, tin, uranium, zinc, and tungsten. There are reserves of coal, oil, and timber, and the rivers of the Snowy Mountains—part of the Great Dividing Range—provide hydroelectric power.

Manufactured goods include textiles, chemicals, and vehicles. Australia has become a major center of television and movie making, and newspaper publishing. It has also become a popular tourist destination, with people flying in to enjoy sun and surf, watersports, wilderness trekking, and lively city entertainments.

⟳ KANGAROOS

There are over 50 species of Australian kangaroo, large and small, gray and reddish-brown, living in forests, grasslands, and coastal regions. All leap on immensely powerful back legs.

⟳ HARBOR BRIDGE

This Sydney landmark, built in 1932, links the north and south of the city.

223

OCEANIA

⟳ IN REMEMBRANCE...
The National War Memorial is linked by Anzac Parade to the new parliament building in Canberra. Anzac Day (April 25th) commemorates members of the Australia and New Zealand Army Corps killed in World War I (1914–18).

⟳ AUSSIE FOOTBALL
Australian Rules football is a tough, fast game with 18 players per side.

People descended from the first Australians are known as Aborigines. Various Aboriginal cultures and languages exist in different parts of Australia. Traditionally the Aborigines are experts at desert survival. The Torres Strait islanders of the far north form another ancient, related ethnic group.

⟳ EXPLORING AUSTRALIA
More and more city-based Australians are beginning to explore their own vast back country, with its extraordinary landscapes.

⟳ NEW AUSTRALIANS
Since 1974, many immigrants have arrived in Australia from Southeast Asia. This Vietnamese mother and child live in the west Melbourne suburb of Footscray.

The Aboriginal peoples experienced persecution and violence in the years following the arrival of the British in the 1770s. They were excluded from citizenship until 1967. Today Aborigines number only about one percent of the population. They face many economic and political problems, and are lodging claims to possession of their ancient lands. There has been a great revival of Australian and international interest in their culture and traditions in recent years.

The great majority of Australians are of English, Scottish, Irish, or Welsh descent. The English language is spoken throughout the country, but with its own accent and many local phrases and expressions. In the last 20 years, Australia has become much more of a multi-ethnic society. It has also been settled by Scandinavians, Poles, Dutch, Germans, Italians, Greeks, Lebanese, Indians, Chinese, Thais, and Vietnamese.

⟳ BARBIE TIME
The barbecue has become a famous Australian tradition—nothing can beat freshly caught seafood or meat grilled in the open air.

⟳ THE FLYING DOCTOR
Australia pioneered airborne medical services. The Flying Doctor Service provides medical advice by radio and aircraft for emergencies on remote farms.

CITIZENS
Aborigines may be greatly outnumbered in their own land, but at least they now face the future as full citizens.

IN THE SURF
These days, Australian life centers on the beach as much as the outback. Swimmers, lifeguards, rowers, and surfers like to show off their muscles to the crowds.

Many Australians enjoy outdoor activities and sports, such as tennis, sailing, swimming, surfing, cricket, rugby, and Australian rules football. Cities such as Sydney and Melbourne have become centers for the arts in recent years. While 85 percent of Australians live in the modern coastal cities or in other towns, there is still a widespread fascination with the folklore and traditions of the outback. Life in the more remote areas can be tough. If there is an accident at a remote sheep station, doctors may have to fly in by plane. A teacher may have to give lessons to his or her pupils from hundreds of miles away, over a two-way radio link.

ABORIGINAL ART
Traditionally, the Aborigines used natural pigments for their paintings on rock faces and on panels of bark. Many paintings featured the animals that the people hunted for food.

ARTIST AT WORK
Recent years have seen great international interest in contemporary Aboriginal art. Today, painters use modern paints and materials, but the abstract patterns they produce often refer back to ancient spiritual beliefs.

SYDNEY OPERA HOUSE
Completed in 1973, this inspiring building rises from Sydney harbor like a series of billowing white sails.

225

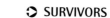

⟳ SURVIVORS
The Aborigines survived in a harsh land by being expert at hunting and desert survival.

⟳ VICTORIAN AGE
As part of the British Empire, Australia developed rapidly during the reign of Queen Victoria (1837–1901).

⟳ ROCK ART
To the ancient Aborigines, the rocks of Australia were part of a sacred landscape. Rock faces were carved, and later painted, with magical markings.

Explorers began to set out into the harsh lands of the interior. During the 1850s, the transportation of prisoners ended and free settlers from the British Isles arrived in their thousands, lured by the discovery of gold. New colonies were founded in Western and South Australia, and Victoria and Tasmania broke away from New South Wales. Many Aborigine populations were killed or treated with violence. In Tasmania, all the original inhabitants were slaughtered by British settlers.

Humans may have first entered Australia over 50,000 years ago, when low ocean levels made it easier to cross from Southeast Asia. Over the ages, waves of Aboriginal peoples moved across the land, following river valleys as they hunted, fished, and traded.

Portuguese, Spanish, and Dutch explorers sailed into Australian waters, but it was the British who settled there. In 1770 Captain James Cook (1728–79) landed at Botany Bay, and explored the east coast, which he named New South Wales.

In 1787 the British founded a prison colony at Sydney Cove. By 1823 New South Wales had become a full colony.

⟳ THE CONVICTS
Transported across the world, often for petty crimes, British prisoners arrived to a regime of brutal punishment.

◑ THE RUSH FOR GOLD
In the 1850s, gold was discovered in New South Wales and Victoria. Prospectors arrived from around the world, hoping to make their fortunes.

◑ NED KELLY (1855–80)
Outlaw, bushranger, and bank robber, the notorious Ned Kelly was hunted by police before a final shoot-out in which he wore home-made iron armor. Kelly was hanged in Melbourne jail.

The separate colonies federated as the Commonwealth of Australia in 1901. During the century that followed, Australia fought as part of the British Empire in World Wars I and II (1914–18 and 1939–45). During World War II, Australia was threatened by the Japanese invasion of Southeast Asia. In the 1950s, there was a new wave of settlement from Britain.

After the 1960s, Australia gradually moved away from its close political and commercial links with Britain. Japan and the United States became its major trading partners. New immigrants from Asia and the Pacific came to Australia, and Aborigines' rights were more fully recognized.

◑ VOICES TO BE HEARD
In the last 20 years Australia's Aborigines, with their flag of black, yellow, and red, have been vocal in their demand for social justice and land rights. Many white Australians are looking again at their country's history.

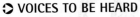

TIMELINE	
BC	
50,000	Possible first Aboriginal settlement
12,000	Waves of settlers
AD	
1606	Dutch discover Australia
1644	Abel Tasman maps Australian coast
1770	James Cook claims New South Wales for Britain
1788	Prison colony founded at Sydney
1825	Tasmania becomes separate colony
1829	Western Australia colonized
1836	South Australia colonized
1840	Transportation of convicts draws to an end (by 1868)
1851	Australian Gold Rush (until 1861)
1851	Victoria becomes separate colony
1855	Self-government (by 1856)
1859	Queensland becomes new colony
1901	Commonwealth of Australia founded
1914	World War I (until 1918): many Australian troops die at Gallipoli
1927	Federal government moves to Canberra
1931	Statute of Westminster: Australia confirmed as independent
1939	World War II (until 1945)
1950s	Large-scale immigration from Europe
1967	Aborigines recognized as citizens
1970s	New immigrants from Asia and the Pacific
1992	Court confirms Aboriginal right to ancestral lands

227

NEW ZEALAND
AND THE PACIFIC ISLANDS

⟳ KIWI

The Pacific Ocean is surrounded by a "ring of fire," a region of intense volcanic activity. Erupting volcanoes under the ocean have thrown up chains of small islands. In the warm waters of the South Pacific, many of these have become rimmed with growths of coral. Sometimes the volcanic rock has then collapsed, leaving a coral ring called an atoll.

New Zealand lies about 1,200 miles to the southeast of Australia. It is home to many unusual animals, including the kiwi, a flightless bird. Its two main parts, North Island and South Island, are separated by Cook Strait. North Island has rich farmland, active volcanoes, geysers, and hot springs. Its major cities are Wellington, the capital, and Auckland. South Island has the snowy peaks of the Southern Alps, the fertile Canterbury Plains, and the cities of Christchurch and Dunedin.

Papua New Guinea is another volcanic country, with remote, forested mountains and lush, tropical valleys—a habitat for the world's biggest butterflies. Mount Wilhelm is the highest point in Oceania. National territory also includes many smaller islands, including the Bismarck archipelago and the northern Solomon Islands.

The nations and territories of the open Pacific are made up of thousands of tiny, scattered islands. Some are low-lying coral reefs and atolls, while others are mountainous, with tropical forest.

⟳ CLOUDS OF STEAM
There are seven spectacular geysers at Whakarewarewa, near Rotorua, on North Island, New Zealand.

⟳ NAVILU ISLAND, FIJI
Fiji is made up of 800 or so small tropical islands, many of them uninhabited.

⟳ FRILLED LIZARD

FACTS

AMERICAN SAMOA
Territory of American Samoa
UNINCORPORATED US TERRITORY
LAND AREA: 77 sq mi.
POPULATION: 0.06 million
CAPITAL: Pago Pago
OFFICIAL LANGUAGES: Samoan, English
CURRENCY: US dollar

FIJI
Republic of Fiji
LAND AREA: 7,055 sq mi.
POPULATION: 0.8 million
CAPITAL: Suva
OTHER TOWNS: Lautoka, Nadi, Ba, Labasa
HIGHEST POINT: Mt Tomanivi (4,340 ft)
OFFICIAL LANGUAGE: English
CURRENCY: Fiji dollar

FRENCH POLYNESIA
Térritoire de la Polynésie Française
OVERSEAS TERRITORY OF FRANCE
LAND AREA: 1,263 sq mi.
POPULATION: 0.2 million
CAPITAL: Papeete
OFFICIAL LANGUAGES: French, Tahitian
CURRENCY: CFP franc

KIRIBATI
Republic of Kiribati
LAND AREA: 277 sq mi.
POPULATION: 0.08 million
CAPITAL: Bairiki
HIGHEST POINT: Banaba summit (266 ft)
OFFICIAL LANGUAGE: English
CURRENCY: Australian dollar

MARSHALL ISLANDS
Republic of the Marshall Islands
LAND AREA: 70 sq mi.
POPULATION: 0.1 million
CAPITAL: Majuro
OTHER TOWN: Ebeye
HIGHEST POINT: Nowhere more than 20 ft
OFFICIAL LANGUAGES: English, Marshallese
CURRENCY: US dollar

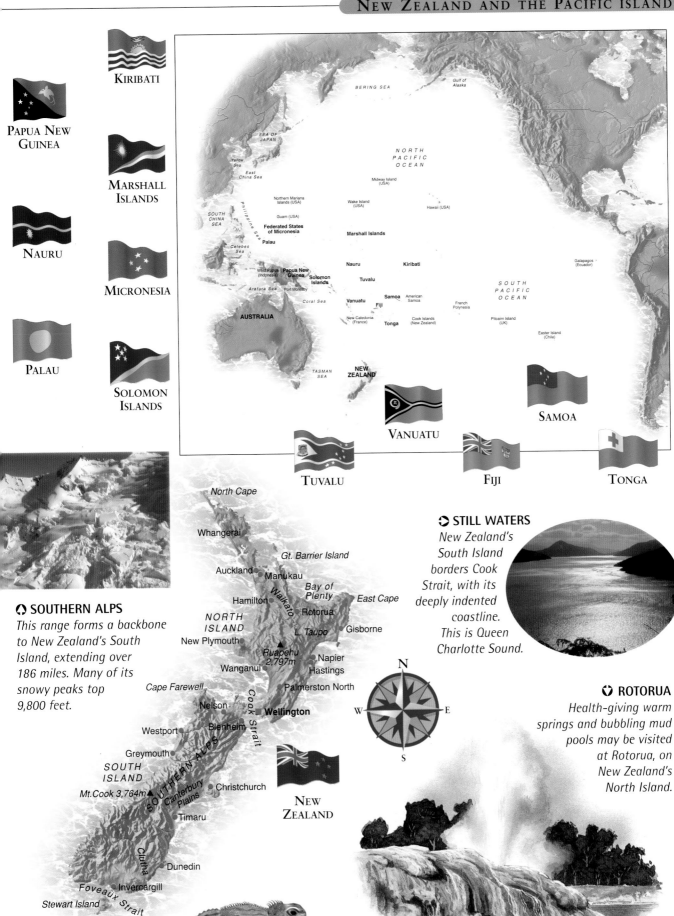

KIRIBATI

PAPUA NEW GUINEA

MARSHALL ISLANDS

NAURU

MICRONESIA

PALAU

SOLOMON ISLANDS

SAMOA

VANUATU

TUVALU

FIJI

TONGA

NEW ZEALAND

BERING SEA

Gulf of Alaska

SEA OF JAPAN

Yellow Sea

East China Sea

NORTH PACIFIC OCEAN

Midway Island (USA)

Wake Island (USA)

Hawaii (USA)

Northern Mariana Islands (USA)

SOUTH CHINA SEA

Philippine Sea

Federated States of Micronesia

Palau

Celebes Sea

West Papua (Indonesia)

Papua New Guinea

Solomon Islands

Marshall Islands

Nauru

Kiribati

Tuvalu

Galapagos (Ecuador)

SOUTH PACIFIC OCEAN

Arafura Sea

Port Moresby

Coral Sea

Vanuatu

Samoa

American Samoa

French Polynesia

New Caledonia (France)

Fiji

Tonga

Cook Islands (New Zealand)

Pitcairn Island (UK)

Easter Island (Chile)

AUSTRALIA

TASMAN SEA

NEW ZEALAND

◆ SOUTHERN ALPS

This range forms a backbone to New Zealand's South Island, extending over 186 miles. Many of its snowy peaks top 9,800 feet.

◆ STILL WATERS

New Zealand's South Island borders Cook Strait, with its deeply indented coastline. This is Queen Charlotte Sound.

◆ ROTORUA

Health-giving warm springs and bubbling mud pools may be visited at Rotorua, on New Zealand's North Island.

North Cape

Whangerai

Gt. Barrier Island

Auckland

Manukau

Hamilton

Bay of Plenty

Waikato

East Cape

NORTH ISLAND

Rotorua

New Plymouth

L. Taupo

Gisborne

Ruapehu 2,797m

Napier

Wanganui

Hastings

Cape Farewell

Palmerston North

Nelson

Cook Strait

Wellington

Westport

Blenheim

Greymouth

SOUTH ISLAND

SOUTHERN ALPS

Canterbury Plains

Christchurch

Mt.Cook 3,764m

Timaru

Clutha

Dunedin

Foveaux Strait

Invercargill

Stewart Island

NEW ZEALAND

N
W   E
S

◆ **TUATARA**

◇ KIWI FRUIT
The juicy green Chinese gooseberry, marketed under a name more associated with New Zealand, has become a major export.

◇ SAND AND SUN
Vanua Levu and its surrounding islands, in northern Fiji, attract tourists to their palm-fringed, tropical beaches.

New Zealand is an independent nation, and has the British monarch as its head of state, reflecting its historical links with the British empire. It rules over two self-governing Pacific territories, Niue and the Cook Islands.

New Zealand has become one of the most important economies on the Pacific "rim." It raises large numbers of sheep and cattle and exports wool, meat (especially lamb), and dairy products. It also produces grain, vegetables, and fruit, including apples and kiwi fruit. Power is generated from hydroelectric schemes and from geothermal plants, which convert the heat from underground volcanic activity into electricity. Tourism is a fast-growing industry.

FACTS

MICRONESIA
Federated States of Micronesia
LAND AREA: 271 sq mi.
POPULATION: 0.1 million
CAPITAL: Palikir
OTHER TOWNS: Weno, Kolonia
HIGHEST POINT: Totolom (2,359 ft)
OFFICIAL LANGUAGE: English
CURRENCY: US dollar

NAURU
Republic of Nauru, Naoero
LAND AREA: 8 sq mi.
POPULATION: 0.01 million
SEAT OF GOVERNMENT: Yaren
HIGHEST POINT: Western Nauru (225 ft)
OFFICIAL LANGUAGES: Nauruan
CURRENCY: Australian dollar

NEW CALEDONIA
Nouvelle Calédonie et Dépendances
OVERSEAS TERRITORY OF FRANCE
LAND AREA: 1,173 sq mi.
POPULATION: 0.2 million
CAPITAL: Nouméa
OFFICIAL LANGUAGE: French
CURRENCY: CFP franc

Papua New Guinea is another independent democracy, formally headed by the British monarch. The plantations of Papua New Guinea produce coffee, tea, rubber, palm-oil, and copra (dried coconut). Villagers clear forest to grow crops such as sweet potato, corn, and bananas for their own needs. The country has rich mineral reserves, including gold, silver, and copper.

◇ PEARL FISHERS
The warm waters of the South Pacific are ideal for oysters—and pearls. Pearls develop around small grains of sand inside oyster shells.

◑ HARVESTING COCONUTS
Dried coconut flesh, or copra, is produced on many Pacific islands. The hairy brown coconuts are the seeds of large green fruits, which grow at the tops of the palm trees.

○ NORTHERN SKYLINE
Auckland is New Zealand's largest city. Founded in 1840, it is an important seaport and industrial center.

○ SHEARING TIME
The New Zealand climate and terrain is ideal for raising sheep. Meat and wool are exported all over the world.

The smaller islands of the Pacific include independent monarchies and republics as well as overseas territories such as New Caledonia and French Polynesia. Scattered locations, small populations, and lack of fertile land offer limited economic opportunities for the islanders. Many grow coconuts and tropical fruits, raise pigs and chickens, and catch fish. Local dishes are often made with breadfruit, cassava, or sweet potatoes. Sugarcane is grown as a cash crop in Fiji, and cocoa in the Solomon Islands. Islands such as Tahiti in French Polynesia have developed a tourist industry. Nickel is mined in New Caledonia. Tiny Nauru has been mined into a desert for its phosphates, which are used in the manufacture of fertilizers. Phosphate supplies in Kiribati have already been exhausted.

○ IN PAPUA NEW GUINEA
Local markets may sell pigs, poultry, yams, taro (a root vegetable), sago (cereal from the sago palm), bananas, and sweet potatoes.

○ WEDDING PARTY, TONGA
Guests gather for a royal wedding in Tonga. The chiefdoms of this Polynesian island group were united as a single kingdom in 1845.

◑ MAORIS

The first inhabitants of the south Pacific were the ancestors of today's Melanesian, Micronesian, and Polynesian peoples. Over several thousand years, they explored the world's largest ocean in their canoes, settling land from the Hawaiian islands in the north to Easter Island in the east, where they carved large, mysterious stone statues.

Their last great expansion took place over a thousand years ago, when a Polynesian people called the Maoris settled New Zealand.

The tattooed Maoris were fierce warriors. They hunted the islands' gigantic flightless birds, called moas (now extinct). Today Maoris make up about nine percent of New Zealand's population. They have preserved a keen sense of their history and culture.

The Dutch explored New Zealand's coasts in 1642. The next European visitor was the English navigator Captain James Cook (1728–79), in 1769.

◑ TREE CARVING
Carvings, customs, and spiritual beliefs link many widely scattered Pacific islands, revealing a common ancestry.

FACTS

SOLOMON ISLANDS
LAND AREA: 10,656 sq mi.
POPULATION: 0.4 million
CAPITAL: Honiara
OTHER TOWNS: Gizo, Kieta, Auki
HIGHEST POINT: Mt Popomanaseu (7,648 ft)
OFFICIAL LANGUAGE: English
CURRENCY: Solomon Islands dollar

TONGA
Kingdom of Tonga;
Pule'anga Fakatu'i'o Tonga
LAND AREA: 290 sq mi.
POPULATION: 0.1 million
CAPITAL: Nukualofa
OTHER TOWNS: Neiafu, Pangai
HIGHEST POINT: 3,432 ft
OFFICIAL LANGUAGES: Tongan, English
CURRENCY: Pa'anga

TUVALU
Southwest Pacific State of Tuvalu
LAND AREA: 9 sq mi.
POPULATION: 0.01 million
CAPITAL: Fongafale
OTHER TOWNS: Vaitupu, Niutao
HIGHEST POINT: Nowhere more than 20 ft
OFFICIAL LANGUAGES: English, Tuvaluan
CURRENCY: Australian dollar

VANUATU
Ripablik blong Vanuatu
LAND AREA: 5,714 sq mi.
POPULATION: 0.2 million
CAPITAL: Port-Vila
OTHER TOWN: Luganville
HIGHEST POINT: Tabwémasana (6,165 ft)
OFFICIAL LANGUAGES: Bislama, English, French
CURRENCY: Vatu

SAMOA
Independent State of Samoa
LAND AREA: 1092 sq mi.
POPULATION: 0.02 million
CAPITAL: Apia
OTHER TOWNS: Lalomanu, Falevai, Tuasivi, Falealupo
HIGHEST POINT: Mt Sisili (6,100 ft)
OFFICIAL LANGUAGES: Samoan, English
CURRENCY: Tala

◑ FIJI TRADITIONS
Fiji was settled by both Melanesians and Polynesians, and later by Indians.

◑ MEETING-HOUSE
The wharerunanga, with its elaborately carved roof and doorposts, is a Maori meeting-house built in the traditional style.

⟐ MAORI CRAFTS
*Intricate, swirling designs
are a part of the Maori
tradition, carved in wood,
whale ivory, or stone.*

⟐ EUROPEAN ENCOUNTER
*In 1769 the English explorer Captain James Cook sailed around New Zealand, charting the
waters and meeting tattooed Maori warriors.*

In the following century, many British settlers
came to New Zealand, attracted by the moderate
climate, green pastures, and gold. They met with
warlike resistance from the Maoris. By 1852 New
Zealand was a self-governing British colony, and
in 1907 it became a Dominion within the British
Empire (having a similar status to Canada).

New Zealand fought in the two World Wars
(1914–18 and 1939–45), and maintained close
ties with Britain. By the 1970s, however, New
Zealand saw itself more as a Pacific nation,
expanding its trade with Japan, the USA, and
Australia. Today's New Zealanders enjoy a
good standard of living and an outdoor
life, sailing, skiing, and playing team
sports such as rugby and cricket.

⟐ THE ALL BLACKS
*In rugby football, New
Zealand's national team has
regularly been a world beater.
Games start with a Maori
chant and dance, the haka.*

⟐ GOING TO CHURCH
*The Tongans had converted
to the Christian faith by
1860. Today, Protestant
churches are
well attended.*

⟑ THE WARRIOR AGE
*The Maoris defended their lands with war canoes.
Fortifications called pa were surrounded by ditches and
fences of stakes, or palisades.*

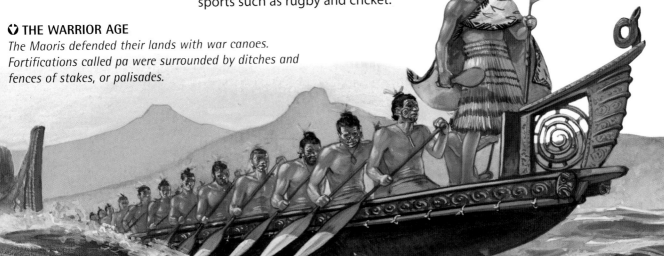

The smaller Pacific islands were colonized in the 1800s, mostly by Germans, French, British, and Americans. Some of the Europeans came to live on the islands, but most merely acted as colonial governors. Workers were brought to Fiji from India, and their descendants became a large part of that island's population. Some colonies passed from British to Australian or New Zealand rule, but by the 1980s large areas of the Pacific were ruled as small, independent states.

◯ FACES OF PAPUA
Papua New Guinea is home to hundreds of different ethnic groups. Many of them wear elaborate face and body decorations.

Ancient customs on the Pacific islands changed greatly during the colonial period. Christian missionaries banned traditional forms of worship, and people found work on plantations or in mines.

◯ HOUSE OF SPIRITS
Most people in Papua New Guinea are Christian, but traditional beliefs in spirits and magic are still widespread.

The last land in the region to be opened up to the outside world was Papua New Guinea. Its forest and mountain communities were so isolated from each other that as many as 800 different languages had grown up there. The tribal costumes worn by many of the communities may still be seen at festivals today. They include spectacular feathers, bone ornaments, and body paint.

The way of life in the Pacific today is a mixture of the traditional and the modern. Social life is still marked by feasting, dancing, and singing. However modern communications have shrunk the great distances between one group of islands and another, and transportation is by aircraft and motor-boat as well as by canoe.

◯ OCEAN RIDER
This canoe is of Samoan design. The Samoan Islands were colonized by Lapita seafarers, ancestors of today's Polynesians, as early as 1000 BC.

◑ TROBRIAND ISLANDER
The people of the Trobriand or Kiriwina Islands are taller and lighter-skinned than most other Melanesians.

TIMELINE

AD

c.900	Polynesians (Maoris) settle New Zealand
c.1200	Rise of Polynesian chiefdoms
1526	Portuguese discover Papua New Guinea
1642	Tasman discovers New Zealand
1769	James Cook explores New Zealand coast (until 1777)
1815	First British settlers in New Zealand
1840	Treaty of Waitangi: New Zealand linked to Australia
1842	Formation of French Polynesia
1845	Maori uprising (until 1847)
1851	New Zealand becomes a separate British colony
1860	Maori uprisings (until 1872)
1884	British and Germans claim New Guinea
1907	New Zealand self-governing
1914	World War I (until 1918): Australia occupies German New Guinea
1939	World War II (until 1945)
1970	Tonga becomes independent
1975	Papua New Guinea and Tuvalu become independent
1978	Solomon Islands become independent
1980	Vanuatu becomes independent
1983	Kiribati becomes independent
1990	Federated States of Micronesia become independent
1991	Marshall Islands become independent
1994	Palau becomes independent

PACIFIC OCEAN

SEPIK TURTLE
This reptile takes its name from the Sepik River in northern Papua New Guinea.

The Pacific Ocean is the largest body of water in the world, with an area of approximately 11.1 million square miles. It is bordered by Asia to the west and the Americas to the east, and is artificially linked to the Atlantic Ocean by the narrow Panama Canal.

SCORPION FISH, FIJI
Camouflage often conceals venomous spines on these tropical fish.

The ocean floor is marked by extreme differences in relief. The Marianas Trench plunges to 36,200 feet, the deepest place on the planet, while massive volcanic mountains rise from the ocean floor to form the Hawaiian island chain.

Beneath the Pacific, the cracked crust of the Earth is moving apart at the rate of 8 inches a year. Intense activity surrounds the plates, or sections of crust, around the Pacific. This is an area of volcanoes and earthquakes, which in turn may create massive waves called tsunamis. Underwater lava creates chains of volcanic islands, often surrounded by coral reefs.

Ocean currents, including the Californian and Kuroshio, circulate clockwise around the North Pacific, while the Humboldt and East Australian currents move anti-clockwise around the South Pacific. Cycles of warming (an effect known as El Niño) and cooling (La Niña) of waters in the Pacific Ocean have a major effect on global climate, creating severe storms.

STONE MYSTERIES
Giant figures were carved on Easter Island, the most easterly of the Polynesian settlements, between AD 1000 and 1600.

BIKINI ATOLL
From the 1950s until the 1980s, places in the South Pacific like this atoll were used as testing grounds for nuclear weapons, amid protests worldwide.

235

ATLANTIC
OCEAN

○ MANTA RAY
Manta rays live near the surface in the open sea. They feed on plankton.

The Atlantic is the world's second-largest ocean. It covers a total area of more than 41 million square miles. Its average depth is 11,745 feet, but depths of more than 29,500 feet occur in some trenches. The many islands in the Atlantic include Greenland, Iceland, and the British Isles.

The ocean's main feature is the Mid-Atlantic Ridge, an underwater mountain range that stretches from north to south. Running through the ridge is a rift valley, where earthquakes are common.

This rift valley is the border between huge plates that are widening the Atlantic by about 1 inch a year. Lava from beneath the Earth's crust flows to the surface in places along the rift valley, creating new crustal rock.

Strong currents flow around the Atlantic Ocean. One famous current, the Gulf Stream, flows from the Gulf of Mexico to northwestern Europe. Its waters bring mild weather to places such as the Norwegian coast. The Atlantic contains important fishing grounds, though some places have been overfished. The Atlantic is also the busiest ocean for shipping.

○ SQUID
Atlantic fishermen regard the many species of squid as pests, because they eat herring and mackerel.

○ OIL RIGS
The Atlantic has vast reserves of oil and natural gas, mined by offshore drilling platforms.

○ VIKING SETTLERS
After sailing across the North Atlantic from Norway to Iceland, and then Greenland, Viking explorers built settlements.

○ TRAWLER
From Atlantic waters come about a third of the world's annual catch of fish and shellfish.

○ HUMPBACK WHALE
Humpback whales live in coastal waters in all the oceans.

GREEN TURTLE
Hunting has greatly reduced the number of green turtles in the Indian Ocean.

INDIAN
OCEAN

The Indian Ocean, the world's third-largest ocean, lies between Africa to the west, Indonesia and Australia to the east, and Antarctica to the south. It covers an area of about 28.5 million square miles. Major islands include Madagascar and Sri Lanka. India and Sri Lanka divide the ocean's northern part into the Bay of Bengal and the Arabian Sea.

The average depth is 12,500 feet, but the deepest point is in the Java Trench, where depths of more than 24,300 feet have been recorded. Like the Atlantic, the Indian Ocean contains ocean ridges.

New crustal rock is being formed along the central rift valleys of the ridges—and earthquakes are common.

The northern part of the Indian Ocean lies in the tropics. Water temperatures are high in some areas, especially in the Red Sea and the Persian Gulf. The ocean currents are determined by the winds. North of the equator, the direction of the currents varies every year when wind directions change because of the monsoon.

MORAY EEL
Moray eels live in tropical waters, lurking in the crevices of coral reefs.

SEA CUCUMBER
Despite their name, sea cucumbers are animals! In the warm waters of the Indian Ocean, they reach lengths of up to 35 inches.

GREAT WHITE SHARK
Great white sharks are among the most dangerous sharks, and have attacked people and small boats.

TRADITIONAL FISHING
In the rich coastal waters of the Indian Ocean, fishermen catch sardines, anchovies, and bummalo, or Bombay duck, among other fish.

237

ARCTIC
OCEAN

ARCTIC
AREA: 4,633,236 sq mi.
AVERAGE DEPTH: 3,675 ft
GREATEST KNOWN DEPTH: 17,880 ft

↻ INUIT
The Inuit live in the Arctic region of North America. In 1999, they took control of a new Canadian territory named Nunavut.

The Arctic is a bitterly cold region and the Arctic Ocean is largely covered with thick ice throughout the year. This ice blocked early explorers trying to find sea routes around North America and northern Asia. Today, ice-breakers can force a passage through the ice. The first expedition to reach the North Pole was led by Commander Robert Edwin Peary (1856–1920) of the US Navy in 1909.

The average depth of the Arctic Ocean is about 3,675 feet and the greatest depth is 17,880 feet. Whales and many fishes, including cod and halibut, live in the Arctic Ocean. Polar bears live on the polar ice, where they hunt seals and fish in the freezing waters.

The Arctic is the region that lies north of the Arctic Circle. It includes the northern parts of Asia, North America, and Europe, together with most of the world's largest island, Greenland. These land areas enclose the world's smallest ocean, the Arctic Ocean. Near its ice-covered center is the North Pole.

↻ ICEBERGS
Icebergs break away from valley glaciers and from Greenland's huge ice sheet. Some drift south into the Atlantic Ocean.

Mainland areas within the Arctic Circle are covered in a treeless wilderness called tundra. The most common animals are caribou and reindeer, which graze there during the short summers. Other animals include bears, foxes, hares, lemmings, and voles. Many birds migrate to the Arctic in summer to breed, feeding on small animals or the swarms of insects that thrive in the marshy summer environment.

Greenland is a dependency of Denmark, but has been self-governing since 1981. With the exception of Antarctica, it is the world's least-populated land. Temperatures on the central ice cap can drop below -85°F, but ocean currents keep the southwest coast relatively mild. The fishing industry is a major employer. As well as the Inuit of Greenland and northern Canada, other Arctic peoples are the Saami (or Lapps) in northern Scandinavia, and the Samoyeds, Tungus, and Yakuts of northern Asia. In the past, most lived by fishing and hunting. But many now live in permanent settlements.

↻ INUITS AND THEIR DOGS
Traditionally, the Inuits used teams of dogs to pull their sleds across the snow. Today, motorized snowmobiles are more commonly used to travel over the ice.

○ DRYING WHITE FISH
Fishing and hunting seals and whales are traditional activities of Arctic peoples. But today, many people live more comfortable lives in permanent settlements.

○ ICEBOUND SHIPS
Ships can become locked in the frozen waters of the Arctic Ocean.

Yukon

Bering Strait

ALASKA (USA)

CHUKCHI SEA

Ambarchik

Kolyma

EAST SIBERIAN SEA

Indigirka

R U S S I A

Barrow   Pt. Barrow

Mackenzie

BEAUFORT SEA

C.Bathurst

New Siberian Islands

LAPTEV SEA

Lena

C A N A D A

Banks Island

McClure Strait

Victoria Island

A R C T I C
O C E A N

Nordvik

Queen Elizabeth Islands

North Magnetic Pole

Severnaya Zemlya

★ North Pole

Dikson

Yenisey

Ellesmere Island

LINCOLN SEA

Franz Josef Land

○ HARP SEALS
Newly born harp seals were hunted for their valuable soft, white pelts.

Foxe Basin

Baffin Island

Baffin Bay

Novaya Zemlya

KARA SEA

Ob'

Davis Strait

GREENLAND (DENMARK)

Svalbard (Norway)

BARENTS SEA

Pechora

Godthåb

GREENLAND SEA

North Cape

Murmansk

Denmark Strait

Archangel

○ BULL CARIBOU
The caribou of North American spend the summer in the Arctic tundra.

ICELAND

NORWEGIAN SEA

Reykjavik

POLAR BEAR

SNOWY OWL

ARCTIC FOX

WALRUS

239

ANTARCTICA

FACTS

ANTARCTICA
AREA: about
5,405,405 sq mi.
POPULATION: none permanent
HIGHEST POINT: Vinson
Massif (16,864 ft)

⟳ **WEATHER BALLOONS**
Weather studies are important, because conditions in Antarctica affect the world's weather.

⟳ **ROALD AMUNDSEN**
Amundsen, a Norwegian explorer, led the first expedition to reach the South Pole on December 14, 1911.

The Antarctic is the region lying south of the Antarctic Circle. It includes most of the world's fifth-largest continent, Antarctica, in the middle of which is the South Pole. Only the tip of the Antarctic Peninsula, jutting out toward South America, lies outside the Antarctic Circle. The waters around Antarctica are sometimes called the Antarctic or Southern Ocean. But most geographers regard these waters as parts of the Pacific, Atlantic, and Indian oceans.

Ice covers about 98 percent of Antarctica, although mountain peaks jut through the ice in places. The average thickness of the ice is 7,200 feet, but in places it is 15,750 feet thick. Antarctica is bitterly cold—the world's lowest air temperature, -128°F, was recorded at the Russian Vostok Station in 1983. Few plants and animals are found on Antarctica. The best-known creatures are penguins—flightless birds that feed mainly on fish in the waters around the continent.

Early explorers in Antarctica faced great hardship. An expedition first reached the South Pole in 1911.

It was led by the Norwegian Roald Amundsen (1872–1928). A British expedition led by Robert Falcon Scott (1868–1912) reached the pole five weeks later, but Scott and all his team perished on the way back. Later explorers used aircraft. The first flight over the South Pole was made in 1929 by Richard E. Byrd (1888–1957), a US naval officer.

Several countries have claimed parts of Antarctica, but none of the claims is recognized under international law. Many people would like to make the continent a huge international park, a protected wilderness safe from development and pollution.

Today, scientists from several countries work in Antarctica. In the 1980s, scientists discovered that the ozone layer above Antarctica was being thinned by chemicals called fluorocarbons. The ozone layer is important because it protects our planet from harmful ultraviolet rays. International action has been taken to reduce the release of fluorocarbons into the atmosphere.

⟳ **TRAWLING NEAR ANTARCTICA**
The waters around Antarctica are rich in marine life, including krill (tiny, shrimplike creatures), squid, seals, fish, and whales.

OZONE LAYER
The ozone layer in the upper atmosphere of the Earth blocks most of the Sun's harmful ultraviolet rays. Since the 1980s, pollution has created "holes" in the ozone layer over Antarctica.

VITAL SUPPLIES
Supplies for scientists are flown or shipped in to Antarctica.

WANDERING ALBATROSS

ICE CAVE
Around the coast of Antarctica, the sea hollows out spectacular caves in the ice.

WHOPPING WHALE
Blue whales, the largest animals ever to have lived, feed on krill in the seas around Antarctica.

PENGUIN PARADE
Adélie penguins, the most common penguins in Antarctica, build nests of pebbles on the coast.

TENTS IN THE SNOW
Scientists use special tents when they are making research journeys across Antarctica.

241

GLOSSARY

ABYSSAL PLAIN The deepest part of the ocean, below the continental slope.

AMMONITES Extinct mollusks whose fossils are common in rocks formed during the Mesozoic era. Like the dinosaurs, they became extinct about 65 million years ago.

ASTEROID A very small planet in orbit around the Sun. Most are found between the orbits of Mars and Jupiter.

ATMOSPHERE The layer of air that surrounds the Earth.

AUTOMATION The use of machines—or robots—to perform tasks that are too repetitive, complex, dangerous, or costly for people to undertake.

BIOME A plant and animal community that covers a large area. Biomes include the tundra, coniferous forests, temperate forests, temperate grasslands, deserts, savanna, and tropical rainforests.

BIRTH AND DEATH RATES The number of births and deaths in a year for every 1,000 people.

BLOCK MOUNTAIN A mountain system formed when a block of land is pushed upward between sets of roughly parallel faults.

CIRCUMFERENCE The distance around a circle.

COLONY A territory ruled by a foreign power.

COMET A heavenly body usually consisting of a nucleus and tail. It is composed of frozen gases of ice and dust, and follows a definite path through space.

COMMUNISM A political system where land, industry, and all property and goods are controlled by the government.

COMPASS Instrument used to measure direction. Magnetic compasses have needles that point to the magnetic North Pole.

CONDENSATION A change of state that occurs when a gas or vapor is turned into a liquid. Invisible water vapor in the air condenses into water droplets when the air is chilled.

CONIFEROUS FOREST Forests of mostly evergreen, cone-bearing trees. Common coniferous trees include fir, larch, pine, and spruce.

CONTINENT A very large land mass. The world has seven continents in all. In order of size they are Asia, Africa, North America, South America, Antarctica, Europe, and Australia.

CORAL A rock formed from the external skeletons of tiny sea creatures called coral polyps.

CUMULONIMBUS CLOUD A high, often anvil-shaped thundercloud formed when warm, moist air rises quickly.

DELTA A flat area at the mouth of a river, formed from muddy sediments deposited by the river.

DEPRESSION A region of low air pressure associated with changeable, and often stormy, weather.

DIALECT A variation of a language used by a group of people in a particular area.

DIAMETER A line which dissects a circle, passing through its center.

DECIDUOUS TREES Trees that shed their leaves during a certain season. Deciduous trees such as elms and oaks in the mid-latitudes shed their leaves in the fall. In monsoon regions, deciduous trees shed their leaves in the dry season.

EARTHQUAKE Sudden movements or tremors in the Earth's crust that make the ground shake.

ENVIRONMENT The external conditions that influence the growth and development of plants, animals, and people.

EROSION The process by which natural forces, including weathering, running water, ice, winds, and the sea, constantly wear down the land and carry the worn material, only to deposit it elsewhere.

ETHNIC GROUP A group of people with common characteristics, such as ties of ancestry, culture, language, nationality, or religion. These characteristics distinguish them from other people in the same country or society.

EVAPORATION A change of state that occurs when a liquid turns into a gas or vapor. For example, heat evaporates water to create invisible water vapor.

FAULT A fracture or break in rocks that make up the Earth's crust, along which the rocks have moved. Sudden movements along faults cause earthquakes.

FOSSIL Evidence of ancient life found in rocks. They include traces of leaves, shells, or bones, together with footprints made by animals. Sometimes, whole animals or plants are preserved.

FOSSIL FUELS Fuels such as coal, oil, and natural gas that are formed from the remains of once-living organisms.

GLOBE A spherical model of the Earth showing the land and seas. Some mounted globes can be rotated around a central axis.

HABITAT The type of place or environment to which a plant or animal is adapted. Habitats are usually defined in terms of their vegetation, altitude, or climate.

HOMO SAPIENS The scientific name for human beings, distinguishing them from early humanlike creatures such as *Homo erectus* and *Homo habilis*.

HURRICANE A severe tropical storm that forms over the oceans north and south of the Equator. When it reaches land, the hurricane often does much damage.

HYDROELECTRICITY Electricity that is generated at power plants by the force of water flowing through turbines at dams.

INDUSTRIAL REVOLUTION An important event in history involving the use of power-driven machines and the growth of factories. It began in the late 18th century in Britain and, by the mid-19th century, had spread through much of western Europe and North America. Progress in industrial development is still continuing in some developing countries.

INTERNATIONAL DATE LINE An imaginary line around 180 degrees east and west longitude. To the east of the line, the day is one day ahead of places to the west of the imaginary line.

MAGMA Molten rock inside the Earth's crust. When magma rises to the Earth's surface and spills out through volcanoes, it is called lava.

MAGNETIC POLE The Earth is like a giant magnet. It has two magnetic poles, north and south, just like the ends of a magnet.

MANGROVE SWAMP Coastal swamp in tropical regions, in which mangrove trees grow in the salty water along the coasts. The stiltlike roots sent down from their branches trap silt, which may build up to form new land.

MAP A representation of the Earth—or a large or small part of it—on a flat surface such as a sheet of paper. Navigators use maps.

METEOR A streak across the sky, also known as a shooting star, caused by a lump of rock burning up as it enters the Earth's atmosphere. Meteoroids that reach the surface are called meteorites.

MID-LATITUDES The mostly temperate climatic zones between the hot tropics and the cold polar regions.

<u>MIGRATION</u> The movement of animals and people from one location to another. People usually migrate to escape from something they do not like, or to go somewhere that seems to be more attractive.

<u>MINORITIES</u> Groups of people who differ in some ways, for example in culture or language, from the main group in a society.

<u>NATURAL RESOURCES</u> Materials that occur naturally and can be used by people, such as energy sources, forests, minerals, and fertile soils.

<u>NUCLEAR POWER</u> Energy that is released from a controlled nuclear reaction in a nuclear power plant.

<u>OZONE</u> An unstable form of the gas oxygen. It is produced when electricity is discharged through air.

<u>PENINSULA</u> Part of the land that juts out into the sea.

<u>PINGO</u> A mound that occurs in polar regions when freezing water beneath the surface pushes up the overlying soil.

<u>PLANET</u> In our Solar System, a heavenly body that orbits the Sun. Astronomers have identified other distant stars that have planets orbiting them.

<u>PLANKTON</u> Microscopic plants and animals that float near the surface of oceans. They are the food for many marine creatures.

<u>PLATEAU</u> An large upland region with a generally level surface.

<u>PRAIRIE</u> A mid-latitude grassland region in North America. It is the equivalent of the pampas in South America and the veld in South Africa.

<u>RIFT VALLEY</u> A valley formed when a block of land sinks between sets of roughly parallel faults.

<u>SATELLITE</u> In astronomy, a body that orbits a planet. Artificial satellites are manufactured objects that orbit the Earth or some other heavenly body. They may be used to send and receive radio signals.

<u>SMOG</u> A fog that is mixed with smoke. Photochemical smog is caused by the action of sunlight on exhaust gases from cars and factories.

<u>SOIL EROSION</u> The removal of the topsoil as the result of human interference with the land, such as deforestation. Soil erosion occurs quickly on exposed areas, especially on sloping land. By contrast, natural erosion is a much slower process.

<u>STEPPE</u> A mid-latitude grassland extending from the Ukraine into Central Asia. The term is often used for grasslands that are drier than prairies, with shorter and coarser grasses.

<u>STRATOSPHERE</u> The part of the atmosphere above the troposphere, extending to about 427 ft above ground level. It contains the ozone layer, which blocks most of the Sun's harmful ultraviolet rays.

<u>SUBSISTENCE FARMING</u> The farming of crops in order to support a farmer and his/her family. Often there is little surplus left to trade. It is the chief activity in many developing countries.

<u>TELECOMMUNICATIONS</u> The communication of information over long distances, by a wide variety of electrical and electronic systems, including telephone, telegraph, radio, television, and satellite.

VOLCANO A hole (or vent) in the ground through which lava, steam, and gases are ejected. The term volcano is also used for the mountains of ash and lava that form around the vent.

WATER VAPOR Invisible moisture in the air. It has the properties of a gas, until it condenses into droplets of water.

WIND The movement of air either across the Earth's surface or within the atmosphere. For example, the jet stream is a powerful wind that blows in the upper atmosphere.

TEMPERATURE The measurement of the hotness or coldness of a gas, liquid, or solid. It is normally measured on the Celsius or Fahrenheit scales.

TORNADO A small, intense storm, or whirlwind, with wind speeds of up to 404 mph.

TRADE The buying and selling of both goods and services.

URBAN AREA A built-up area such as a town or city and the suburbs around it.

245

INDEX
OF PLACE NAMES

247

INDEX

The publishers would like to thank the following sources
for the use of their photographs in this book:

Page 15 (C/R)Rex Features; 15 (C/L) Keith Lye; 34 (B/L) courtesy Legoland; 37 (T/L) AKG,London; 41 (C/L) courtesy Nederlandse Philips Bedrijven BV; 41 (T/L) Frank Spooner; 42 (T/L) AKG,London; 42 (B) Frank Spooner; 42 (T/R) Frank Spooner; 49 (T/L) Rex Features; 50 (C/L) AKG,London; 51 (C) Rex Features; 54 (T/C) Rex Features; 55 (C/L) Spectrum Colour Library; 55 (B/L) & Rex Features; 56 (B/R) AKG, London; 57 (C/R) Rex Features; 57 (T/L) Stock Market; 58 (T/L) AKG, London; 58 (T/R) Spectrum Colour Library; 59 (T/L) AKG, London; 59 (B/R) & (B/L) Rex Features; 62 (B/L) Dover Publications; 63 (B/L) courtesy Volkeswagon; 64 (T/R) Rex Features; 66 (T/L)AKG, London; 67 (C/L) SIPA/Rex Features; 70 (B/L) Stock Market; 70 (B/L) courtesy SEAT; 72 (B/L) Stock Market; 72 (B/R) Stock Market; (72) courtesy Spanish Tourist Office; 72 (B/L) Stock Market; 73 (C/L) Rex Features; 74 (B/L) AKG, London; 75 (T/L) AKG, London, (C/L) SIPA/Rex Features; 76 (C/L) Hilary Fletcher; 78 (B/L) Spectrum Colour Library; 78 (B/L) Stock Market; 78 (T/L) & 79 (B/L) Rex Features; 79 (B/R) D.Parker/Science Photo Library; 80 (T/R) Spectrum Colour Library; 80 (B/L) AKG, London; 81 (B/R) Rex Features; 82 (C/L) Frank Spooner; 82/83 AKG, London; 87 (T/L) & 86 (T/L) Spectrum Colour Library; 89 (C) Panos; 88 (B/L) Mary Evans Picture Library; 91 (T/R) AKG, London; 91 (C/L) Gamma/Frank Spooner Pictures, (B/L) Spectrum Colour Library; 93 (T/L) Spectrum Colour Library; 93 (B/R) & (L/C) Spectrum Colour Library; 94 (C/R) Panos; 94 (B/L) Hilary Fletcher; 95 (T/L) & (C/L) Spectrum Colour Library, (B/R) Hilary Fletcher; 96 (C/L) Spectrum Colour Library; 96 (T/R) & 97 (T/L) Spectrum Colour Library; 97(C/R) SIPA/Rex Features; 103 (T/R) Frank Spooner; 107 (B/R) Graham King, (B/L) Hilary Fletcher;108 (T/R) Hilary Fletcher, (B/R) Keith Lye; 94 (C/R) Panos; 111 (T/L) Stock Market, 110/111 (C) Hilary Fletcher; 111 (T/R) Gamma/Frank Spooner; 112 (B) 113 (C), (T/R) Hilary Fletcher; 112 (C/L) & 113 (C/R) Gamma/Frank Spooner; 115 (C/L) & (C/R) Gamma/Frank Spooner; 117 (B/R) Gamma/Frank Spooner; 118 (T/C) Graham King; 119 (B/L), (T/L) & (T/R) Panos; 120 (C/L) &121 (T/R) Graham King; 122(C) Stock Market; 123 (B/R) Hilary Fletcher; 123 (T/R) Frank Spooner; 125 (T/L) Gamma/Frank Spooner; 125 (B) & (T/R) Hilary Fletcher; 126 (B/R) Mary Evans Picture Library;126 (B/L) Panos; 127 (T/L) Gamma/Frank Spooner; 128 (T/C) & 129 (C) Graham King; 128 (B), 129 (B/L), & (T/R) Graham King; 130 (C/R) Graham King; 131 (B/L), (C/L), Graham King; 131 (T/L) &130 (B/R) & (T/R) Graham King, 131 (R) Panos ; 132 (T/L), (T/R) & 133 (C) (T/Graham King; 132 (B/L) Graham King, 132 (R/C) Jon Keyte; 133 (T/R); 134 (B/L) &135 (T/L) Graham King; 135 (T/R) & (B/L) Graham King; 137 (T/L), 136 (T/C) Panos; & (T/R) Graham King; 137 (B/L) Hutchison Library; 137 (T/C) Hutchison Library; 138 (B/L) & 139 (T/L) Graham King, (C) Panos; 139 (L/C) Frank Spooner, (C/R) Panos; 140 (T/L) AKG, London, (T/L) Panos; 140 (C/R) 141 (C/R) & 141 (B) Panos; 141 (C/L) Hutchison Library; 143 (C/R), (T/R), (T/L) & 142 (B) Graham King; 142 (C/L) Jon Keyte; 143 (C/L) & (B/L) Graham King; 144 (C/R) Hutchison Library, (T/R), (C), 145 (B/L) Graham King; 145 (T/L), 144 (B/L) 146 (T/C) & 147 (B/R); 146 (B/L) & 147 (T/L) Gamma/Frank Spooner, (C) Jon Keyte; 152 (T/L) Rex Features; 153 (T/R) Spectrum Colour Library, 153 (C/L) Spectrum Colour Library; 155 (T/R) Rex Features; 160 (B/L) Keith Lye; 163 (B/R) Keith Lye; 164 (B/C) & 165 (T/R) Keith Lye; 167 (C/R) Keith Lye; 168 (C/L) & 169 (B) Keith Lye; 168 (T/R) Hilary Fletcher, 169 (T/R) Frank Spooner; 170 (B/C) Keith Lye; 171 (C) & (B) Hilary Fletcher; 172 (B) Hilary Fletcher; 177 (T/L) Hilary Fletcher, (T/R) E/T. Archive, (C/R) Hutchison Library; 178 (R/C) Keith Lye, (T/R) Hutchison Library; 179 (R/C) Hilary Fletcher; 181 (T/R) Hilary Fletcher; (T/C) Stock Market; 182 (B/R) & 183 (B/R) Hutchison Library; 183 (L/C) Rex Features; 185(T/R), 184 (B/L) & 184/5 (B) Gamma/Frank Spooner; 185 (C/L) courtesy Sony, (C) courtesy Nikon; 187 (B/L) V & A Museum/E.T.Archive; 194 (C/L) Hutchison Library; (T/C) Gamma/Frank Spooner; 195 (T/R) Hutchison Library, (B/L) Frank Spooner; 198 (B) Hilary Fletcher; 199 (T/L), & (B/L) Hilary Fletcher; 200 (C/R) Hilary Fletcher; 201 (T/L) Hilary Fletcher; 206 (T) Hutchison Library; 212 (B) Keith Lye; 213 (C/R) Hutchison Library; 213 (B/R) Keith Lye; 215 (T/L) Keith Lye; 216 (T/R) & 217 (T/R) Hutchison Library; 222 (C/L) Gamma/Frank Spooner; 223 (C/R) Hutchison Library; 224/5 (C) Frank Spooner, 224 (C/L) Hutchison Library; 226 (B) Mary Evans Picture Library; 227 (T/L) Corbis; 231 (T/L) Gamma/Frank Spooner; 231 (B/L) Hutchison Library; 235 (B/L) Rex Features; 237 (B) Hutchison Library.
All other photographs from Miles Kelly archives.

The publishers would like to thank the following artists whose work appears in this book:

David Ashby/Illustration Ltd; Richard Bonson; Vanessa Card; Kuo Kang Chen; Andrew Clark; Wayne Ford; Chris Forsey; Mike Foster/Maltings Partnership; Terry Gabbey/A.F.A.; Jeremy Gower; Gary Hincks; Sally Holmes; John James/Temple Rogers; Roger Kent/Illustration Ltd; Alan Male/Linden Artists; Jane Pickering/Linden Artists; Eric Rowe/Linden Artists; Peter Sarson; Rob Sheffield; Guy Smith/Mainline Design; Tony Smith; Christian Webb/Temple Rogers; Mike White/Temple Rogers; John Woodcock.